WEST INDIES

Scale
Miles 60 to a Degree
60 120 180 240
410

ATLANTIC

OCEAN

Tropic of Cancer

CARIBBEE

ISLANDS

HAMA ISLANDS

Lucayos

Eleuthera
S.t Salvador
or Catt I 1492
Watlins I

Providence

Long I

Crooked I

Maguana

Atwoods Keys

Anagua I

Caicos B

North Riff

I

S.t Jago

C Mayze

Torutgas

Monte
Christo

C Francis

Scots Bay

G of Samana I

Passage

C S.t Nic

holas

P d Guanives

S Iago

C. del Engano

S Juan

Virgin Islands

Anguda

Anguilla

S.t Martin

S.t Bartholomew

Barbuda

C Anns

HISPANIOLA

S Domingo

PORTO RICO

Saba

Windward

Petit
Guavas

C Tabran

Firmos

Saona

Mona

Crab I

S.ta Cruz

Estatia

S.t Kits

Redondo

Nevis

Antego

MAMAICA

S.t Jagu

Navaza

P.t Morant

Port Royal

Tierra I

Alta

LEEWARD

ISLANDS

Montse.t

Deseada

Guadalupe

Marigalante

Dominica

Port Louis

Great   Antilles

Ares I

Martinico

CARIBEAN

WINDWARD

S.t Lucia

SEA

Little   Antilles

ISLANDS

Barbadoes

Conguibacoa

Aruba

Curissoro

Bonaire

I de Aves

Granadillos

S.t Vincent

C de la Vela

Orchilla

I Blancy

Granada

P.Samba

Lit. Caracas

Roca

Tartuga

Tabago

P Canoa

R de la
Hacha

Coro

Gulf of
Trieste

La Guiava

Margarite

pta de la Galera

rtagene

cenchica

Sta Martha

Maracaybo

Caracas

Comana

Verird

S.t Joseph

Trinidad

mbay Keys

STA MARTHA

Lake
Maracaybo

CARACOS

Gulf of Paria

P.t R.

Moco Moco

Cenit

los Rojas

Truxillo

NEW

Oronoque

B.o

Mopox

TERRA

FIRMAN

ANDULASIA

C Naga

Sta Fe

Apuero

Merida

VENEZUELA

Ariaoa

N Middelbury

RE 19

aret Bay

Nueva Segovia

GUI

NEW GRANADA

Truxillo

F Looic
about

Pamptona

career at the head of a company of Artillery raised for the particular defence of this State I had better pretensions to the allowance that others to whom it was actually made — Yet has it not been extended to me A H

A Hamilton

Statement of my pretensions &c with remarks

THE ILLUSTRATED BIOGRAPHY

ALEXANDER
HAMILTON

RICHARD SYLLA

STERLING
New York

STERLING
New York

An Imprint of Sterling Publishing, Co., Inc.
1166 Avenue of the Americas
New York, NY 10016

ISBN 978-1-4549-2275-9

Distributed in Canada by Sterling Publishing Co., Inc.
c/o Canadian Manda Group, 664 Annette Street
Toronto, Ontario, M6S 2C8, Canada
Distributed in the United Kingdom by GMC Distribution Services
Castle Place, 166 High Street, Lewes, East Sussex, BN7 1XU, United Kingdom
Distributed in Australia by NewSouth Books,
45 Beach Street, Coogee, NSW 2034, Australia

For information about custom editions, special sales, and premium
and corporate purchases, please contact Sterling Special Sales
at 800-805-5489 or specialsales@sterlingpublishing.com.

Manufactured in Canada

2 4 6 8 10 9 7 5 3

www.sterlingpublishing.com

Design by Lorie Pagnozzi

A complete list of picture credits appears on page 266.

THIS BOOK IS DEDICATED TO THE MUSEUM OF AMERICAN
FINANCE, WHICH PRESERVES ONE OF ALEXANDER HAMILTON'S
GREATEST LEGACIES: HIS KEY INSIGHT INTO THE POWER
OF MODERN FINANCE TO MAKE BETTER OUR LIVES.

VIEW OF THE SPOT WHERE G

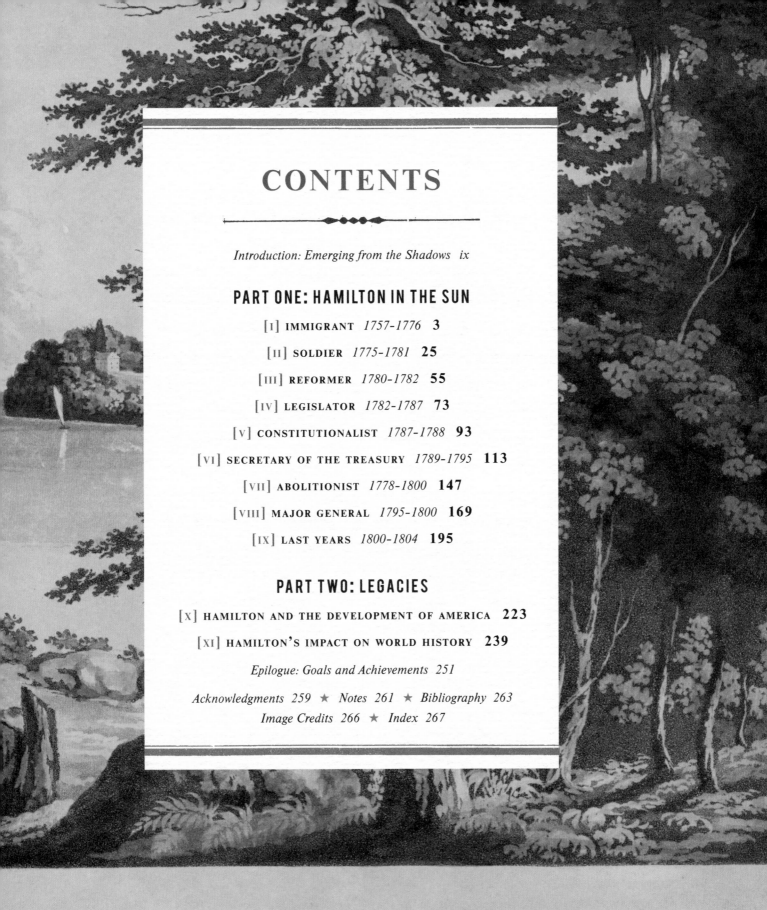

CONTENTS

HAMILTON FELL, AT WEEHAWK.

"Hamilton is perhaps the least loved founding father."

—DARREN STALOFF, *HAMILTON, ADAMS, JEFFERSON*

EMERGING FROM THE SHADOWS

Seldom has popular interest in a historical figure changed as dramatically as it has with Hamilton since historian Darren Staloff pegged him a decade ago as the least loved of the founders. Hamilton has gone from least loved to, if not most loved, then certainly most talked about, the founder with the most buzz.

The catalyst for the change? Broadway—but not the Manhattan thoroughfare from which you can spy Hamilton's tomb in the graveyard of Trinity Church. No, Broadway in the theatrical sense: Lin-Manuel Miranda's smash-hit musical, *Hamilton,* premiered in 2015 and promises to have a very long run in New York City and elsewhere. Inspired by Ron Chernow's biography, *Alexander Hamilton*, Miranda's musical makes for an innovative work of genius. In that sense, it mirrors its subject. Those who study Hamilton often describe him as a statesman of genius and a financial innovator.

But this isn't the first time or even the second in American history that Hamilton has burst forth from the shadows. In the early 1770s—following an obscure and illegitimate birth in the West Indies and an upbringing marked by tragedies that left him a penniless orphan—Hamilton migrated as a teenager to Britain's continental North American colonies. Despite his checkered start, relatives, friends, and employers in the Caribbean noticed his drive, intellect, maturity, and gift for writing. He had something special about him. In the fall of 1772 they sponsored his migration there to further his education, providing the teenager with funds and letters of introduction to their friends in New York and New Jersey. Hamilton was just fifteen years old.

The young man spent a year in a New Jersey prep school and then entered what is now Columbia University. By 1775, halfway into his second year of college, he had produced two lengthy polemical pamphlets espousing the American

ALEXANDER HAMILTON BY
JOHN TRUMBULL, 1792.

THE FRONT AND BACK
OF A MINIATURE
PORTRAIT, DRAWN
FROM LIFE IN 1773,
SHOWING HAMILTON
AT AGE FIFTEEN.

cause in the colonies' increasingly heated relationship with Britain. Most readers didn't realize they came from the pen of an eighteen-year-old. Less than two months later, what had been a war of words and trade embargos became a war of bullets and bayonets. In New York, Hamilton and his fellow students dropped their studies to begin military drills. In 1776, Hamilton's leadership abilities prompted New York State to appoint him captain of an artillery company. From that moment, his career took off. For the next twenty-eight years, until his untimely death, Hamilton played a part in virtually every major event that created America and set the course of its early development.

He became a great modernizer. He made and left his marks on the country's independence, government, legal traditions, military establishment, and, perhaps most important, its financial systems. We live today in a Hamiltonian nation. Not all who recognize Hamilton's great influence liked what he did, however. That's why he stood, until recently, as the least loved of the founders and probably why he slides into and out of the shadows of history that followed his brief life.

★ ★ ★ ★ ★

As General George Washington's principal aide de camp during the early years of the American Revolution, Hamilton became acquainted with many of the leading figures of the day. Newspapers published his outspoken views on the weakness of America's national government and the need for reform, spreading his thoughts and reputation.

Hamilton played a part in virtually every major event that created America.

In early 1781, Hamilton was given charge of a light infantry company, and his successful mission to capture a key British fortification during the decisive Battle of Yorktown in October 1781 made him an instant military hero. He seemed to sense, though, after seven long years of fighting, that the British defeat at Yorktown wouldn't play well in London and that the British were likely to agree to negotiations to end the war. Hamilton resigned his commission and returned to New York to join his wife, Elizabeth Schuyler Hamilton, who was expecting their first child. He also returned to an intensive study of the law, his intended career before the war.

Hamilton achieved more than most people do in several lifetimes. By mid-1782, in near-record time, he qualified as a lawyer and became the receiver of continental taxes for New York State. Soon after, New York appointed him a delegate to the Confederation Congress. He cofounded the Bank of New York. On several notable occasions, he took a stand against slavery, cofounding the New York Society for Promoting the Manumission of Slaves in 1785, for example. Public knowledge of his abolitionist values no doubt lurked behind some of the strong opposition he faced from southern slaveholding leaders in Congress when he wielded power as secretary of the Treasury. But like many others of his time, he wanted foremost to hold together the fragile new nation that slavery could so easily split apart—and did in 1861. For the sake of national unity, he didn't push an abolitionist agenda as he helped form the new nation.

He wanted foremost to hold together the fragile new nation that slavery could so easily split apart.

The weaknesses of the national government became increasingly apparent in the mid-1780s. Tribulations in and among the states eventually culminated in the Philadelphia convention of May 1787. Chaired by Washington and with Hamilton, James Madison, and others as delegates, the convention drafted a new constitution over the summer of 1787 to deal with sorely needed national reforms. To take effect, nine of the thirteen states had to ratify it, but its prospects in New York looked dim. Hamilton seized on a clever idea. He organized a series of newspaper essays to explain and defend the proposed constitution. He recruited Madison and John Jay to help, and from the fall of 1787 to the spring of 1788, 85 essays were published under the pseudonym "Publius." Hamilton wrote 51 of them, and *The Federalist Papers* have become a classic text of political science.

In 1789, the fledgling government met in New York City with Washington as first president. He appointed Hamilton as the first secretary of the newly created Treasury Department. Hamilton served in the office from September 1789 to January 1795; in that time he made the greatest of his many contributions to American nation building. Drawing on his time as Washington's principal aide de camp during the war, Hamilton functioned something like Washington's prime minister and, more than any other American leader, turned the Constitution's words into a living, breathing system that modernized and invigorated U.S. political and economic life. Hamilton's financial reforms created a strong, fiscally sound federal government to replace the weak national government of the Articles of Confederation. They also jolted the American economy by promoting the banks, securities markets, and corporations that propelled economic growth. As Treasury

> *Hamilton helped launch what has become the world's most powerful nation and the largest, most dynamic, richest economy. Ironically, he almost went broke in the process.*

secretary, Hamilton helped launch what has become the world's most powerful nation and the largest, most dynamic, richest economy the world has seen. Ironically, he almost went broke in the process. His government salary of $3,500—as compared to Washington's presidential $25,000—couldn't support his growing family. By early 1795, he stepped down as Treasury secretary, knowing that he could earn far more money as a lawyer.

Hamilton's post-cabinet career didn't match the grand creativity of his years in the Treasury, but it wasn't uneventful. When the French Republic insulted American diplomats and threatened to declare war on America in 1798, Congress called for a military buildup that included a new army. Washington agreed to serve as titular head of it but insisted that Hamilton receive operational control. President John Adams, to his chagrin, had to yield to Washington's demands rather than buck the revered father of the country. The affair revealed the high regard that Washington had for Hamilton's talents, but war with France never came, and Major General Hamilton had to disband his army in 1800.

Hamilton unwisely vented his frustrations with Adams in public before the 1800 elections. The discord between the two pillars of the Federalist Party contributed to Adams's narrow defeat by the Democratic-Republican Party, led by Thomas Jefferson, but the political turmoil didn't end there. Jefferson and Aaron Burr received the same number of electoral votes. At the time, a tie in electoral votes called for a contingent, or runoff, election in the House of Representatives. Hamilton frenetically lobbied Federalist congressmen to support Jefferson, and, after 35 tied contingency votes, Jefferson finally secured the presidency.

The Federalist Party fell from power, and so Hamilton began to recede into the shadows. In 1801, he founded the *New-York Evening Post* as an outlet for Federalist Party views. Today's *New York Post* remains America's oldest continuously published daily paper. That year Hamilton also began construction on the Grange, a country house in upper Manhattan. He lived there less than two years. When Burr mortally wounded him in the now-infamous 1804 duel, Hamilton died a relatively poor man. Friends and admirers had to take up a collection to pay his debts so that Hamilton's family could remain at the Grange.

> *From life he wanted fame.*

The man who did the most to make the fortunes of his country cared little for money or wealth. From life he wanted fame, which, as he described it in *Federalist No. 72*, was "the ruling passion of the noblest minds, which would prompt a man to plan and undertake extensive and arduous enterprises for the public benefit, requiring considerable time to mature and perfect them." Fame, in other words, meant immortality. All the great founders—Franklin, Washington, Adams, Jefferson, Madison, and Hamilton—craved it. Franklin and Washington both had achieved it by the time they died in the 1790s. Admired by many but hardly revered, Hamilton died soon after. Adams, Jefferson, and Madison—all political opponents of Hamilton and all presidents—lived for decades longer, shaping future interpretations of their legacies.

ALEXANDER HAMILTON BY JOHN TRUMBULL, 1806.

★ ★ ★ ★ ★

Hamilton's reputation spent the next six decades in the shadows. The great split that he worked so hard to prevent in the nation's early days ironically brought him back into the light. The secession and armed rebellion of the Confederacy in 1861 met with and eventually fell to the federal power that Hamilton had advocated. The Republican Party of Abraham Lincoln emancipated slaves and forged a Hamiltonian agenda, including federal aid for infrastructure, land-grant colleges, uniform national currency, a national banking system, and tariffs on imports to protect American industry.

In the decades of the Reconstruction and the Gilded Age that followed, the Republican Party, led by businessmen and bankers, dominated national politics. Their leaders, notably Senator Henry Cabot Lodge and President Theodore Roosevelt, replaced Jefferson with Hamilton as the founder who mattered most. Presidents Harding, Coolidge, and Hoover, along with their long-serving Treasury secretary Andrew Mellon, revered Hamilton and erected a statue of him in front of the Treasury Department.

By that time, however, Hamilton's star was beginning to slide into darkness yet

SECRETARY OF THE
TREASURY ANDREW
MELLON PLACES A
WREATH BEFORE
THE STATUE OF
HAMILTON IN JANUARY
1927 OR 1928.

again. The late nineteenth and early twentieth centuries witnessed the rise of big business, such as John D. Rockefeller's Standard Oil Company and U.S. Steel, and the alleged Money Trust on Wall Street, led by bankers such as J. Pierpont Morgan. This essentially unchecked corporate growth disturbed Americans suspicious of large concentrations of private power. Progressive-era intellectuals traced these developments back to Hamilton and counted them the long-term consequences of his policies.

In fact, they were. Industrial corporations such as Standard Oil achieved success because they achieved economies of scale. They also created lots of jobs. Hamilton saw these possibilities more than a century earlier, which is why he wanted to develop banks and capital markets. With those modern institutions, he reasoned, entrepreneurs could pool limited funds to build efficient enterprises—and his plan worked.

But to farmers, workers, and small businesses, the power of large corporations and the wealth accumulated by those who controlled them seemed threatening. Politicians responded to these concerns, enacting antitrust laws and creating regulatory authorities. Woodrow Wilson—one of just two Democrats to hold the presidency between 1861 and 1933—offers a prime example of these shifting sands. Shortly before becoming president he pronounced Hamilton a great man but not a great American—presumably because Hamilton was an immigrant who supposedly over-admired British institutions, was too pro-business, and expressed a less-than-perfect confidence in democracy. Wilson's administration introduced new antitrust laws and boosted the regulation of business. It also curried favor with southern Democrats by reversing the progress that African Americans had made in the federal civil service under Republican administrations.

If Hamilton's star faded in the first decades of the twentieth century, it went into almost total eclipse after Franklin D. Roosevelt took office in 1933. The Great Crash in

1929 and the Great Depression that followed gave big business, Wall Street financiers, and Hamilton by implication a collective black eye. FDR elevated Jefferson as a great democrat and Democrat, the ideal founder who believed in the wisdom of the people and distrusted the behavior of businessmen, bankers, and financiers. Roosevelt installed a grand marble memorial to Jefferson in the capital, placing him on par with Washington and Lincoln. The gambit cleverly united southern segregationists and northern workers as the base of the Democratic Party. But most of Roosevelt's New Deal embodied the federal power and action that Hamilton had espoused. FDR explained the paradox by saying that he was pursuing Jeffersonian ends by Hamiltonian means.

For most of American history, the Democrats, whether in or out of power, carried the Jeffersonian mantle, while the other party—successively the Federalists, Whigs, and Republicans—carried the Hamiltonian one. FDR's telling quip encapsulates the change that unfolded during the remainder of the twentieth century, resulting in neither of the major parties liking Hamilton. President Lyndon Johnson caused much of this split when, as a Democrat, he pushed a Hamiltonian agenda. On the one hand, as a disciple of FDR and the New Deal, Johnson created Medicare and Medicaid, Great Society programs that used federal power to improve Americans' lives. On the other, by backing the civil rights movement and advocating for the civil rights acts of 1964 and 1968 and the Voting Rights Act of 1965, he alienated the segregationist South and broke up the old New Deal coalition.

Republicans saw the opening that Johnson created and pounced to create a southern strategy of states' rights, covert racism, and opposition to federal power. In other words, the Republicans became a Jeffersonian party, while the Democrats stuck with the FDR ruse that they were really a Jeffersonian party.

Poor Hamilton! The political left doesn't like him because he favored big business and big finance, both of which have too much power in modern America, making us feel uneasy. From the Nixon administration to the present, Republicans have narrowed their eyes at him because he favored big government and the use of federal power, also sources of unease. Is it any wonder that our man spent nearly a century in the shadows or that he became the least loved of the founders?

Now, however, in one of those strange twists of American history, the smashing success of a Broadway musical has sparked new curiosity about Hamilton's life and values. Pursuing that curiosity will show us why the country seems to lack direction now just as it did in the early 1770s when an apprehensive teenager arrived from the West Indies and first burst forth from the shadows.

{ PART ONE }

★

HAMILTON IN THE SUN

"I wish there was a War."

ALEXANDER HAMILTON TO EDWARD STEVENS, 1769

{I}

IMMIGRANT

1757-1776

H e may have accomplished great feats as a soldier, lawyer, statesman, finance minister, and politician, but at the beginning of his relatively short life—and again at its end—Alexander Hamilton was a loser.

Father.

He was born on January 11, 1757, in Charlestown on the island of Nevis in the West Indies.* His father, James Hamilton, was the fourth son of the laird, also named Alexander, of the Grange in Stevenston, Scotland, on which stand the ruins of Kerelaw Castle. Under British laws of primogeniture, the eldest son inherited his father's entire estate. Other sons and heirs had to fend for themselves. As a result, James, born around 1718, pursued a life as a merchant in the West Indies, moving to St. Kitts, next to Nevis, in the early 1740s.

HAMILTON OF
GRANGE

Mother.

Alexander Hamilton's mother, Rachel Fawcett, descended from Huguenots, French Protestants forced to flee France in 1685 after King Louis XIV revoked the Edict of Nantes, which had granted Protestants religious freedom. Rachel was born in the late 1720s to John Fawcett, a Nevis physician, and his wife, Mary Uppington Fawcett. In 1740, John and Mary Fawcett separated, a split that Rachel repeated later in her

OPPOSITE: THE
BOSTON TEA
PARTY.
LEFT: THE COAT
OF ARMS OF THE
HAMILTONS OF
STEVENSTON.

---

*Historians disagree about the year of Hamilton's birth. Some argue that he was born on that date in 1755. Michael Newton, in the latest and most thorough research, doubts the 1755 date and deems 1757 more likely.

HAMILTON'S
BIRTHPLACE IN
CHARLESTOWN
ON NEVIS.

own life. Mother and daughter moved to St. Croix—then a Danish colony, now part of the U.S. Virgin Islands—and John Fawcett died in 1745, leaving his estate to Rachel.

That inheritance made the young Rachel Fawcett quite an attractive prospect as a wife, and her mother promoted the idea of a match to Johan Lavien, a well-to-do German planter. (Some historians theorize that Lavien was Jewish, but we have no evidence for that.) Lavien and Rachel married, probably in 1745, and the next year Rachel gave birth to a son, Peter. But Johan Lavien's fortunes slumped, and the marriage soon soured.

Around 1750, Lavien charged Rachel with adultery and had her sent to prison. Upon her release, Rachel left her husband and son, and she and her mother relocated to St. Kitts. There she met and took up with James Hamilton. The couple moved to Nevis, living together as husband and wife, and had two children: James Jr., born in 1754 or 1755, and Alexander in 1757. Rachel couldn't obtain a divorce from Lavien, though, so she and James Hamilton weren't legally married. That made James Jr. and Alexander bastards, a word that haunted her youngest son in his later years.

Lavien finally instituted divorce proceedings against Rachel in

> *That made James Jr. and Alexander bastards, a word that haunted her youngest son in his later years.*

1759, and Danish officials granted it. Under the terms, neither Rachel nor her "whore children" had any claim on Lavien's estate, nor could Rachel remarry.

In 1765, James Hamilton's employer sent him to St. Croix—where Rachel's sister, Ann, and her husband, James Lytton, still lived—to collect a business debt. Thinking the task would take some time, James Hamilton moved his family to St. Croix and succeeded in collecting the debt by early 1766.

Then, for reasons not entirely clear, James Hamilton abandoned his family in 1766 or 1767—never to return. Perhaps Rachel's divorce from Lavien made it difficult for him to find work on St. Croix. Whatever the reason, he lived in the West Indies without much business success for the next three decades, communicating with his increasingly famous son sporadically, sometimes through James Jr., who also remained in the Caribbean.

After James Sr. deserted the family, Rachel opened a small store on St. Croix. She eked out a modestly comfortable living with profits from the store, additional aid from her Lytton relatives, and income from hiring out slaves.

Rachel had inherited three slaves when her mother died in 1756, but these weren't the same people (five women, four children) she owned on St. Croix when she herself died, so either she sold her mother's former slaves or they died in the meantime. Either way, we know that Hamilton grew up in a slaveholding family on slaveholding islands and witnessed the unfairness and cruelty of that institution that he denounced as an adult.

Whatever comforts Rachel and her two sons had accrued came to an abrupt end in 1768. Rachel died in February of an unidentified disease. She was forty years old. Probate records show that the nine slaves were her major asset, but none of her estate went to the Hamilton boys. Danish law ruled them illegitimate, so Peter Lavien, her legitimate son, inherited her estate.*

After Rachel's death, James Lytton's son, Peter—the boys' cousin but roughly the same age as their late mother—became their legal guardian. Compounding the tragedy already marking their young lives, Peter Lytton committed suicide in July 1769, and his father, James, died a month later.

James Jr. and Alexander, bastard orphans, now had no family on St. Croix. Thomas Stevens, another St. Croix merchant-planter and the father of Alexander's childhood friend Edward Stevens, kindly took them into his home.

One of the suppliers of goods to their mother's store was the firm of David Beekman and Nicholas Cruger, New York-based merchants who had an office on St. Croix. Cruger spent a great deal of time in the Caribbean office and, after Hamilton's mother died, hired him as a clerk. On November 11, 1769, Hamilton penned a letter—the first writing we have from his hand—to his friend Edward Stevens, who had just gone to New York to further his education. Two months shy of his thirteenth birthday, the young Hamilton pours fourth his heart and reveals the inner workings of his mind:

> *my Ambition is prevalent that I contemn the grov'ling and condition of a Clerk or the like, to which my fortune &c. condemns me and would willingly risk my life tho' not my Character to exalt my Station. I'm confident, Ned that my Youth excludes me from any hopes of immediate Preferment nor*

THE ST. CROIX-BASED MERCHANT NICHOLAS CRUGER HIRED YOUNG ALEXANDER HAMILTON AS A CLERK, OFFERING HIM A LINK TO THE WORLD BEYOND THE CARIBBEAN.

Hamilton's first job.

---

* At this point, James Lytton, the boys' uncle, told the probate court that they were fifteen and thirteen years old, respectively. Historians unearthed the Danish St. Croix probate records in the early twentieth century and, doing the math, posited that Alexander must have been born in 1755. But Alexander believed he was born in 1757 and said as much to his own family and anyone who asked during the rest of his life. The point of contention rests on whether we trust the man himself or the testimony of his sixty-six-year-old uncle, who was living on St. Croix when the boys were born on Nevis more than a decade earlier. It seems reasonable to trust Hamilton on this.

do I desire it, but I mean to prepare the way for futurity. Im no Philosopher you see and may be jusly said to Build Castles in the Air. My Folly makes me ashamd and beg youll Conceal it, yet Neddy we have seen such Schemes successfull when the Projector is Constant I shall conclude saying I wish there was a War.

Even at the tender age of twelve, Hamilton saw war as a chance for a disadvantaged but ambitious person to advance. Six short years later, his wish was granted.

★ ★ ★ ★ ★

Now chiefly tourist destinations, Nevis and St. Croix then consisted mainly of sugar-producing estates run by local and absentee owners. Virtually all arable land succumbed to that great cash crop, which meant that almost everything else, including food, had to be imported. That's why firms such as Beekman and Cruger thrived: They exported sugar and imported whatever else the islanders needed.

A 1756 census puts Nevis's population at some 9,500 people: 8,400 slaves and a white populace of 1,100 split nearly equally among men, women, and children. So Hamilton spent his early years on a mostly black island. His mother owned slaves, and the island's slave market lay not far from his home. He knew black people at home and saw others buying and selling them. His view that the "natural faculties" of black people were probably as good as whites' came from concrete experience rather than lofty, detached ideals.

Also near Hamilton's Nevis home stood Fort Charles, a garrison for British soldiers

HAMILTON'S LETTER TO HIS CHILDHOOD FRIEND EDWARD STEVENS.

"I mean to prepare the way for futurity."

The West Indies in the late eighteenth century.

THE HAMILTON FAMILY TREE

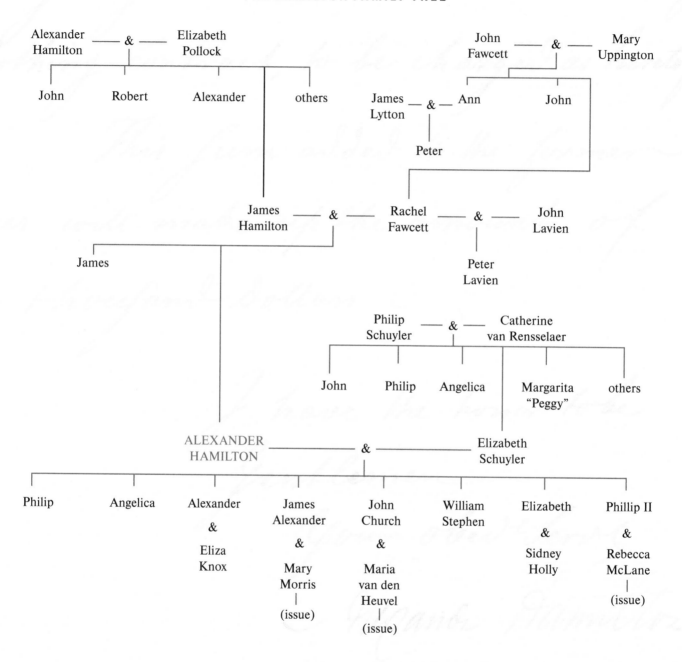

Alexander Hamilton — & — Elizabeth Pollock

John   Robert   Alexander   others

John Fawcett — & — Mary Uppington

James Lytton — & — Ann   John

Peter

James Hamilton — & — Rachel Fawcett — & — John Lavien

James

Peter Lavien

Philip Schuyler — & — Catherine van Rensselaer

John   Philip   Angelica   Margarita "Peggy"   others

ALEXANDER HAMILTON — & — Elizabeth Schuyler

Philip   Angelica   Alexander & Eliza Knox   James Alexander & Mary Morris | (issue)   John Church & Maria van den Heuvel | (issue)   William Stephen   Elizabeth & Sidney Holly   Phillip II & Rebecca McLane | (issue)

stationed to defend against French incursions as well as the ever-present danger of slave revolts. Watching their drills catalyzed Hamilton's lifelong fascination with military affairs.

The West Indies offered limited opportunities for education, however. White children were essentially homeschooled and self-taught. Hamilton's mother taught him French, a skill that later proved valuable. A Jewish woman ran a small school on Nevis that Hamilton attended, and the story goes that she taught him the Ten Commandments in Hebrew when he was so small that she had to stand him on a table to recite them to others. Books then counted more as luxury objects, and his mother owned some three dozen, which Hamilton devoured. After she died, they went to auction, with proceeds going to Hamilton's half brother, Peter Lavien. Alexander's cousin and guardian, Peter Lytton, bought them so Hamilton could keep them.

The most important part of Hamilton's early education took place at Beekman and Cruger on St. Croix. In 1771, Nicholas Cruger became ill and decided to recuperate for several months in New York. By that time, he had developed such confidence in his clerk that he left the young man fully in charge of the St. Croix business. A series of letters from those months, written to and on behalf of Cruger, survives and shows that he ran matters quite well. His letters touch on nearly all the subjects covered in the curriculum of a modern business school: accounting, economics, finance, information systems, insurance, international business, marketing, and management. As in so many other ways, Hamilton proved himself ahead of his time.

Cruger's admiration for Hamilton's business acumen found a match in the Reverend Hugh Knox's esteem for the young man's intellectual and literary talents. Knox, a Presbyterian minister educated at the College of New Jersey (now Princeton), arrived in St. Croix early in 1772. He befriended Hamilton, tutored him, and shared his antipathy to slavery. Knox also discerned Hamilton's extraordinary abilities. In the literary form of a letter to his father, the young clerk penned a flowery account of a hurricane that devastated St. Croix at the end of August 1772. Its eloquence and piety so impressed Knox that he sent it to the local newspaper for publication.

His letters touch on nearly all the subjects covered in the curriculum of a modern business school.

Knox and Cruger, probably in concert, resolved that a lad of Hamilton's talents deserved a proper education on the mainland, and they sponsored his migration for that purpose. Hamilton's cousin Ann Lytton Venton also agreed to help. Thomas Stevens—father of Hamilton's friend Edward, already studying at King's College in New York—probably lent a hand as well.

THE COUNTRYSIDE OF ST. CROIX WITH FIELDS, PALM TREES, SUGAR MILLS, AND MOUNTAINS.

With letters of introduction from his St. Croix sponsors to their friends on the mainland and with financing arranged through Cornelius Kortright's New York–based mercantile firm, Hamilton set sail for America in October 1772. He landed in Boston later that month and made his way to New York City. He left behind—except as painful memories—the separations and divorces, desertions and abandonments, early deaths and suicides that had plagued his upbringing.

Alexander Hamilton was on his way to fame.

*Hamilton arrives
in America.*

Reverend Knox intended that Hamilton attend Elizabethtown Academy in New Jersey, a feeder school for Princeton, his Presbyterian alma mater. In New York, Hamilton met Hercules Mulligan, an Irish-born tailor. (Mulligan's brother worked in the Kortright firm that held and dispensed Hamilton's sponsorship funds.) The tailor and the former clerk soon became lifelong friends. When Hamilton applied to Princeton in 1773, Mulligan, who knew Princeton's president, John Witherspoon, accompanied him. Hamilton requested that Princeton allow him to proceed at his own pace. Princeton rejected his application.

Instead, Hamilton enrolled at King's College (now Columbia University), an Anglican school, staying with Mulligan's family part of the time while studying there. Knox had provided Hamilton with letters of introduction to William Livingston and Elias Boudinot, heads of prominent families who hosted the young man in Elizabethtown. Livingston later became the first American and longest-serving governor of New Jersey, and Boudinot served in both the confederation and federal congresses before President George Washington appointed him to direct the U.S. Mint.

At the Livingston and Boudinot homes, Hamilton converged with many current and future leaders of the country. Among them: Livingston's son, Brockholst (later a U.S. Supreme Court justice), and Livingston's son-in-law John Jay (later chief justice of the United States, among many other offices). But Hamilton knew his first duty was to learn, and he threw himself into his studies, qualifying for college in less than a year.

He threw himself into his studies, qualifying for college in less than a year.

He entered King's College in the fall of 1773 as a "private" student because the Princeton rejection came too late for him to start the academic year. Formal admission to King's came the following year. At first, he focused on becoming a physician, but he soon shifted his sights to a legal career, remaining at King's until late 1775 or early 1776.

Hamilton enters college.

Hamilton never graduated from King's College, although Columbia counts him among its most distinguished alumni. Instead, when the war that he so fervently wanted years earlier arrived in 1775—and even before it arrived—he threw himself into the revolutionary spirit then brewing, taking up the cause of American independence first as a pamphleteer, then as a soldier.

The infamous Boston Tea Party had taken place in December 1773, shortly after he started college. Protesting a tax on tea sold in the colonies along with an act that gave the British East India Company a virtual monopoly on colonial tea imports, a mob of Boston patriots calling themselves the Sons of Liberty and disguised as Mohawk Native Americans boarded three ships—the *Dartmouth, Eleanor*, and *Beaver*—carrying East India Company tea and threw it all into the harbor.

The Boston Tea Party.

Parliament responded to this affront in 1774 by passing legislation known as the

A MINIATURE OF
HAMILTON BY CHARLES
WILLSON PEALE.

War of pamphlets.

Coercive and Intolerable acts, which closed the port of Boston and suspended self-government in Massachusetts. Alarmed, other colonies implemented acts designed to boycott imports from Britain and sent representatives to what became known as the First Continental Congress. Held in Philadelphia in September 1774, that meeting further endorsed the boycotts and discussed other measures to protest British high-handedness.

To the British and their colonial supporters, the Continental Congress reeked of illegal republicanism. One of their number in New York, Reverend Samuel Seabury, wrote a pamphlet in November 1774 under the pseudonym "A. W. Farmer," castigating the Congress for endorsing the boycotts and countenancing the punishments threatened against violators. Americans were British subjects, said Seabury, so they had an obligation to obey the king and Parliament.

Hamilton, not quite eighteen years old, responded to Seabury the next month with a lengthy pamphlet titled "A Full Vindication of the Measures of Congress." In it, he argues that the British were violating "the natural rights of mankind" by enacting taxes and laws applicable to Americans without their consent. He contended that the British threatened to reduce Americans to slavery, and he repeated that theme over and over again, judiciously revealing his feelings about the institution.

Hamilton defended the boycotts because they would diversify the American economy by encouraging manufacturing and economic independence—goals he developed later in his career. More important, if the British mended their ways and redressed American grievances, war—the only alternative—could be avoided. But if war came, odds were that the Americans would win because "Our superiority in number would overbalance our inferiority in discipline."

Recognizing the power of Hamilton's essay, Seabury responded in January 1775 by merely repeating his argument that Americans had to obey king and Parliament. Protocol required petitioning for redress of their grievances. But of course the colonists had tried that already without much success.

THE SONS OF LIBERTY DUMP EAST INDIA COMPANY TEA FROM THE *DARTMOUTH*, *ELEANOR*, AND *BEAVER* IN THE BOSTON TEA PARTY ON DECEMBER 16, 1773.

The able Doctor, or America Swallowing the Bitter Draught.

Hamilton counterresponded with an even longer essay, "The Farmer Refuted." Once again, he founded his argument on the natural rights of mankind, one of which holds that a people must consent voluntarily to both the government and laws that bind them together. Anything less made them slaves. To Seabury's suggestion that Americans reread their colonial charters to refresh themselves of their obligations, Hamilton responded with mighty eloquence: "The sacred rights of mankind are not to be rummaged for, among old parchments or musty records. They are written, as with a sun beam, in whole *volume* of human nature, by the hand of the divinity itself; and can never be erased or obscured by mortal power."

But he still liked the odds if it came to war. The British had an army of professional soldiers at their disposal, true, but American patriotism and the right strategies could defeat them.

There is a certain enthusiasm in liberty that makes human nature rise above itself in acts of bravery and heroism.... The circumstances of our

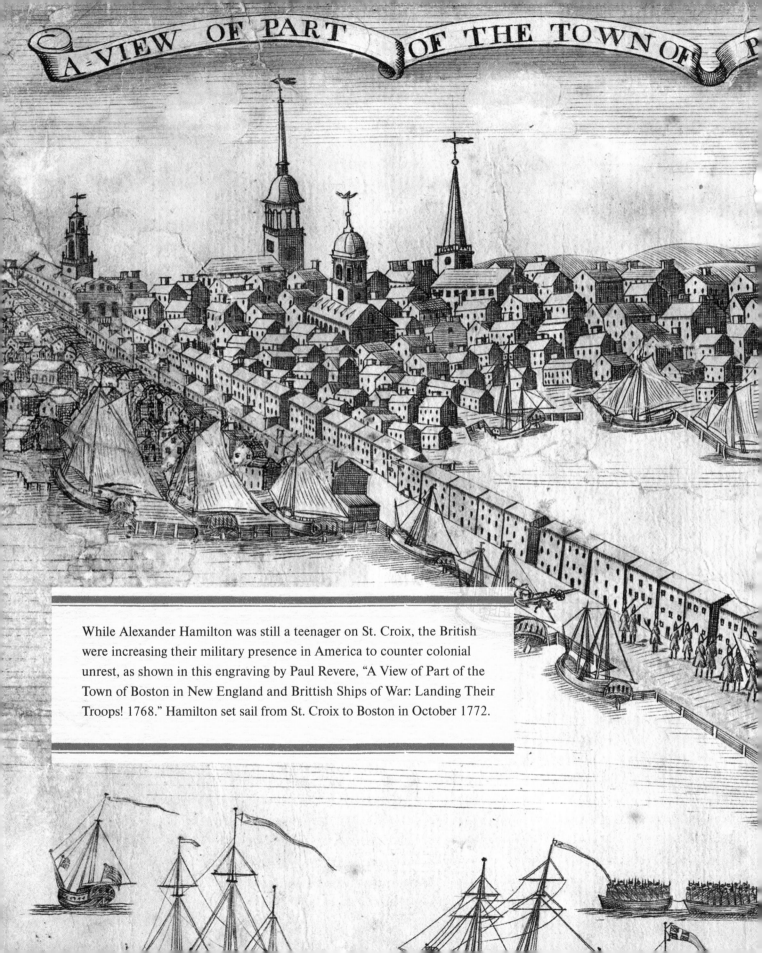

While Alexander Hamilton was still a teenager on St. Croix, the British were increasing their military presence in America to counter colonial unrest, as shown in this engraving by Paul Revere, "A View of Part of the Town of Boston in New England and Brittish Ships of War: Landing Their Troops! 1768." Hamilton set sail from St. Croix to Boston in October 1772.

On April 19, 1775, while Hamilton was studying at what is now Columbia University, shots rang out on Lexington Common in Massachusetts, triggering the American War of Independence.

PS ¦ OF WAR: LANDING THEIR TROOPS! 1768

A

FULL VINDICATION

OF THE

Meafures of the Congrefs,

FROM

The CALUMNIES of their ENEMIES;

IN ANSWER TO

A LETTER,

Under the Signature of

A. W. FARMER.

WHEREBY

His *Sophiftry* is expofed, his *Cavils* confuted, his *Artifices* detected, and his *Wit* ridiculed;

IN

A GENERAL ADDRESS

To the Inhabitants of America,

AND

A Particular Addrefs

To the FARMERS of the Province of New-York.

Veritas magna eft & prævalebit.
Truth is powerful, and will prevail.

NEW-YORK:
Printed by JAMES RIVINGTON. 1774.

"The sacred rights of mankind are not to be rummaged for, among old parchments or musty records. They are written, as with a sun beam, in whole volume of human nature, by the hand of the divinity itself; and can never be erased or obscured by mortal power."

HAMILTON'S
REBUTTAL TO
SEABURY'S REBUKE
OF COLONIAL
BOYCOTTS.

country put it in our power to evade a pitched battle. It will be better policy to harass and exhaust the soldiery by frequent skirmishes and incursions than to take the open field with them, by which means they would have the full benefit of their superior regularity and skill. Americans are better qualified for that kind of fighting which is most adapted to this country than regular troops.

He also noted that Britain's enemies, particularly France, would aid the American cause in their own interest. Barely eighteen years

Hamilton sagely predicted how the War of Independence unfolded over the following seven bloody years.

CHAPLAIN JACOB DUCHÉ LEADS THE FIRST PRAYER AT THE FIRST CONTINENTAL CONGRESS, IN PHILADELPHIA, SEPTEMBER 1774.

THE BATTLE OF LEXINGTON,
APRIL 19, 1775.

old, Hamilton sagely predicted how the War of Independence unfolded over the follow-ing seven bloody years.

The revolution begins.

Less than two months after his second essay appeared, the battles of Lexington and Concord in Massachusetts marked the start of the American Revolution, and events quickened. In May, a patriot mob thronged King's College to harm—perhaps even kill—the college's president, Dr. Myles Cooper, a loyalist like Samuel Seabury. Cooper had taught Hamilton, and, though Hamilton disliked Cooper's politics, he disliked mob rule

even more. So he stood in the college's doorway urging the mob to desist. The delay allowed another student to rouse Cooper and spirit him away.*

Around that same time, Hamilton ceased his studies and enlisted as a private in one of New York's nascent militia companies. He drilled and undertook other training. George Washington, recently named by Congress to command the Continental Army,

---

* Shortly afterward Cooper sailed for England.

came through New York on his way to Cambridge, Massachusetts, to take charge of American forces outside Boston. We don't know whether Hamilton saw or met him then, but a year later he stood with Washington's forces to defend New York City.

In August 1775, the *Asia*, a British warship, sailed into New York Harbor and threatened to seize or destroy the battery of cannons at the lower tip of Manhattan. Under fire from the *Asia*, Hamilton and others hauled the cannons to safety.

In January of the following year, New York's provincial government formed an artillery company. Hamilton, known to colony leaders from his pamphleteering, received the appointment to lead it with the rank of captain. He gathered enlistments of ninety men, studied the principles of artillery, and trained his company. By that summer they were ready for action—no matter what lay in store.

WASHINGTON IN
1775 AROUND THE
TIME HE TOOK
COMMAND OF THE
CONTINENTAL ARMY.

"That he is ambitious I shall readily grant, but it is of that laudable kind which prompts a man to excel in whatever he takes in hand."

—GEORGE WASHINGTON ON ALEXANDER HAMILTON, TO JOHN ADAMS, SEPTEMBER 25, 1798

{II}

SOLDIER

1775-1781

────────────◆◆◆────────────

Alexander Hamilton played a more important role in the War of American Independence than most people, including historians and other scholars, give him credit for. Some of this neglect happened understandably because his accomplishments as a soldier pale against his later achievements. He also served for much of the war as a staff officer rather than a line officer, the latter fighting principally on the front lines.

In between two brief stints as a line officer, Hamilton served for four years, from March 1777 to April 1781, as an aide de camp to the commander in chief, General George Washington. During those years, many—including Washington himself—came to recognize the young man as the general's primary aide de camp.

Washington counted him as one of his trusted military advisors and sent him on especially important missions. Early on, Washington discovered that he and Hamilton thought alike about the war and the world and that Hamilton could express in clear, elegant prose the general's ideas, messages, orders, and reports. When Hamilton joined Washington's staff in early 1777, the general had just turned forty-five. His young aide had just turned twenty. Their partnership lasted until Washington's death almost twenty-three years later, and that partnership did much to shape the early history of America and launch the country on its modern trajectory.

HAMILTON AND
WASHINGTON
MEET.   ★ ★ ★ ★ ★

GENERAL HOWE EVACUATES BRITISH
TROOPS FROM BOSTON, MARCH 1776.

*General
Washington
moves the
Continental
Army.*

While Captain Hamilton threw himself into organizing and training his New York State artillery company in the spring of 1776, General Washington had forced the British to retreat from Boston. They soon set their eyes on New York City, so Washington moved the Continental Army southwest. Hamilton's company came under the command of Henry Knox, Washington's artillery commander, and at this point Hamilton's name appears in orders that Washington issued.

As the heat of summer intensified, so did hostilities between the opposing sides. In late June and early July, more than a hundred British ships entered New York Harbor, landing some 30,000 troops on Staten Island. On July 2, 1776, the Second Continental Congress, which had assembled in Philadelphia, voted to declare independence from Britain; two days later the group formally adopted and issued the Declaration of Independence, having it printed and distributed throughout the new nation. John Hancock, president of the Second Continental Congress, sent a copy to Washington to share with his troops in New York City. Several days later, Washington ordered his men to assemble to hear the proclamation read. Provoked by the document, a mob of incensed

ALEXANDER HAMILTON

HENRY KNOX,
WASHINGTON'S
ARTILLERY COMMANDER,
BY CHARLES PEALE
POLK, AFTER CHARLES
WILLSON PEALE.

THE SONS OF LIBERTY
TOPPLE THE EQUESTRIAN
STATUE OF KING GEORGE III
AT BOWLING GREEN IN
MANHATTAN, JULY 1776.

HAMILTON IN THE UNIFORM OF THE NEW YORK ARTILLERY BY ALONZO CHAPPEL.

MINIATURE OF GEORGE
WASHINGTON BY CHARLES
WILLSON PEALE, C. 1775-76.

*The British build
up troops in
New York City.*

patriots toppled the statue of King George III on Bowling Green in lower Manhattan; its metal was melted and made into bullets. Several days later, Hamilton's company fired from the Battery on two British warships sailing up the Hudson—to little effect.

In late August, the British moved thousands of troops to Brooklyn, surrounding New York Harbor. They battered American forces there on August 27 and forced an American retreat from Brooklyn Heights across the East River to Manhattan on the night of August 29. The British attacked and landed forces in mid-Manhattan, above the city of that time, on September 15. That maneuver nearly trapped Hamilton's unit, still stationed to the

Aaron Burr led Hamilton's unit to safety.

AMERICAN FORCES RETREAT ACROSS GOWANUS CREEK IN THE BATTLE OF LONG ISLAND, AUGUST 1776.

ALEXANDER HAMILTON

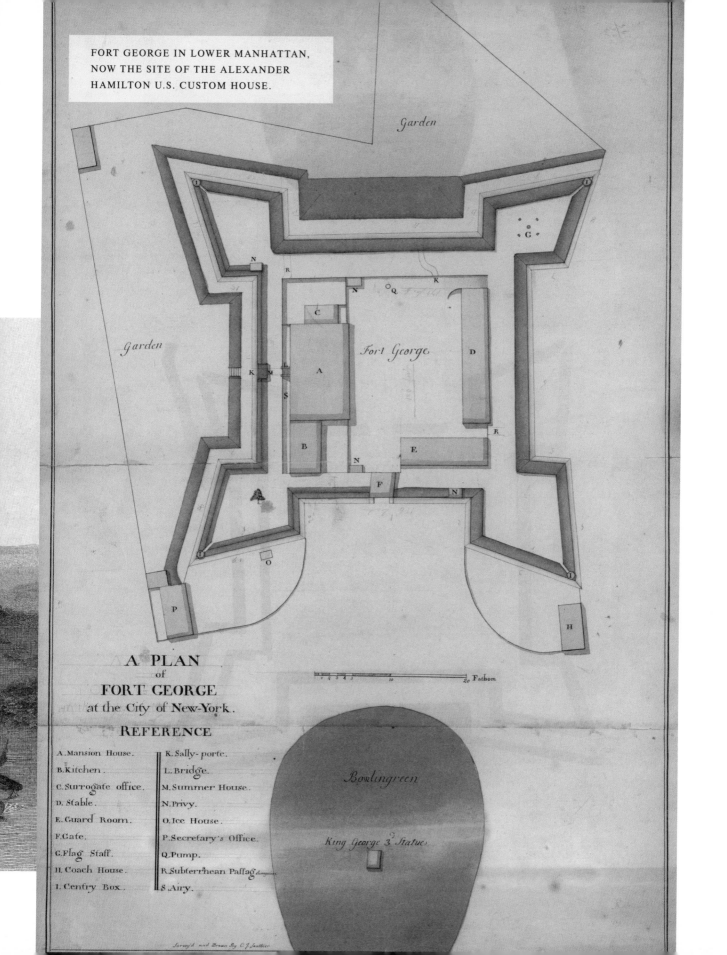

FORT GEORGE IN LOWER MANHATTAN,
NOW THE SITE OF THE ALEXANDER
HAMILTON U.S. CUSTOM HOUSE.

Garden

Garden

Fort George

A PLAN
of
FORT GEORGE
at the City of New-York.

REFERENCE

A. Mansion House.	K. Sally-porte.
B. Kitchen.	L. Bridge.
C. Surrogate office.	M. Summer House.
D. Stable.	N. Privy.
E. Guard Room.	O. Ice House.
F. Gate.	P. Secretary's Office.
G. Flag Staff.	Q. Pump.
H. Coach House.	R. Subterrhean Passag....
I. Centry Box.	S. Airy.

Bowlingreen

King George 3 Statue

Survey'd and Drawn By C. J. Sauthier.

south, but Aaron Burr led Hamilton's unit to safety by linking them up with the main force of the American army, which had retreated to Harlem Heights, in upper Manhattan. The British attacked Harlem Heights the next day, but the Americans held their ground.

The British tightened their stranglehold on New York City by landing additional forces in the Bronx on October 12. Increasingly in harm's way, Washington shifted most of his army, including Hamilton's unit, north to White Plains. He left units at Fort Washington, in what is now Manhattan's Washington Heights neighborhood, a strong defensive position. On October 28, the British attacked at Chatterton's Hill near White Plains. But Washington knew where the British would want to strike next. From the stronghold of New York City, they easily could invade New Jersey and advance south to the glittering prize of Philadelphia. Early that November, he moved his army across the Hudson, still leaving the units at Fort Washington, which the British captured on November 16 before crossing the Hudson, in swift pursuit.

The battles of New York in late 1776 proved disastrous for the American side. After them, the British controlled New York City until late 1783. More immediately, Washington found himself in a defensive, retreating position. Hamilton's artillery company allowed for Washington's successful retreat by delaying British forces from crossing the Raritan River at New Brunswick in New Jersey on December 1 as Washington moved the army farther south to Princeton. Hamilton's company followed.

As they marched through Princeton, the unit attracted attention. "It was a model of discipline," said one eyewitness. "At their head was a boy, and I wondered at his youth; but what was my surprise when, struck with his slight figure, he was pointed out to me as that Hamilton of whom we already had heard so much." Another described Hamilton as a "a mere stripling, small, slender, almost delicate in frame, marching beside a piece of artillery, with a cocked hat pulled down over his eyes, apparently lost in thought."

These delaying tactics—always staying just out of reach from the advancing British forces—allowed Washington's increasingly tattered army to escape across the Delaware

River into Pennsylvania. The British and their Hessian mercenaries were marching hot on American heels, but they hadn't been able to land a death blow that would have ended the American Revolution in December 1776.

Then Washington, showing his military genius, saved the American cause. In the middle of a fierce winter storm, he led his army across the Delaware on Christmas night to launch a surprise attack on a substantial force of Hessian mercenaries stationed at Trenton. On the morning of December 26, Henry Knox's artillery company helped rout the Hessians in the Battle of Trenton, a victory that captured 900 enemy soldiers and boosted American morale enormously.

Washington crosses the Delaware.

A week later, British general Charles Cornwallis led some 5,000 troops to Trenton. But American artillery halted their advance in the Battle of Assunpink Creek. That night, January 2, 1777, Washington executed another brilliant move by marching the

The Battle of Trenton.

THE PASSAGE OF THE DELAWARE BY THOMAS SULLY.

WASHINGTON ADVANCES TOWARD TRENTON ON DECEMBER 26, 1776. HAMILTON (FAR LEFT ON HORSE) AND HIS ARTILLERY COMPANY ARE CROSSING THE FOREGROUND OF THE PAINTING.

CHARLES CORNWALLIS
AFTER JOHN
SINGLETON COPLEY.

ALEXANDER HAMILTON

bulk of his forces to Princeton, where he surprised and defeated the British garrison the next day. Hamilton's artillery unit participated in the fighting, and the story goes that he exacted his revenge against the College of New Jersey by firing his guns at Nassau Hall, then occupied by British forces.

WASHINGTON RALLYING THE AMERICANS AT THE BATTLE OF PRINCETON BY WILLIAM TYLEE RANNEY.

WASHINGTON AND
THE CONTINENTAL
ARMY'S WINTER
ENCAMPMENT AT
MORRISTOWN,
NEW JERSEY.

*Hamilton becomes
Washington's
aide de camp.*

After the crucial victories at Trenton and Princeton, the Continental Army moved to their winter encampment in Morristown, New Jersey. Hamilton was recuperating from an illness in January 1777 when Washington sent him an invitation to join his "family" as an aide de camp. The American cause was re-energized; Washington knew he needed additional aides; and for some months he had been observing Hamilton's proficiency. Hamilton accepted the invitation in February and took up his new duties with a double promotion to lieutenant colonel around March 1. Long an outsider, Hamilton suddenly became an insider.

Hamilton suddenly became an insider.

The rest of the war unfolded slowly. Battles now came fewer and farther between—in part because, after Trenton and Princeton, the British developed a cool respect for American capabilities and a calculated cautiousness in dealing with them. But the Americans had adopted a Fabian strategy* of avoiding pitched battles, frontal assaults, and decisive battles that could be lost in favor of wearing down the enemy by harassment, skirmishes, and maintaining their ability to fight another day. In other words, the revolution became a war of attrition.

....
* The strategy takes its name from Fabius Maximus, a Roman consul and general who developed this tactic and employed it against Hannibal when the Carthaginian invaded Italy in the Second Punic War.

IN AUGUST 1777, BRITISH
GENERAL WILLIAM HOWE
SAILED INTO CHESAPEAKE
BAY IN ORDER TO
CAPTURE PHILADELPHIA.

Hamilton had recommended exactly this strategy in "The Farmer Refuted" back in 1775. After his forces faced near annihilation in the Battle of Brooklyn, Washington made it his strategy as well, but the tactic carried a major risk: Impatient military and political leaders would wonder why the army wasn't doing more to win the war and would question its leader's abilities.

In July and August 1777, Washington received critical intelligence that British general John Burgoyne, then in Quebec, was planning a southward invasion. The American general ordered some of his best commanders and forces to move northward to intercept the move. In August, General William Howe sailed from New York into Chesapeake Bay and landed some 17,000 British troops just fifty miles from Philadelphia, America's largest city and of course the seat of Congress. Washington's troops tried to stop the British advance at Brandywine Creek on September 11, 1777, but faulty intelligence about enemy positions forced them to retreat.

The Battle of Brandywine.

Now the British had a clear path to capture Philadelphia. A week after Brandywine, Washington assigned Hamilton and others to destroy flour mills along the Schuylkill River before the British could take them. British cavalry intercepted them, though, and the destruction party fled across the river. Seeing the potential for disaster that lay before them, Hamilton warned Congress to flee Philadelphia immediately, which the legislators did after planning to regroup in Lancaster, Pennsylvania.

The British take Philadelphia.

The British lingered, however, and didn't take Philadelphia until September 26. Before that happened, Washington put Hamilton in charge of a mission to confiscate provisions, blankets, horses, and other items useful to the Continental Army—or the enemy if not taken—from denizens of the city. The soldiers kept accounts of the seizures and issued receipts for them that later became part of the national debt. The Continental Army repeated this practice on numerous occasions, which shows how poorly supplied the American forces were during the revolution. These hugely unpopular seizures stoked Hamilton's thinking about public finance and military forces.

The Battle of Germantown.

The British now controlled Philadelphia. Washington had to act. After assigning Hamilton to draft the battle plan, Washington attacked one of their outposts north of the city at Germantown on the morning of October 4. But fog and stout defense of a stone house manned by the British delayed American troops from pursuing the retreating enemy long enough for reinforcements to arrive. Once again the Americans had to retreat.

The Battle of Saratoga.

But alongside the two defeats of Brandywine and Germantown came a great victory to the north. On September 19 and October 7, near Saratoga, New York, American forces commanded by General Horatio Gates defeated the British force led by General Burgoyne, who had marched south. He surrendered on October 17. That victory importantly convinced the French that the Americans actually could win the war, prompting them to provide substantial financial support, followed later by military and naval support. The tide finally had turned.

The tide finally had turned.

When Washington learned of the Saratoga victory in late October, he made plans to reinforce his main army with troops from Gates's northern army in order to face Howe in Philadelphia. He needed to regain the capital. Washington dispatched Hamilton north to deliver his orders to Gates and other commanders. Hamilton reached Albany by horseback on November 5. Along the way, he conveyed orders for several thousand militia and Continental troops around New York City to join Washington in Pennsylvania. But Gates resisted. In a draft of a letter to Washington, Gates complains: "I believe it is never practiced to Delegate that Dictatorial power to One Aid de Camp sent to an Army 300 Miles distant." Hamilton, not yet twenty-one years old, persisted, though, and proved himself a tough bargainer.

Hamilton gathers troops for Washington.

The young aide de camp had a similar experience with General Israel Putnam, also ordered to send reinforcements. Putnam delayed obeying and complained to Washington about Hamilton. The commander in chief backed his aide de camp, writing to him:

"I approve entirely of all the Steps you have taken and have only to wish that the exertions of those you have had to deal with had kept pace with your zeal and good intentions." Nevertheless, those unnecessary delays prevented Washington from striking further blows upon the British in Philadelphia before winter fell. The war therefore entered another bloody year of fighting.

Hamilton's exertions wore him down, and he became gravely ill in mid-November, spending several weeks in bed at Peekskill, New York. It took until late December for him to recover, at which point he set off to rejoin Washington at the army's winter encampment at Valley Forge, Pennsylvania.

What he found shocked him.

★ ★ ★ ★ ★

Hamilton arrived at Valley Forge on January 20, 1778. What he found shocked him. The army lacked basic necessities. Scenes of suffering and death played out everywhere. Men were deserting, and some feared mutinies. On his own and on Washington's behalf, Hamilton pleaded with various leaders for help. Otherwise the war might come to a swift end as the American army simply melted away.

Valley Forge.

WASHINGTON REVIEWING HIS TROOPS AT VALLEY FORGE.

But Washington was facing more than just severe conditions in a harsh winter. His recent defeats—Brandywine Creek and Germantown—combined with Gates's victory at Saratoga led a cabal of army officers and sympathetic members of Congress to consider replacing Washington with Gates as commander in chief. Washington fought back. He challenged the men who wanted to strip him of his powers to explain themselves. Working with Hamilton, he composed a long report in the form of a letter to a committee of Congress coming to Valley Forge to investigate conditions. This sixteen-thousand-word letter offered a systematic statement of what had to happen to carry on the war and make the American army more effective.

Washington defends his position.

The committee received the letter on January 29, meaning that Hamilton had written it in little more than a week. Historian Thomas Fleming has called it "nothing less than America's first great state paper." It duly impressed the members of the congressional committee, and the challengers to Washington's authority lost much ground.

Washington had to defend himself, but Congress was facing bigger problems than an ineffective military commander. Washington had repulsed the British at Boston, but he had lost New York City and Philadelphia, America's two most important northeastern cities. His efforts at Brandywine and Germantown had failed, and supporters could look

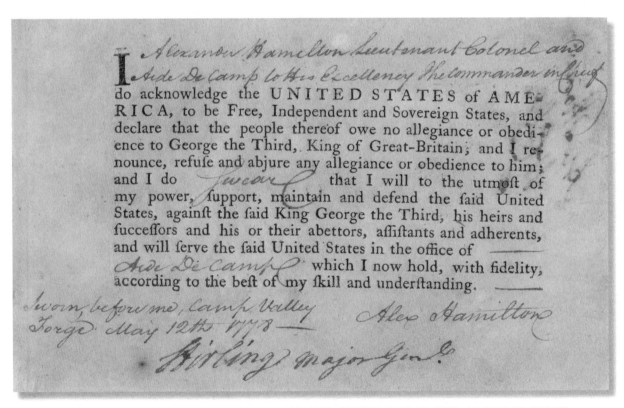

HAMILTON'S OATH OF ALLEGIANCE, SIGNED MAY 12, 1778, AT VALLEY FORGE.

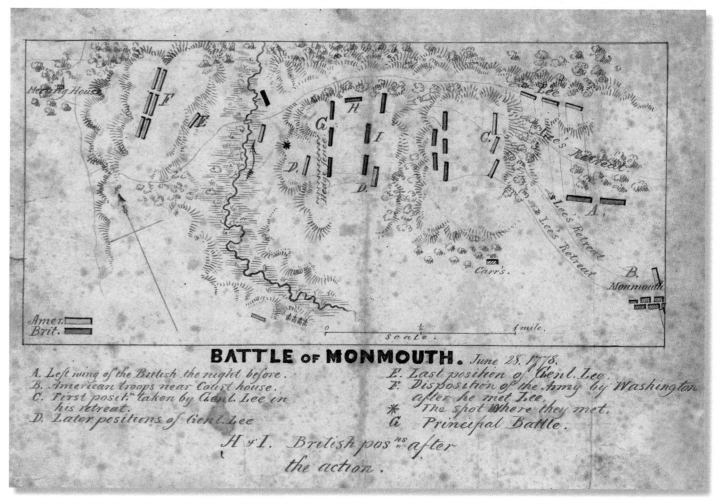

PLAN OF THE BATTLE OF MONMOUTH, JUNE 28, 1778.

only to Saratoga for a rallying point. It looked more than likely that the rebels would lose. In order to uproot and then neutralize loyalists, Congress issued an oath to be taken by officers and enlisted men in the army.

Further improvement came with the arrival of Baron Friedrich von Steuben at Valley Forge on February 23, 1778. Steuben, a former Prussian army officer, had volunteered his services to the fledgling nation. In March, Washington authorized him to drill the relatively undisciplined army on a daily basis. Steuben spoke no English, but he did speak French, as did Hamilton and a few other officers, so they translated his orders for the men.

Steuben got results, which paid dividends in the Battle of Monmouth on June 28, 1778. The British, now under the command of General Henry Clinton, who had replaced William Howe, departed Philadelphia and were marching across New Jersey

The Battle of Monmouth.

back to New York City. Washington attacked them near Monmouth Court House and sent General Charles Lee at the head of an advance party to delay the British advance while Washington gathered the main force for a full attack. After initiating contact with the enemy, Lee retreated. On hearing this, Hamilton raced to Lee's location to stop him. Hamilton's horse was shot out from under him, and he sustained serious injury in the fall. Washington took personal charge of the battle, and his newly disciplined troops inflicted serious damage on the enemy. Some considered it an American victory, but the remainder of the British army marched on to New York.

After the Battle of Monmouth, more than two years passed before another major engagement between the warring sides. In the interim, Washington focused on retaking New York City, which he believed would end the war. That feat required serious naval power, however, which the Americans lacked. But the French-American alliance had become official in 1778, offering an avenue of possibility because the French fleets rivaled those of Britain.

One such fleet sailing under the command of Charles Hector, comte d'Estaing, appeared off the coast of New Jersey in July 1778. Washington sent Hamilton to meet the French admiral, who deemed his ships too large to enter New York Harbor safely. Instead they sailed to Rhode Island and coordinated to attack British forces there in August. That plan went awry, though, when the French fleet suffered damage in a storm.

Washington made similar plans for a combined French-American operation to take New York by land and sea in 1779 and 1780. Hamilton again served as intermediary between Washington and his allies. But the French fleets never arrived, so plans were shelved. A French fleet did deliver several thousand men under General Jean-Baptiste de Vimeur, comte de Rochambeau, to Newport, Rhode Island, in mid-1780. Both in letters and in meetings, Hamilton coordinated much of the information between the American and French commanders.

The British undertake a southern campaign.

With New York City as their principal base of operations, the British grew increasingly frustrated at not being able to lure Washington into a decisive confrontation there. Changing tactics, they embarked on a southern campaign, sending fleets and troops to capture Savannah, Georgia, in December 1778 and Charleston,

THE COMTE DE
ROCHAMBEAU
REVIEWS HIS
TROOPS, 1780.

South Carolina, in May 1780. Over Washington's misgivings, Congress sent his rival, General Horatio Gates, to counter the southern strategy. With a smaller force, Cornwallis defeated Gates at the Battle of Camden, South Carolina, on August 16, 1780. Gates beat an ignominious retreat that ended his military career.

Washington dispatched Nathanael Greene to replace Gates as southern commander. American militias defeated loyalist forces at Kings Mountain in South Carolina in October, and Greene arrived in North Carolina in December. He sent Daniel Morgan to harass the British in South Carolina, and Morgan won a great victory at Cowpens, South Carolina, on January 17, 1781. Cornwallis chased Greene until they met at the Battle of Guilford Court House in North Carolina on the Ides of March, 1781. The British won the battle, but their victory was pyrrhic. Cornwallis moved his bloodied forces to the coast, winding up in Yorktown, Virginia, by late summer. Greene then retook most of the Carolinas from the British and American loyalists.

As the southern campaign unfolded, Washington continued harassing the British in New York City. He had Hamilton engage in several prisoner-exchange negotiations that achieved little success because the British still considered the Americans rebels rather than citizens of a sovereign nation. Hamilton used what free time he had to

*Benedict Arnold
betrays West Point.*

study and write letters and essays on various problems that he had encountered as a soldier.

The plan to take New York almost fell apart in September 1780, when General Benedict Arnold turned traitor. Arnold had a reputation as an accomplished battlefield commander, but Congress had granted commands that he wanted to others. He also bristled at allegations of corruption. Washington sympathized with Arnold's plight and in early August 1780 granted Arnold's request to take command of the fort at West Point, on the Hudson River north of New York City. Washington had no idea that Arnold only wanted the post so he could deliver it to the British in return for a reward. He tried to do just that in September by delivering the plans of the fort to a British officer, John André, who disguised himself in civilian clothing to pass through American lines of defense. But Americans captured André, who had stashed the plans in his boots, and soon executed him as a spy.

Arnold got wind of André's capture and fled to the British base in New York City just before Washington, Hamilton, the Marquis de Lafayette, and others, returning from a meeting with Rochambeau, arrived at West Point to meet with Arnold and inspect the fort. They quickly learned of Arnold's treason. Arnold joined the British army and soon wrought havoc on Virginia, which Cornwallis also hoped to vanquish, moving his own forces there in 1781 to join Arnold's.

While war scarred the new nation, Hamilton's private life underwent a dramatic change. In February 1780, with the army encamped for the winter at Morristown, Hamilton met Elizabeth Schuyler, daughter of General Philip Schuyler, an upstate New York landowner who had commanded the Northern Department of the Continental Army from 1775 to 1777. The couple charmed each other, and Hamilton soon asked for Elizabeth's hand in marriage. She consented, and they received her parents' permission.

Hamilton falls in love.

As the army's campaign season began, many love letters passed between the couple. In them, Hamilton refers to his fiancée as a "saucy little charmer," "little nut brown maid," "my angelic Betsey," "my sweetheart." He muses that "Love is a sort of insanity" and even asks her: "Do you soberly relish the pleasure of being a poor man's wife?" Her letters don't survive, but clearly she felt a similar passion for him. In June 1780, Hamilton wrote his friend John Laurens:

> *Next fall completes my doom. I give up my liberty to Miss Schuyler. She is a good hearted girl who I am sure will never play the termagant; though not a genius she has good sense enough to be agreeable, and though not a beauty, she has fine black eyes—is rather handsome and has every other requisite of the exterior to make a lover happy. And believe me, I am lover in earnest, though I do not speak of the perfections of my Mistress in the enthusiasm of Chivalry.*

The wedding took place at the Schuyler Mansion in Albany on December 14, 1780. Hamilton, age twenty-three, had a family of his own again for the first time in many years.

The marriage invigorated his ambitions. During his four years as Washington's aide de camp, he longed for a field command or other higher office. Others had recommended him for such appointments, but Washington needed the young man's knowledge, intelligence, and voice, so he never received any of the appointments. As Washington later wrote to John Adams, Hamilton's

opportunities, as the principal and most confidential aid of the Commander in chief, afforded him the means of viewing every thing on a larger scale than those whose attentions were confined to Divisions and Brigades, who knew nothing of the correspondences of the Commander in Chief, or of the various orders to, or transactions with, the General Staff of the Army. . . . That he is ambitious I shall readily grant, but it is of that laudable kind which prompts a man to excel in whatever he takes in hand. He is enterprising, quick in his perceptions, and his judgment intuitively great: qualities essential to a Military character.

Hamilton's "foreignness" and dubious background also didn't help his cause—an irony considering the trajectory of his close friend Gilbert du Motier, Marquis de Lafayette, roughly the same age.

The wealthy French nobleman hailed from a family with long military traditions, became captivated by the American revolt, and then joined it. He paid for the ship that brought him and other French volunteer officers to America in 1777. In gratitude, Congress appointed him—at age nineteen!—to the rank of major general. It may have been intended as an honorary appointment, but Lafayette took up arms and fought in the battles of Brandywine and Monmouth, and he too became one of Washington's favorites. In 1781, Washington sent Lafayette to Virginia to counter Arnold's havoc there. An outsider like Hamilton, Lafayette had risen to great heights in the Continental Army because of his noble birth, wealth, and formal military training. The equally if not more talented Hamilton remained a staff officer.

Hamilton leaves Washington's side.

But Hamilton was watching carefully for an opportunity. It came in February 1781 after he and his wife, Betsy, had returned to headquarters at New Windsor, New York. Passing Hamilton on the stairs, Washington asked to speak to him, and Hamilton replied that he would as soon as he delivered the letter in his hand to another aide. On his way back, Lafayette stopped Hamilton for a brief conversation—whereupon Washington accused Hamilton of keeping him waiting and disrespecting him. Hamilton replied: "I

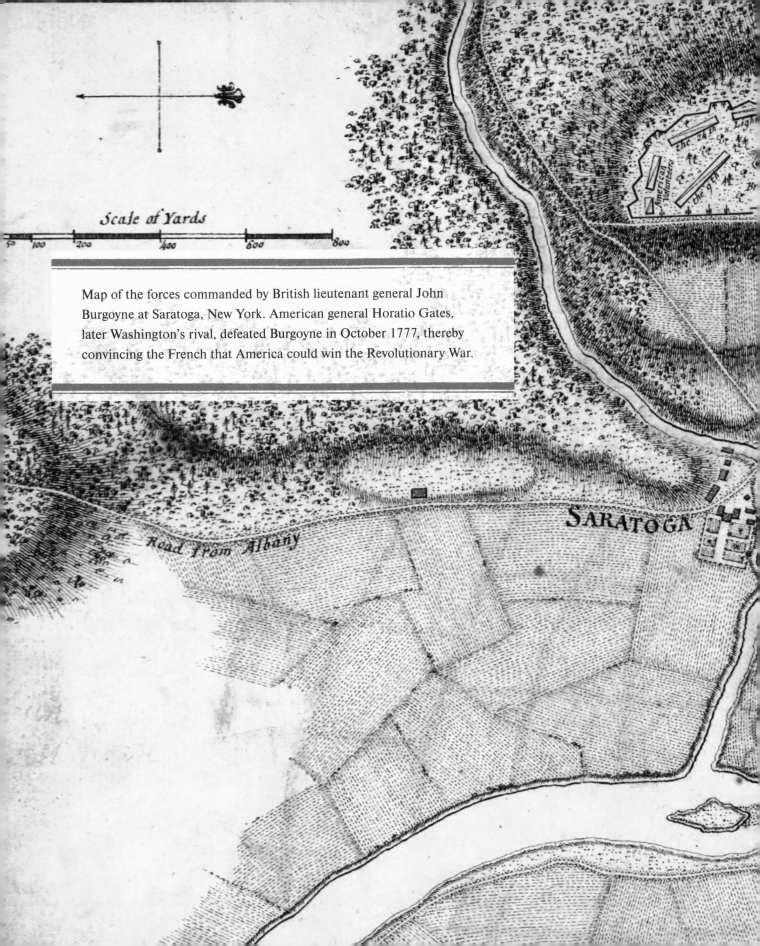

Scale of Yards

50 100   200   400   600   800

Map of the forces commanded by British lieutenant general John Burgoyne at Saratoga, New York. American general Horatio Gates, later Washington's rival, defeated Burgoyne in October 1777, thereby convincing the French that America could win the Revolutionary War.

Road from Albany

SARATOGA

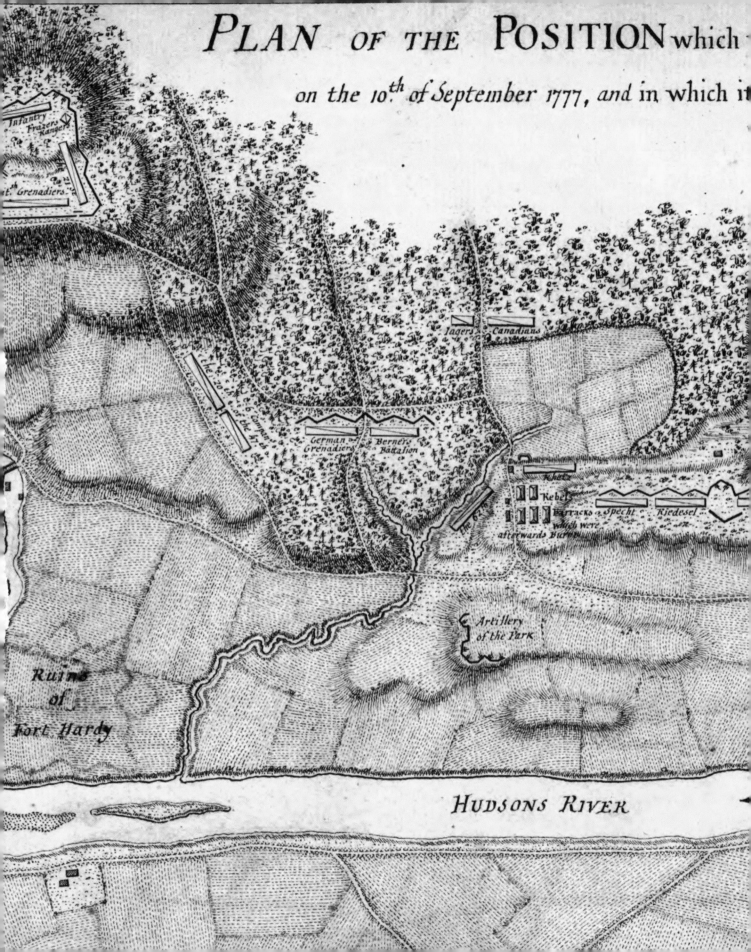

Infantry
Frazers Rangers

Grenadiers

Jagers   Canadians

German
Grenadiers   Berner
Battalion

Rebel
Barracks   Specht   Riedesel
which were
afterwards Burnt

Artillery
of the Park

Ruins
of
Fort Hardy

HUDSONS RIVER

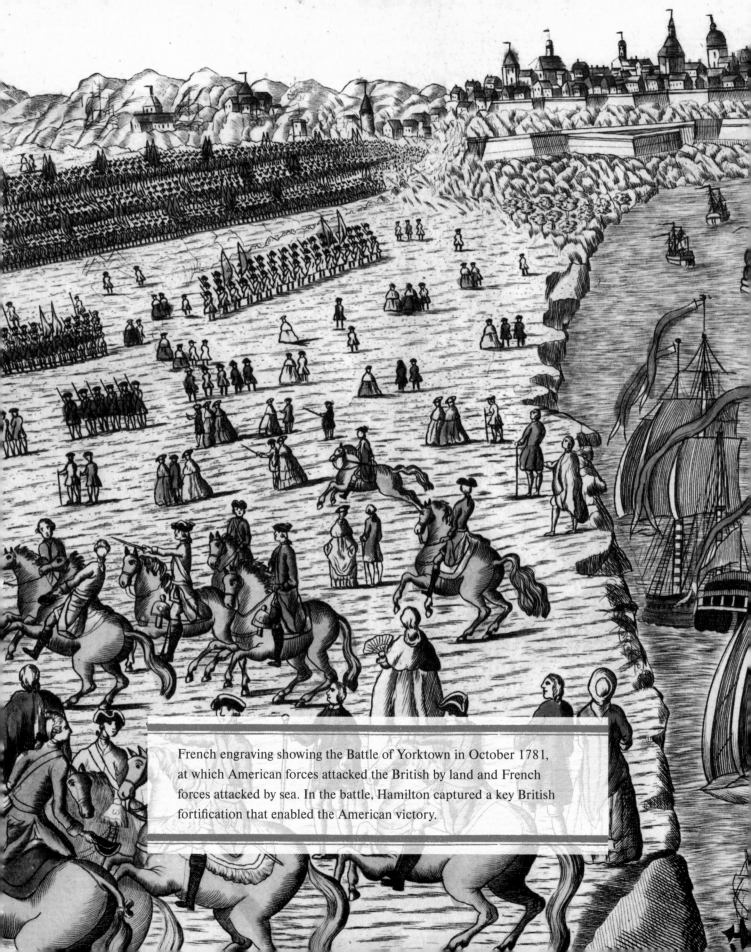

French engraving showing the Battle of Yorktown in October 1781, at which American forces attacked the British by land and French forces attacked by sea. In the battle, Hamilton captured a key British fortification that enabled the American victory.

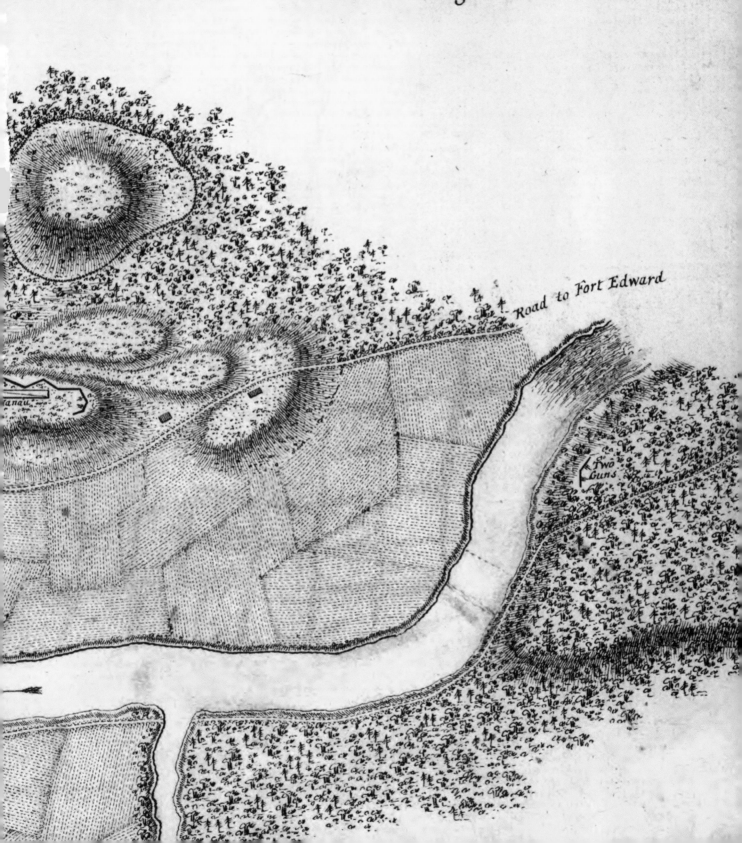

he ARMY under L.ᵗ GEN.ˡ BURGOYNE took at SARATOGA,

remained till THE CONVENTION was signed

ELIZABETH SCHUYLER
HAMILTON BY RALPH
EARLE, 1787.

am not conscious of it, sir; but since you have thought it necessary to tell me so, we part."

Hamilton resigned. He remained on staff for more than two months, however, until Washington found a suitable replacement. In May, Hamilton entered the regular army, and at the end of July he obtained the line command of a light infantry battalion.

In mid-August, Washington learned that Admiral François de Grasse's French fleet was moving from the Caribbean to Chesapeake Bay. At the same time, Cornwallis, following orders from General Clinton in New York, was building a defensive position at Yorktown, Virginia. The opportunity that Washington had wanted was presenting itself: a French fleet blocking British relief or escape and combined American and French forces to crush them on land. The only change in plan? The showdown would take place at Yorktown rather than New York City.

The French fleet arrived at the mouth of Chesapeake Bay and prevented British attempts to evacuate Cornwallis's army. Washington and Rochambeau sailed and marched their armies to Virginia to surround Yorktown. From late September to mid-October, the opposing forces skirmished and traded bombardments. The British drew in their lines.

By October 14, all that remained to make the British position totally untenable was capturing two redoubts, or outer fortifications, standing in the way of the American and French artillery. That night, under the command of Lafayette, French forces crept out to capture one of the redoubts. Hamilton's battalion went after the other. Hamilton led several hundred soldiers with unloaded bayonet rifles—to avoid an accidental discharge that might betray their actions—to the fortification, which they stormed and took in a matter of minutes. The French took a bit longer but also accomplished their mission.

The Americans and French moved their artillery forward, which began heavy bombardments on October 15. On the night of the 16th, Cornwallis tried a last-gasp measure to save his army, ferrying them across the York River to Gloucester, from where they might escape. But bad weather scotched their plan.

On the morning of the 17th, the British waved a white flag and entered negotiations to surrender. Parties from both sides signed the articles of capitulation on October 19, and that afternoon the British marched out and laid down their weapons. Capturing the redoubts had played a crucial role in winning the Battle of Yorktown. Hamilton finally achieved the military glory that he craved.

"I am not conscious of it, sir; but since you have thought it necessary to tell me so, we part."

The Battle of Yorktown.

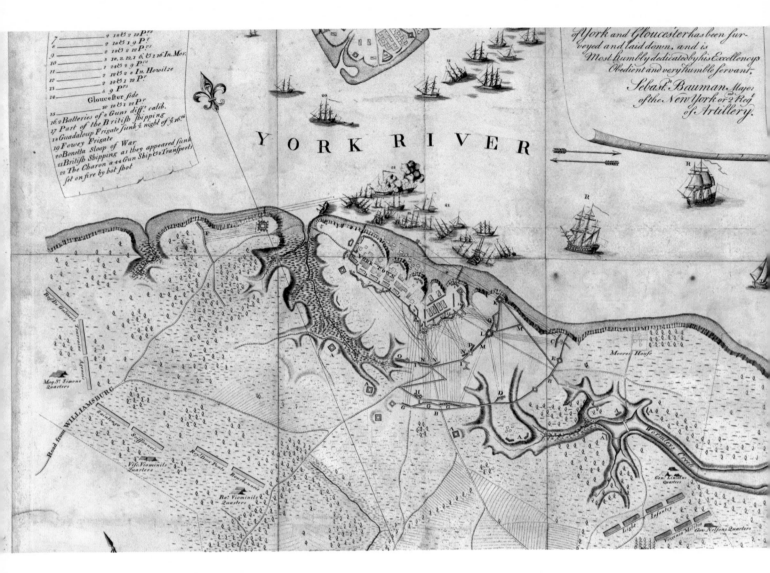

PLAN OF THE BATTLE OF YORKTOWN.

Cornwallis's surrender came six and a half years after those famous shots rang out in Lexington and Concord. Yorktown marked the last significant land battle of the war, but of course no one knew that at the time. Washington returned the Continental Army to the north and held it outside New York City for another eighteen months until news of a preliminary peace treaty reached American shores.

Shortly after Cornwallis surrendered in Virginia, Hamilton,

SURRENDER OF LORD CORNWALLIS BY JOHN TRUMBULL. CORNWALLIS
DIDN'T ATTEND THE CEREMONY, SO WASHINGTON REMAINS IN
THE BACKGROUND ON THE BROWN HORSE TO THE CENTER RIGHT.
HAMILTON IS THE FOURTH MAN STANDING FROM THE RIGHT.

ever the cunning strategist, seems to have foreseen that operationally the war had ended.
He resigned from the army and returned to his pregnant wife in Albany. Their first child,
Philip, named for his Schuyler grandfather, was born on January 22, 1782. By that time
Hamilton had turned his sights back to the law.

"Our whole system is in disorder."

—ALEXANDER HAMILTON, AUGUST 9, 1781

{III}

REFORMER

1780-1782

No significant battles took place between Monmouth in the summer of 1778 and Yorktown in the fall of 1781. This lack of action along with British military successes in the southern states proved frustrating to the American cause. But the cloud had a silver lining.

It gave Hamilton time to study politics, economics, and finance, which allowed him to formulate solutions to the challenges of building a new nation. He shared his thoughts with national leaders in three long letters written between winter 1779 and spring 1781. Then he went public with his ideas by writing six newspaper essays collectively called *The Continentalist*. These writings foreshadowed his actions as a constitutional reformer in the 1780s and as secretary of the Treasury in the 1790s. They established his agenda, which in turn became the nation's agenda in the last two decades of the eighteenth century.

★ ★ ★ ★ ★

Financial history shows that the medieval and Renaissance Italian city-states—republics with representative governments rather than monarchies—first implemented the key components of modern finance. Those city-states became very prosperous as a result. Indeed, the English word *bank* derives from the Italian *banco*, a bench or small table, on which those first bankers opened their account books of deposits and loans.

The Italians may have set the wheels in motion, but the Dutch Republic aligned all the vital mechanisms, which gives it the distinction of developing the world's first

A short course in political and financial history.

Italian city-states.

The Dutch Republic.

WASHINGTON CONSULTS
WITH MORRIS AND HAMILTON
IN NEW YORK CITY.

SCENE FROM A COUNTING HOUSE IN
GENOA, LATE FOURTEENTH CENTURY.

modern economy. The Dutch established public borrowing and debt securities in the late 1500s to finance their war of independence from Spain. The Dutch East India Company formed in 1602 and issued tradable shares in 1609, the same year that the Bank of Amsterdam and the Amsterdam Stock Exchange opened for business. The Dutch had bankers, called *kassiers* (cashiers), and a stable currency in the Dutch guilder. As a result, the Netherlands experienced enormous prosperity in the seventeenth century, the Dutch Golden Age.

England. The English spent most of that century envying the Dutch, to whom they paid the ultimate compliment in the Glorious Revolution of 1688. Parliament deposed King James II and invited the Dutch head of state, Prince Willem III of Orange, to rule England as King William III. For England, the change marked the definitive transition from the divine right of kings to a constitutional monarchy with power shared between monarch and Parliament. Almost a century later, in this political structure, the British government resisted yielding absolute control of its colonies in North America.

William III brought Dutch finance to England, and the British (after the union of England and Scotland in 1707) added to it. They borrowed money to fight their seemingly endless wars with France, and Parliament levied taxes to assure the bondholders. The Bank of England, a private corporation with more powers than the publicly owned Bank of Amsterdam, had formed in 1694 to finance the government and manage the national debt. The English reformed and stabilized the pound sterling. Securities markets emerged to trade government debt and corporate shares. This financial revolution, an

KING WILLIAM III BY
GODFREY KNELLER, 1680.

improvement on what the Dutch had achieved a century earlier, helped Britain win every one of its wars with France from 1688 to 1815. It also laid the groundwork for the Industrial Revolution, which clanked into gear in the latter half of the eighteenth century, and it eventually created an empire on which the sun never set. You can see a pattern emerging: Modern financial systems lead to national power and economic growth.

France in turn tried to emulate the British. In 1715, John Law, a financially astute Scot, convinced Philippe d'Orléans, regent of France for King Louis XV, that he could modernize France's financial system along Dutch and British lines. But after a promising start, Law made mistakes, and his efforts failed catastrophically in what became known as the Mississippi Bubble, which burst in 1720. As a result, France had to wait until the nineteenth century to enjoy the benefits of modern financial success.

Isolating the main ingredients of success in the Anglo-Dutch model generates four points that also apply to other successful nations:

The financial revolution helped Britain win every one of its wars with France from 1688 to 1815.

- Political systems and governments establish the rule of law and commit to economic growth and prosperity for all.

- Financial systems provide money and credit for governments, businesses, and individuals.

- Entrepreneurs have access to that financing.

- Managerial capabilities develop to run the new enterprises.

Imagine the four points like a baseball diamond: Home plate represents good government. First base becomes an effective financial system. Round second with entrepreneurs having the capital to build their enterprises, which then creates a need for management to run them on third base—all of which score the home run of sustained economic growth.

"JOHN LAW
AS A SECOND
DON QUIXOTE"
BY ANTOINE
HUMBLOT, 1720.

Now zoom in on the financial systems corner of the diamond, which breaks down into six crucial pillars:

- Strong public finances and effective management of public debt.

- Stable currency, a standard of deferred payment, and a store of value.

- A central bank to control and serve the financial system and act as the government's banker.

- A system to provide bank money (deposits on which checks can be written and currency notes) and to provide loans to businesses and individuals.

- Securities markets to initiate and trade bonds issued by governments and stocks and bonds issued by businesses.

- Corporations, which allow individuals to pool resources to create large, legally recognized, perpetual organizations with limited personal liability to make owning corporate shares attractive to investors.

Hamilton mastered this short course in political and financial history on his own during that lull in the revolution between 1778 and 1781. With a better government and modern financial institutions, he realized, the U.S. government would become strong and the American economy would grow.

The Italians, Dutch, and British had stumbled into or copied the right set of institutions that gave them power and prosperity. Always in a hurry, Hamilton worked hard over the next fifteen years to accomplish in America the reforms that took the Europeans decades—even centuries—to execute. In other words, he became the world's first statesman to comprehend all the necessary facets of sustained economic growth and put them into play.

He became the world's first statesman to comprehend all the necessary facets of sustained economic growth and put them into play.

★ ★ ★ ★ ★

By 1781, the Revolutionary War had dragged on for five grueling years. Congress's Continental Currency—first issued in 1775 and issued to excess by 1779—was quickly becoming worthless. Congress pegged these "Continentals" one-to-one to the Spanish

The Continental Currency Crash.

peso . . . but never indicated when that redemption might happen. Congress didn't have enough Spanish dollars—as the pesos generally were called in the English-speaking world—to redeem the Continentals they had printed, so the money swiftly morphed into a fiat currency that hemorrhaged value.

When Hamilton wrote his first surviving letter on finance in late 1779 or early 1780, he noted that it took 20 paper dollars to buy 1 silver dollar.* In March 1780, Congress revalued the Continentals at a rate of 40 paper to 1 silver. A year later, that rate was plummeting to 100 to 1.

The power to tax.

Individual states also issued paper currencies, which did little better. Unlike the Confederation Congress, the states could levy taxes. In fact, they were *supposed* to do that to meet their own fiscal needs as well as Congress's national needs—mainly financing the war at this point. State taxes were supposed to support the value of paper currencies, their own and the Continentals, by making them acceptable for tax payments. But state taxes and revenues collected proved woefully inadequate. It turns out that Americans didn't like taxation with representation any more than they liked taxation without representation.

> *Americans didn't like taxation with representation any more than they liked taxation without representation.*

Borrowing, an alternative to taxation and printing money, proved difficult both at home and abroad. Hyperinflation undermined lender confidence. After all, rebel governments demonstrating fiscal irresponsibility tend not to have good credit!

First letter.

Hamilton's first letter notes that prices were rising much faster than the quantity of paper money that Congress and the states were issuing. He had stumbled onto the modern concept of the velocity of money, or how fast people spend it. Rising inflation makes people realize that money is declining in value, so they spend it as fast as they can before prices rise further. It's all well and good to note the behavior, but Hamilton wisely turned to solutions: "The most opulent states of Europe in a war of any duration are commonly obliged to have recourse to foreign loans and subsidies. How then could we expect to do without them." In other words, Congress needed cash from abroad. That much was obvious, but how to shore up the nation's finances with that loan?

> *The only plan that can preserve the currency is one that will make it the immediate interest of the monied men to cooperate with the government*

* We know neither the exact date nor the addressee—likely a member of Congress—of this letter. Only the draft of the letter exists in the Hamilton Papers at the Library of Congress.

TIN PATTERN FOR A SILVER DOLLAR PLANNED
BY THE CONTINENTAL CONGRESS, 1776.

$3 CONTINENTAL CURRENCY NOTE, 1776.

in its support. This country is in the same predicament in which France was previous to the famous Mississippi scheme projected by Mr. Law. Its paper money like ours had dwindled to nothing, and no efforts of the government could revive it, because the people had lost all confidence in its ability. Mr. Law who had much more penetration than integrity readily perceived that no plan could succeed which did not unite the interest and credit of rich individuals with those of the state; and upon this he framed the idea of his project, which so far agreed in principle with the bank of England. The foundation was good but the superstructure too vast. The proprietors aimed at unlimited wealth and the government itself expected too much; which was the cause of the ultimate miscarriage of the scheme and of all the mischiefs that befell the Kingdom in consequence.

It will be our wisdom to select what is good in this plan and in others that have gone before us, avoiding their defects and excesses. Something on a similar principle in America will alone accomplish the restoration of paper credit, and establish a permanent fund for the future exigencies of government.

The principles of modern finance.

Article 1st The plan I would propose is that of an American bank, instituted by authority of Congress for ten years under the denomination of The Bank of the United States.

2d A foreign loan makes a necessary part of the plan, but this I am persuaded we can obtain if we persue proper measures. I shall propose it to amount to 2000000 £ Sterling. This loan to be thrown into the Bank as part of its stock.

3 A subscription to be opened for 200.000.000 of dollars and the subscribers erected into a company called the company of the Bank of the United States.

This is an amazing statement for several reasons. Hamilton was an American military officer and just twenty-three years old when he wrote the above. He had never been to Europe, and he never went there, yet he knew a great deal about European financial affairs. He also mentions the Bank of the United States by name, an institution that he created more than a decade later as secretary of the Treasury. This letter also touches on most of the key elements of a modern financial system.

So where did Hamilton find the example on which he based his ideas? Compare what he says above with this:

Political writers upon the affairs of France at this period... abundantly certify the incredible advantage produced by the operations of Mr. Law's bank; and the chain of events which followed, in the years 1719, and 1720... shew to what prodigious height credit arose upon the firm foundation laid by Mr. Law.

But alas! The superstructure, then, became so far beyond the proportion of the foundation, that the whole fabric fell to ruin, and involved a nation, just emerging from bankruptcy and ruin, into new calamities, almost equal to the former.

Note in particular the sentence that contains the words "superstructure" and "foundation" and the similar descriptions and interpretations of the Mississippi Bubble. The latter quote comes from James Steuart's *An Inquiry into the Principles of Political Oeconomy*, published in London in 1767. Hamilton owned a copy of Steuart's book* and clearly knew the work, a point that many Hamilton scholars have missed. From this comparison and many other similar ones, we discover that Hamilton used Steuart as the main source of his early economic and financial knowledge.

The shadow of James Steuart.

Hamilton's proposal to use a foreign loan to capitalize the Bank of the United States also included establishing a sound currency to replace the discredited Continentals and state-issued paper currencies. The bank would issue an entirely new currency convertible into specie, or coin money. With this new money, confidence would rise. Private investors would augment the bank's capital and share in its profits with the government, and the bank would lend to both the government and individuals. "We may therefore by means of this establishment carry on the war three years," Hamilton noted. A public authority would review the bank's books, and Congress wouldn't grant it exclusive privileges that might "fetter the spirit of enterprise and competition on which the prosperity of commerce depends."

Plan for the Bank of the United States.

Significantly, this new bank—really a central banking corporation—wouldn't have monopoly privileges, leaving the door open to form more banks and a fully fledged banking system. The only financial pillar that Hamilton didn't mention was a securities market to trade the bank's stock and government debt to increase the liquidity of both, an idea that became part of his grand plan a decade later.

★ ★ ★ ★ ★

---

* Donated by his descendant Alexander Hamilton III to Columbia University in 1955.

AN
INQUIRY
INTO THE
PRINCIPLES OF POLITICAL OECONOMY:
BEING AN,
ESSAY ON THE SCIENCE
OF
Domeſtic Policy in Free Nations.

IN WHICH ARE PARTICULARLY CONSIDERED

POPULATION, AGRICULTURE, TRADE, INDUSTRY,
MONEY, COIN, INTEREST, CIRCULATION, BANKS,
EXCHANGE, PUBLIC CREDIT, AND TAXES.

By Sir JAMES STEUART, Bart.

Ore trahit quodcumque poteſt atque addit acervo.   Hor. Lib. 1. Sat. 1.

IN TWO VOLUMES.

VOL. I.

LONDON:
Printed for A. Millar, and T. Cadell, in the Strand.
MDCCLXVII.

Second letter.

Hamilton's second essay, dated September 3, 1780, tackled the problem of the inadequacies of the American government. He addressed it to James Duane, a New York delegate to Congress, who, according to the letter, had asked him for his "ideas of the defects of our present system, and the changes necessary to save us from ruin." Clearly the nation's founding fathers realized the country was off to a floundering start. In this letter, Hamilton's theories of political economy advance to a higher level. The fundamental problem was this: The national government, lacking the power to tax, therefore lacked the strength and means to meet public needs. The government needed to have the power of the purse:

The government needed to have the power of the purse.

OPPOSITE: THE TITLE PAGE OF STEUART'S
INQUIRY, WHICH INFLUENCED HAMILTON'S
THINKING ON POLITICAL ECONOMICS.

The confederation . . . gives the power of the purse too intirely to the state legislatures. It should provide perpetual funds in the disposal of Congress. . . . All imposts [tariffs] upon commerce ought to be laid by Congress and appropriated to their use, for without certain revenues, a government can have no power; that power, which holds the purse strings absolutely, must rule.

Hamilton outlined two possible remedies. First, he contended that Congress, having declared American independence and considering itself the new nation's government, ought to act like a sovereign government and assert its powers. But Congress was "too timid and indecisive in their resolutions, constantly making concessions to the states, till they have scarcely left themselves with the shadow of power."

Hamilton calls for a constitutional convention.

Hamilton's second, more realistic solution was for Congress to call "immediately a convention of all the states with full authority to conclude finally upon a general confederation, stating to them beforehand explicitly the evils arising from a want of power in Congress, and the impossibility of supporting the contest on its present footing." This was the first call by any U.S. leader for a constitutional convention.*

Hamilton elaborated in his letter to Duane on the appropriate power of Congress:

Congress should have complete sovereignty in all that relates to war, peace, trade, finance, and to the management of foreign affairs, the right of declaring war of raising armies, officering, paying them, directing their motions in every respect, of equipping fleets and doing the same with them, of building fortifications arsenals magazines &c. &c., of making peace on such conditions as they think proper, of regulating trade, determining with what countries it shall be carried on, granting indulgences, laying prohibitions on all the articles of export or import, imposing duties granting bounties & premiums for raising exporting or importing and applying to their own use the product of those duties, only giving credit to the states on whom they are raised in the general account of revenues and expences, instituting Admiralty courts &c., of coining money, establishing banks on such terms, and with such privileges as they think proper, appropriating funds and doing whatever else relates to the operations of finance, transacting everything

....
* After the Annapolis Convention of 1786, at which Hamilton served as a delegate and for which he wrote the report, Congress issued the call for the Constitutional Convention, which took place in Philadelphia in 1787.

with foreign nations, making alliances offensive and defensive, treaties of commerce, &c.

Compare the above passage with the Constitution, which specifies the powers of Congress, and you'll find considerable overlap. In fact, the only points missing are those covering post offices and roads, authors' and inventors' rights, where the seat of the federal government might lie, a "necessary and proper" clause, and the establishment of a national bank. Otherwise, Hamilton's letter functionally becomes Article I, Section 8 of the Constitution.

The powers of Congress.

★ ★ ★ ★ ★

Then it happened. The Continental currency collapsed. In response, Congress appointed Robert Morris, one of the country's leading merchants and patriots, as superintendent of finance. Shortly thereafter, Hamilton sent his third essay to Morris in April 1781. Hamilton wrote the letter as he was transitioning from Washington's aide to his field command in the army. He stressed the importance of finance to the revolution: "Tis by introducing order into our finances—by restoring public credit—not by gaining battles, that we are finally to gain our object." Then he shared some ideas he had on financial administration.

Third letter.

First he estimated the revenue capacity of the country, comparing it with an estimate of necessary civil and military expenses. No great shock: The latter greatly exceeded the former, leaving a deficit. Foreign loans might help, but they certainly couldn't heal the shortfall. Hamilton's solution once again was a national bank. He discussed the pros and cons of national banks in theory and in history, including how banking development and the expansion of credit promoted both state power and economic growth:

The national deficit.

The tendency of a national bank is to increase public and private credit. The former gives power to the state for the protection of its rights and interests, and the latter facilitates and extends the operations of commerce among individuals. Industry is increased, commodities are multiplied, agriculture and manufactures flourish, and herein consist the true wealth and prosperity of a state.

Hamilton's letter functionally becomes Article I, Section 8 of the Constitution.

Most commercial nations have found it necessary to institute banks and they have proved to be the happiest engines that ever were invented for advancing trade. Venice Genoa Hamburgh Holland and England are examples of their utility. They owe their riches, commerce, and the figure they have made at different periods in a great measure to this source. Great Britain is indebted for the immense efforts she has been able to make in so many illustrious and successful wars essentially to that vast fabric of credit raise on this foundation. 'Tis by this alone she now menaces our independence.

In this letter, Hamilton had figured out why the war had dragged on for so long: The British were better financed and had better credit. This point underscored his plan to make better finance and a credit-based economy one of the cornerstones of American power.

The rest of Hamilton's letter consists mostly of articles that comprise the national bank's charter and a discussion of same. The bank would be a corporation, for example, which seemed so obvious to Hamilton and to a businessman such as Morris that it "needs no discussion"—although in America, as elsewhere, few corporations existed then.

The letter ends with a brief look at the national debt once the war ended. It wouldn't pose a problem, Hamilton said, because good financial administration and the country's growth would enable America to pay the debt in a matter of decades. In fact, the debt had benefits:

The national debt.

A national debt if it is not excessive will be to us a national blessing; it will be a powerfull cement of our union. It will also create a necessity for keeping up taxation to a degree which without being oppressive, will be a spur to industry. . . . We labor less now than any civilized nation of Europe, and a habit of labour in the people is as essential to the health and vigor of their minds and bodies as it is conducive to the welfare of the State. We ought not to Suffer our self-love to deceive us in a comparison upon these points.

Here we catch a glimpse of one reason that Hamilton later became the least loved of the founders. He spoke his mind frankly, in this case saying that he didn't think

ROBERT MORRIS, THE SUPERINTENDENT
OF FINANCE FOR CONGRESS.

He didn't think Americans worked very hard.

The Bank of North America.

Americans worked very hard. If they had to pay taxes to service the national debt incurred as the price of their liberty, they would have an incentive to work harder. To Hamilton, that was good for them and the country regardless of whether they liked it.

The letter to Morris was a private communication, but it shows the same candor that marks Hamilton's public speeches and writings. His often polemical public work, whether over his own name or various pseudonyms, provoked strong reactions—both favorable and unfavorable. The other founders paid greater heed to what they said and wrote as it affected their public images. This tendency haunted Hamilton in later years.

Morris replied to Hamilton that he had been thinking along similar lines, although the Bank of North America that he proposed had a less ambitious scale and scope than the national bank that Hamilton recommended. Much of the capital for the Bank of North America—which Congress chartered in 1781—came from a loan that year from France, which, as Hamilton foresaw, wanted to destabilize Britain. Morris used the loan to purchase most of the bank's shares for the U.S. government, a necessity because private investors, given the shakiness of America's finances, largely refrained from buying the shares that Morris offered.

The bank opened in Philadelphia in 1782 and offered considerable aid to the government during the two-year transition from war to peace. Morris then sold the government's shares to private investors, and the Bank of North America continued as an ordinary commercial bank.*

★ ★ ★ ★ ★

The Continentalist.

Even if the men to whom Hamilton had sent his three essays sympathized with his ideas, the American people needed persuading. So Hamilton incorporated his main ideas for reforming the government and its finances into a series of six essays titled *The Continentalist*, for publication in newspapers. Four of these essays appeared in July and August 1781, before he marched to Yorktown, and the final two in April and July 1782, as he was studying the law again.

The Continentalist embodies the two main themes of the earlier letters: the untenable

* After a number of mergers over the years, America's first bank now forms part of Wells Fargo.

weakness of the existing national government and the urgent need for reformation, including the power to generate revenue. These keys would unlock victory in the war and forge a stronger union of the states. He ended the last essay with an eloquent statement of two visions of America's future:

> There is something noble and magnificent in the perspective of a great Foederal Republic, closely linked in the pursuit of a common interest, tranquil and prosperous at home, respectable abroad; but there is something proportionably diminutive and contemptible in the prospect of a number of petty states, with the appearance only of union, jarring, jealous and perverse, without any determined direction, fluctuating and unhappy at home, weak and insignificant by their dissensions, in the eyes of other nations. Happy America! If those, to whom thou hast intrusted the guardianship of thy infancy, know how to provide for thy future repose; but miserable and undone, if their negligence or ignorance permits the spirit of discord to erect her banners on the ruins of thy tranquillity!

Having determined what needed to happen, Hamilton devoted the rest of his life to achieving the first of these visions.

These keys would unlock victory in the war and forge a stronger union of the states.

"There is something noble and magnificent in the perspective of a great Foederal Republic."

FRONT AND BACK OF A THREE-PENCE NOTE ISSUED BY THE BANK OF NORTH AMERICA, AUGUST 6, 1789.

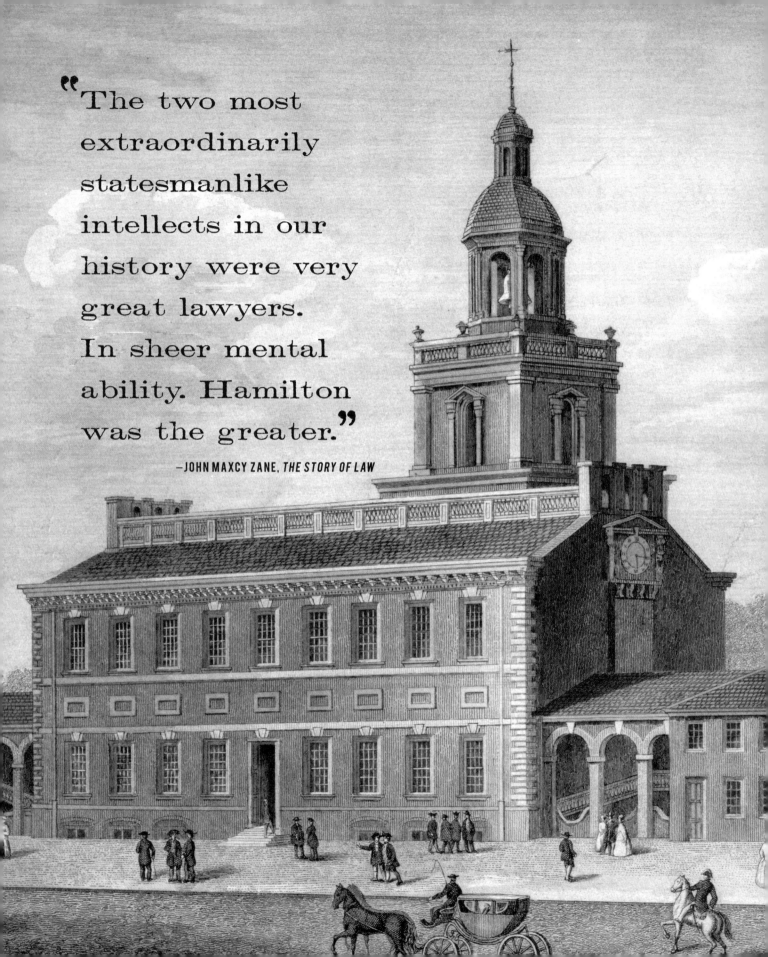

"The two most extraordinarily statesmanlike intellects in our history were very great lawyers. In sheer mental ability. Hamilton was the greater."

—JOHN MAXCY ZANE, *THE STORY OF LAW*

{IV}

LEGISLATOR

1782-1787

————⬥◆⬥————

After enduring a dire childhood in the West Indies and then six punishing years of war, Hamilton enjoyed seven years of what we might call normal life. Throughout these years, he used every opportunity he had to plan and implement the better government that he had invoked in his *Continentalist* essays. Other nationalists joined him, but they faced a tough slog against the entrenched interests of state politicians.

Shortly after Cornwallis surrendered at Yorktown, Hamilton joined his beloved wife, Betsy, at her parents' home in Albany. As he awaited the arrival of their first child, Hamilton was pushing himself through a self-guided crash course in the law, and he made outstanding time. Normally that course of study would have lasted three years, followed by an apprenticeship to a practicing lawyer, but New York State granted a special dispensation to anyone who had interrupted his studies to serve in the army. In July 1782, he flew over the first hurdle of the bar exam, and in October he qualified as a fully fledged lawyer. The newlyweds' first child, Philip, was born in January 1782. In a jocular mood, Hamilton wrote to Lafayette, his friend and comrade-in-arms, who had returned to France after Yorktown:

Hamilton moves to Albany and takes up the law.

The birth of Philip Hamilton.

> *I have been employed for the last ten months in rocking the cradle and studying the art of fleecing my neighbours. I am now a Grave Counsellor at law, and shall soon be a grand member of Congress. The Legislature at their last session took it into their heads to name me pretty unanimously one of their delegates. I am going to throw away a few more months in public life and then I retire to a simple citizen and good paterfamilias.*

THE STATE HOUSE IN
PHILADELPHIA IN 1776.

*Hamilton becomes
a tax receiver.*

ROBERT MORRIS BY CHARLES WILLSON PEALE.

But fate had other plans in store for him.

Robert Morris, the country's superintendent of finance, offered Hamilton the position of continental receiver of taxes for New York. Morris had created the position, among others, to expedite collecting funds from the states for national purposes. Clearly the elder statesman had heeded the letter that Hamilton had sent him in 1781. But the younger man initially rejected the offer. The job would interrupt his efforts to pass the bar, and it promised little pay: one-quarter of 1 percent of what he could collect. New York City still remained in British hands, so no revenue stream there. Then as now, plenty of people resisted paying taxes for national purposes, so the proposition looked grim at best. Then Morris tweaked his offer. Hamilton would earn his commission on what the state was *supposed* to pay, not what he could collect. That made the prospect more interesting. Hamilton accepted.

The appointment lasted just a few months until Hamilton went off to Congress in November 1782. Until that happened, though, he lobbied the state legislature and governor to pay the national requisitions and reminded everyone who failed to do so by naming names in the newspapers. In essence, he had become a government collections agent, nor was it the last time that he aired essentially private matters in public. Hamilton and Morris corresponded frequently, and their communication reveals Hamilton's take on the state's politicians. Two of them also served, five years later, as delegates to the Constitutional Convention: "Judge [Robert] Yates is upright and respectable in his profession" and "[John] Lansing is a good young fellow and a good practitioner of the law; but his friends mistook his talents when they made him a statesman. He thinks two pence an ounce upon plate a *monstrous tax*. The county of Albany is not of my opinion concerning him." Once again Hamilton is writing

Ye as Alexander Hamilton esquire in conformity with an Act of the United States in Congress assembled passed the 2 of November 1781, hath been duly appointed by Commission under my Hand and Seal, Receiver of the continental Taxes within the State of New York. And whereas it is doubtful whether a Receiver of the continental Taxes hath yet been recognized by the Legislature of that State, In order to obviate Difficulties that might arise on that Account I do hereby especially authorize and empower the said Alexander Hamilton Esq. to make Application to and receive from the executive Authority of the said State, the Treasurer or such other Person or Persons as are, or may be appointed and enabled to pay unto the Superintendant of the Finances, or his Order for the Use of the United States the first quarterly Payment of the Quota of the said State in eight million of Dollars Specie required by Congress for the Service of this present Year, and upon the Receipt of the whole or any Part of the said first quarterly Payment which became due to the United States on the first Day of this present Month in the Sum of ninety three thousand, three hundred and ninety nine and one half Dollars Specie to give his Receipts or Discharges which shall be equally valid against the United States as if given by me. Given under my Hand and Seal of the Treasury at the Office of Finance in the City of Philadelphia this fifteenth Day of April 1782

Rob Morris

Thomas Tillotson Esquire having been appointed by
The Superintendant of Finance to succeed me in the Office of the Receiver of the Continental Taxes within this State I do hereby assign to him the foregoing warrant to do whatsoever in virtue thereof I the Underwritten am authorized to do

Albany November 10. 1782

Alex Hamilton
late Receiver

THE DOCUMENT
THAT ROBERT
MORRIS ISSUED,
APPOINTING
ALEXANDER
HAMILTON
RECEIVER OF
CONTINENTAL
TAXES IN NEW
YORK, 1782.

thoughts better expressed by mouth. Another Yates fared worse in the crosshairs of Hamilton's pen:

[Abraham] Yates ... is a man whose ignorance and perverseness are surpassed by his pertinacity and conceit. He hates all high flyers, which is the appellation he gives to men of genius. ... The people have been a long time in the habit *of choosing him in different offices; and to the title of prescription, he adds that of being a preacher to their taste. He* assures *them, they are too poor to pay taxes.*

Hamilton also failed to exercise restraint when it came to more powerful men. George Clinton—the long-serving governor whom Hamilton grew to detest—drew a mixed review in 1782:

The present governor has declined in popularity, partly from a defect of qualifications for his station and partly from causes that do him honor—the vigorous execution of some necessary laws that bore hard on the people. ...
He is, I believe, a man of integrity and passes with his particular friends for a statesman; it is certain that without being destitute of understanding, his passions are much warmer, than his judgment is enlightened. ...
We are not to be surprised, if instead of taking the lead in measures that contradict a prevailing prejudice, however he may be convinced of their utility, he either flatters it or temporizes; especially when a new election approaches.

Hamilton had a dangerous talent for sketching and ridiculing his contemporaries. He also abhorred democratic politics, which tend to flatter people's opinions—particularly of themselves—and play to their prejudices instead of helping them understand their true interests. As democracy transformed from a way of making collective decisions into a political cipher used to goad the masses, posterity appreciated Hamilton less and less for expressing his reservations about it. Being a tax collector also didn't help.

★ ★ ★ ★ ★

Hamilton's time in the Confederation Congress damaged his image both then and later at the hands of biographers and historians. The states failed to ratify a 5 percent tariff on imports to fund Congress. That would have been the nation's first tax and the government's first direct source of tax revenue. The money would have gone to paying interest on loans, which had fallen into arrears, and to paying the army, which hadn't happened in some time. Hamilton had something like it in mind as he wrote his letters and essays in 1780 and 1781, bemoaning the lack of public credit and the failure to give the army what it needed to win the war.

The nation's first tax battle.

The men spoke menacingly of "fatal effects" if no action took place.

Congress proposed the tax in 1781. By late 1782, when Hamilton took his seat there, twelve states had approved it. But the Articles of Confederation required unanimous consent from all thirteen states for such a sweeping grant of power to Congress. Rhode Island remained the lone holdout. Just as Congress began to plea with the Ocean State, Virginia withdrew its ratification. The tax died on the table.

Or did it? In late December, disgruntled army officers traveled from the encampment near Newburgh, New York, to Philadelphia to plead their grievances. The men spoke menacingly of "fatal effects" if no action took place. But rather than taking the army's wording as a threat, Robert Morris and his assistant, Gouverneur Morris (no relation), seized the opportunity to revive the import tax by combining the army's pleas for justice with similar calls from public creditors, who had lent money to the government but hadn't seen repayment yet. The Morrises and their allies pressured Congress to pass a new tax and the rest of Morris's financial plan. Upping the ante, Morris himself threatened to resign if Congress failed to act.

A lack of funds for the army payroll.

Thus began the Newburgh Conspiracy, which unfolded over the next three months. Hamilton certainly shared the Morrises' goal. If he didn't play a central role in the machinations, as some historians allege, he certainly sympathized with them. We know this because the Morrises maintained tight secrecy about the scheme, but Hamilton kept a steady correspondence about it with George Washington, keeping the commander informed. In return, Washington offered his own views and advice on what to do.

The Newburgh letters.

Then events took an ominous turn. In early March, officers loyal to Horatio Gates—Washington's old rival, constantly on the prowl for a chance to oust his competitor—spread rumors that Congress wouldn't support the army. They circulated two anonymous "addresses" to the officers, one calling for a meeting to discuss the army's relationship with Congress and another calling for the army to remain active, even when peace arrived, until Congress paid the troops their due. Calling for a meeting like this without

The Newburgh Conspiracy.

Washington's permission violated military regulations and seriously undermined Washington's power. The threat not to disband the army bordered on mutiny and violated the long-standing tradition of military subordination to civilian authority.

Washington's Newburgh Address.

Washington carefully defused the situation with a call for the officers to meet on March 15. At that meeting, he castigated the men behind the two addresses and appealed to the troops' sense of duty and honor. He also promised to make his own plea to Congress to address their woes. At the end of his address, he pulled a letter by a friendly congressman from his coat and read it aloud, stumbling over some of the words. As he reached for his reading glasses, he famously said that he had grown gray and virtually blind in the service of his country. That clever touch of stagecraft persuaded most of the men, who had come to admire their dignified commander, to put aside their grievances and drop any thoughts of mutiny or threatening Congress. News of the signing of the peace treaty in Paris arrived around the same time, prompting most of the soldiers to return home.

> *Remnants of the army surrounded the statehouse, demanding to be paid.*

Congress passed a new tariff bill the following month and sent it to the states again for approval. Hamilton thought it too watered down and unlikely to take effect, so he voted against it. The bill failed. In June, remnants of the army appeared in Philadelphia and surrounded the statehouse where Congress met, demanding to be paid. Congress asked Pennsylvania authorities for protection but received none, so they left the state and reconvened in Princeton. Hamilton spent July there awaiting the signed peace treaty with the British, which Congress had to approve.

The treaty failed to arrive, and at the end of July Hamilton returned to Albany. His one term in Congress—marked by almost no progress toward the goals of his agenda—had ended.

They were eventful, trying months, but he had the benefit of having his wife by his side for a good portion of his time in Philadelphia. When his term ended, they reunited once again in Albany.

A SUBTLE DEPICTION OF
THE RIVALRY BETWEEN
WASHINGTON AND GATES.

★ ★ ★ ★ ★

Head Quarters at Newburgh 15th
March 1783.

"Gentlemen

By an anonymous summons, an
attempt has been made to convene you together — how inconsistent with the Rules of propri-
ety! — how unmilitary! — and how subversive of all
Order and discipline! — let the good sense of the
army decide. —

In the moment of this summons,
another anonymous production was sent into circulation; addressed more to the feelings & passions,
than to the reason & judgment of the army. — The Author of the peice, is entituled to much credit for
the goodness of his pen: — and I could wish, he
had, as much credit for the rectitude of his Heart —
for, as men see thro' different Optics, and are induced by the reflecting faculties of the Mind, to
use different means, to attain the same End; the
Author of the Address, should have had more Chari-
ty, than to mark for Suspicion, the man who should
recommend ⸺ moderation & longer forbearance —
or, in other Words, who should not think as he thinks,
and act as he advises. — But he had another plan
in view, in which candor & Liberality of Sentiment,
Regard to Justice, & love of Country, have no part —
And he was right, to insinuate the darkest suspicions,
to effect the blackest designs — . —
That the

THE STATE HOUSE IN PHILADELPHIA, WHERE CONGRESS MET AND WHICH THE
CONTINENTAL ARMY SURROUNDED SHORTLY AFTER THE NEWBURGH CONSPIRACY.

The Treaty of Paris.

Everyone knew it was coming, but the mechanics of drafting and executing the peace treaty between Britain and America had rolled along through much of 1783. Officials didn't sign it in Paris until September. After seven tense years of occupation, British forces finally withdrew from New York City in November. Hamilton received a promotion to full colonel in October, and then he and his wife returned to the newly liberated city in December, taking up residence at 57 Wall Street. They called it home for the next seven years, and during that time they had three more children: Angelica in 1784, Alexander in 1786, and James Alexander in 1788.

*The Hamiltons return
to New York City.*

At the end of 1783, Hamilton's trajectory as a New York City lawyer began to skyrocket. Patriots had suffered mightily during the war when the British occupied the city. Now they wanted revenge. The state legislature responded by passing harsh laws to

ALEXANDER HAMILTON

punish British subjects and American loyalists. The Confiscation Act allowed patriots to seize loyalist property. The Trespass Act allowed patriots to sue loyalists who had occupied their property during the war for damages, such as lost rents. Another act prevented loyalists from collecting patriots' debts and allowed those debts to be paid with worthless paper money.

Hamilton believed in the fair rule of law. He also considered it a mistake to drive loyalists from the country, thereby losing their talents and their capital. In early 1784, he wrote two long letters "from Phocion" (a statesman in ancient Athens), arguing not only that these punitive laws were a bad idea but that they directly violated the Treaty of Paris, which Congress had just approved. The treaty held that creditors on either

Patriots versus loyalists.

AMERICAN COMMISSIONERS OF THE PRELIMINARY PEACE NEGOTIATIONS WITH GREAT BRITAIN BY BENJAMIN WEST, 1783. THE BRITISH REFUSED TO POSE, SO WEST COULDN'T FINISH THE PAINTING.

The TIMES Anno 1783

side "meet with no lawful impediment to the recovery of the full value in sterling money" of previously contracted debts and that Congress would "earnestly recommend" that the state legislatures restore all properties previously confiscated from British subjects and loyalists and refrain from further confiscations or prosecutions.

So what to do? In a now-famous 1784 legal case, *Rutgers v. Waddington*, Hamilton represented the loyalist, Waddington, who during the occupation had operated a brewery owned previously by Rutgers, a patriot who had fled but was suing for back rent and damages. Hamilton argued that Congress's endorsement of the peace treaty outranked New York State law. Further, the judiciary had a solemn duty to evaluate conflicts such as these and resolve them. He may not have known it, but Hamilton had provided one of the first arguments for judicial review of legislation, which soon became a pillar of American constitutionalism.

But he didn't base his case on the untested concepts of federal versus state law or judicial review. He offered several other interpretations of the law and the facts of the case, giving the judges a veritable menu of options

Patriots had suffered mightily during the war when the British occupied the city. Now they wanted revenge.

Hamilton had provided one of the first arguments for judicial review of legislation.

JOHN BULL (BRITAIN) THROWS UP HIS ARMS IN DESPAIR AS THE DEVIL, FARTING, FLIES AWAY WITH AMERICA WHILE THE NATIONS OF EUROPE WATCH.

WASHINGTON ENTERS NEW YORK CITY, NOVEMBER 25, 1783, AFTER THE BRITISH EVACUATION.

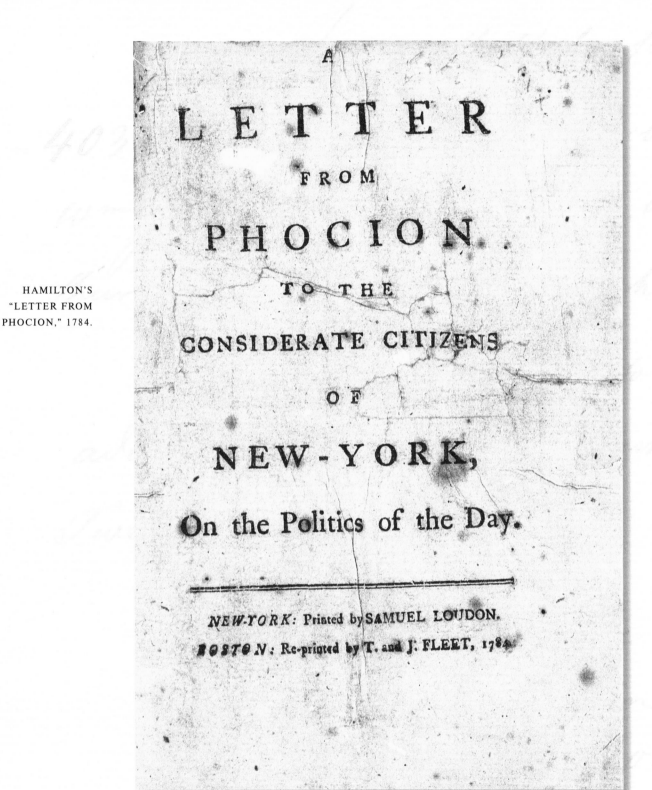

ALEXANDER HAMILTON

HAMILTON ADDRESSING
THE COURTROOM.

from which to choose. Ultimately they selected an outcome that allowed Waddington to settle for ten cents on the dollar. The victory set an important precedent, but patriot New Yorkers fumed at the decision.

Hamilton remained unfazed. On this, as on so many other occasions, he demonstrated that he would rather be in the right than popular.

Even while practicing law, Hamilton never let banking stray far from his thoughts. He had urged Congress and Robert Morris to charter the nation's first bank in 1780 and 1781. John Barker Church—husband of his wife's older sister, Angelica—and his business partner, Jeremiah Wadsworth, had made their fortunes by supplying the French forces in America during the war. Church and Wadsworth also had invested heavily in the Morris-backed Bank of North America. Now they planned to compound their profits by starting a bank in New York. Hamilton of course was in on the action.

In 1784, banks were all the rage. That February, a group of New Yorkers led by Robert Livingston planned to open the Bank of the State of New York, much of its capital consisting of land mortgages. Livingston applied for a charter, but Hamilton and city merchants recognized the folly of capitalizing a bank with hard, immovable assets. Hamilton lobbied to halt Livingston's bank, and the merchants hatched their own plan to found a bank based on specie reserves, like the Bank of North America. Hamilton soon joined the merchants' group. A lawyer who knew more about banking and finance than the others, he drew up the bank's constitution. He also purchased shares and became director of the new bank, which applied for a charter of incorporation. Confronted by two applications for charters in a state that had never had a corporate bank, Albany declined to charter either of them.

The Livingston group dropped its plan, but the Bank of New York opened, unincorporated, anyway. At the same time, Bostonians launched a similar institution, the Massachusetts Bank, so by mid-1784 America had three banks. "The happiest engines

HAMILTON READING THE CONSTITUTION OF THE BANK OF NEW YORK, WHICH HE COFOUNDED IN 1784.

that ever were invented for advancing trade," as Hamilton had called them in his letter to Morris three years earlier, were off to a roaring start. The state finally granted the Bank of New York a charter in 1791, but by then Hamilton had become secretary of the Treasury and Congress had approved his plan for the Bank of the United States, which was authorized to open a branch in New York. Seeing that possibility as a threat, the state legislature quickly granted the Bank of New York a charter so the state had a bank all its own.*

★ ★ ★ ★ ★

America had won the War of Independence, but old ghosts still troubled the new nation. In 1787, when Hamilton was serving as a state representative, New York nearly went to war with Vermont.

The nation's first tax battle.

In 1763, Britain had recognized the Connecticut River as the boundary between the New York and New Hampshire colonies. That didn't stop New Hampshire, however, from selling land west of the river to settlers. During the War of Independence, those settlers declared their independence from New York and adopted the name Vermont.

In March 1787, New Yorkers holding title to land in Vermont asked the legislature to invoke their property rights—by force if necessary. Hamilton opposed the request on principle and for more pragmatic reasons. Like the thirteen colonies, Vermont had declared its independence; like Britain, New York opposed it. But if New York pressed its claims to land in Vermont, that might drive Vermonters into the hands of the British, who still controlled Canada, just to the north. That possibility posed an even greater threat to the new country that only recently had secured its own independence. The obvious solution: Vermont should join the Union as a new state, which Hamilton made a condition for recognizing Vermont's independence.

The Vermont Republic.

> *Old ghosts still troubled the new nation.*

* The Bank of New York operated for more than two centuries under that name. In 2007, it merged with Mellon Financial to become the Bank of New York Mellon, one of the top financial holding companies in America.

Hamilton's argument persuaded the New York Assembly to recognize Vermont's independence in April—but the New York Senate didn't agree. The matter hung in limbo. The new U.S. Constitution, with its stronger federal powers, went into effect in 1789, and the next year New York agreed to a negotiated settlement. That settlement established the border between the two states, and Vermont compensated New Yorkers who had title to Vermont land. In 1791 Vermont petitioned to join the Union, and Congress duly admitted it.

A MAP BY JAMES WHITTLE AND ROBERT LAURIE SHOWS THE BOUNDARIES OF THE STATES IN 1794.

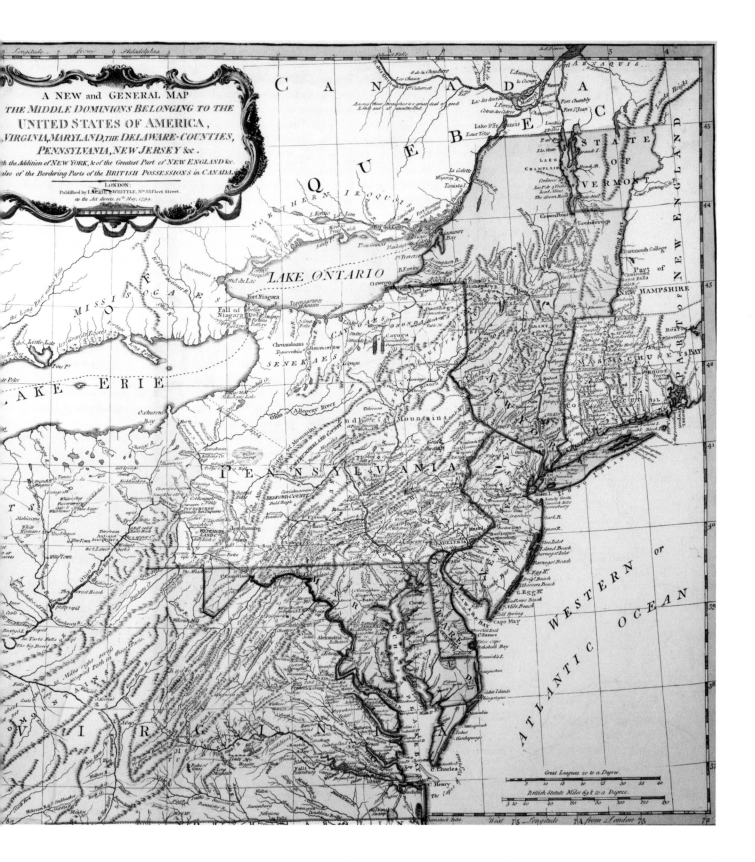

A NEW and GENERAL MAP of THE MIDDLE DOMINIONS BELONGING TO THE UNITED STATES OF AMERICA, VIRGINIA, MARYLAND, THE DELAWARE-COUNTIES, PENNSYLVANIA, NEW JERSEY &c. With the Addition of NEW YORK, & of the Greatest Part of NEW ENGLAND &c. also of the Bordering Parts of the BRITISH POSSESSIONS in CANADA.

LONDON:
Published by LAURIE & WHITTLE, No. 53 Fleet Street
as the Act directs, 12th May, 1794.

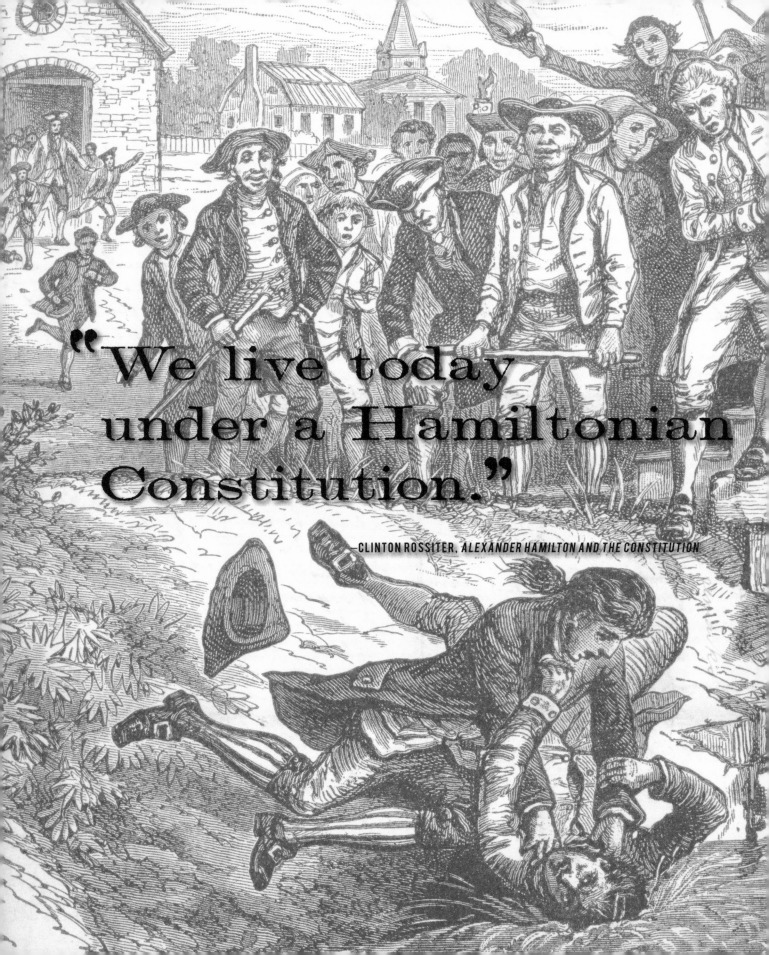

"We live today under a Hamiltonian Constitution."

—CLINTON ROSSITER, *ALEXANDER HAMILTON AND THE CONSTITUTION*

{V}

CONSTITUTIONALIST

1787-1788

———————◆◆◆———————

amilton's brief stint as a tax collector, his term in the Confederation Congress, and his time in the New York Assembly didn't alter his views about how America needed to change. The national government had to be stronger. It needed its own revenue to service debts and defend the country, and it needed a banking system. He had first proposed a convention to plan a better version of the government as well as financial reform back in 1780 as war raged in the South and victory looked dim. Then Yorktown pulled America's chestnuts from the fire.

The downside to peace and British recognition of American independence, he soon realized, was a dissolving sense of urgency to implement the reforms that he and other nationalists such as Washington, Madison, and Jay saw as necessary. Hamilton's calls for a convention fell on deaf ears, and a national tax to allow Congress to pay the army and public creditors fell flat.

But America had more than inaction on its hands. In the depressed postwar economy of the 1780s, states imposed tariffs and other trade restrictions on one another and then retaliated. States with good ports—Massachusetts, New York, South Carolina—financed themselves with import taxes. When New Jersey and Connecticut bought goods that traveled through New York City, they had to pay New York taxes. Resentment boiled.

Tariff strife between the states.

Repeating past mistakes, some states tried to stave off the downturn by issuing paper money. Rhode Island became the most notorious example. A group of debtors seized the reins of power in Providence and issued large batches of paper money, decreeing that creditors had to accept it or forfeit the debts. To Hamilton and other nationalists, this smacked of outright fraud. National creditors persuaded some state legislatures to have

More worthless paper money.

A SCENE FROM THE SHAYS REBELLION
IN SPRINGFIELD, MASSACHUSETTS.

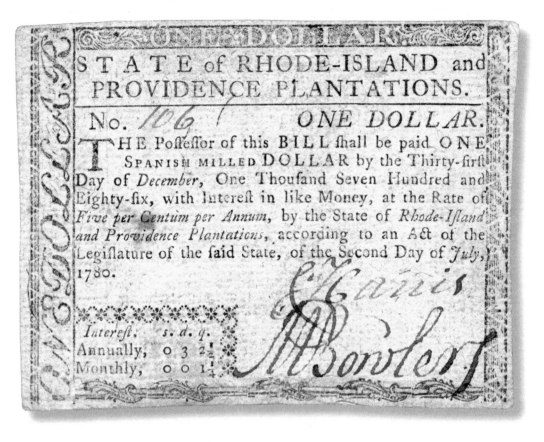

A $1 NOTE
ISSUED BY
RHODE ISLAND
IN THE 1780S.

Resentment boiled.

*The Annapolis
Convention.*

their states pay what Congress owed them. A nice gesture, to be sure, but that only weakened the union they were trying to strengthen.

Amid this dire situation began a series of events that shortly achieved what Hamilton and the nationalists had craved for years. Madison—a Virginia legislator whom Hamilton had befriended when both served in Congress from 1782 to 1783—used the festering disputes between states to persuade Virginia's House of Delegates to call the states together to frame "such regulations of trade as may be judged necessary to promote the general interest."

The New York State Assembly appointed Hamilton and several other delegates to attend. The meeting took place at Annapolis, Maryland, in September 1786, but only twelve commissioners showed up, representing just five states: New York, New Jersey, Pennsylvania, Delaware, and Virginia. Four others, New Hampshire, Massachusetts, Rhode Island, and North Carolina, had agreed to send delegates, but they didn't make it in time. Another four, Connecticut, Maryland, South Carolina, and Georgia, never responded. After waiting for four days for the stragglers to arrive, the commissioners agreed to write a report to the five states that sent them before disbanding.

Hamilton drafted the Annapolis address, which the commissioners endorsed unanimously. Among other points, it argued that the nation's problems involved much more

than commerce and required a "future Convention with more enlarged powers." It asked
the five states to validate their recommendation and to "procure the concurrence of the
other states in the appointment of Commissioners, to meet at Philadelphia on the second Monday in May next, to take into consideration the situation of the United States,
to devise such further provisions as shall appear to them necessary to render the constitution of the Foederal Government adequate to the exigencies of the Union."

At the same time, a new rebellion raised its head. A faction of disgruntled farmers
and debtors in Western Massachusetts couldn't pay state taxes and their debts, losing

*The Shays
Rebellion.*

ANNAPOLIS, MARYLAND, WHERE THE 1786 CONVENTION FAILED TO ACHIEVE THE NECESSARY POLITICAL REFORMS.

their farms and homes in foreclosures. Daniel Shays, a soldier of the revolution still unpaid for his military service, led the rebels. They shut down courts, threatened sheriffs executing foreclosures, and even attacked the government armory in Springfield.

Horrified by the Shays Rebellion, Boston merchants collected funds to form a militia of 3,000 men. Led by General Benjamin Lincoln—the officer who accepted the British surrender at Yorktown—the militia marched west and routed the rebels.

The Constitutional Convention.

News of the rebellion spread through the country like wildfire. It and other disturbances proved that the Articles of Confederation were bootless, a point Hamilton had been making for years to anyone who would listen. The Shays Rebellion prompted Congress to set aside its timidity and call for the states to meet in Philadelphia in May 1787. Hamilton had been pushing for this meeting for more than six years, and New York appointed him a delegate to what became known as the Constitutional Convention.

News of the rebellion spread through the country like wildfire.

★ ★ ★ ★ ★

DANIEL SHAYS FOMENTED A REBELLION THAT HELPED REFORM THE AMERICAN GOVERNMENT.

PENNSYLVANIA, ff.

By the *President* and the *Supreme Executive Council* of the Commonwealth of *Pennsylvania*,

A PROCLAMATION.

WHEREAS the General Assembly of this Commonwealth, by a law entituled 'An act for co-operating with "the state of Massachusetts bay, agreeable to the articles of "confederation, in the apprehending of the proclaimed rebels "DANIEL SHAYS, LUKE DAY, ADAM WHEELER "and ELI PARSONS," have enacted, "that rewards additional to those offered and promised to be paid by the state "of Massachusetts Bay, for the apprehending the aforesaid "rebels, be offered by this state;" WE do hereby offer the following rewards to any person or persons who shall, within the limits of this state, apprehend the rebels aforesaid, and secure them in the gaol of the city and county of Philadelphia, —— viz For the apprehending of the said Daniel Shays, and securing him as aforesaid, the reward of *One hundred and Fifty Pounds* lawful money of the state of Massachusetts Bay, and *One Hundred Pounds* lawful money of this state ; and for the apprehending the said Luke Day, Adam Wheeler and Eli Parsons, and securing them as aforesaid, the reward (respectively) of *One Hundred Pounds* lawful money of Massachusetts Bay and *Fifty Pounds* lawful money of this state : And all judges, justices, sheriffs and constables are hereby strictly enjoined and required to make diligent search and enquiry after, and to use their utmost endeavours to apprehend and secure the said Daniel Shays, Luke Day, Adam Wheeler and Eli Parsons, their aiders, abettors and comforters, and every of them, so that they may be dealt with according to law.

GIVEN in Council, under the hand of the President, and the Seal of the State, at Philadelphia, this tenth day of March, in the year of our Lord one thousand seven hundred and eighty-seven.

BENJAMIN FRANKLIN.

ATTEST
JOHN ARMSTRONG, jun. Secretary.

A PENNSYLVANIA PROCLAMATION SIGNED BY BENJAMIN FRANKLIN OFFERING A REWARD FOR THE CAPTURE OF DANIEL SHAYS.

ALEXANDER HAMILTON

Proposition of Coll. Hamilton of New York, in the Convention for establishing a constitution of Government for the United States.

1. The supreme legislative power of the United States of America to be vested in two different bodies of men; the one to be called the Assembly; the other the Senate, who together shall form the legislature of the United States, with power to pass all laws whatsoever, subject to the negative hereafter mentioned.

2. The Assembly to consist of persons elected by the People to serve for three years.

3. The Senate to consist of persons elected to serve during good behaviour; their election to be made by electors chosen for that purpose by the People; in order to this the States to be divided into election districts. On the death, removal or resignation of any Senator, his place to be filled out of the district from which he came.

4. The supreme executive authority of the United States to be vested in a governor to be elected during good behaviour; the election to be made by electors chosen by the People in the election districts aforesaid — the authorities and functions to be as follows — to have a negative upon all laws about to be passed, and the execution of all laws passed — to have the direction of war when authorized or begun — to have with the advice and approbation of the Senate the power of making all treaties — to have the sole appointment of the heads or chief officers of the departments of finance and foreign affairs — to have the nomination of all other officers, ambassadors to foreign nations included, subject to the approbation or rejection of the Senate — to have power of pardoning

THE OUTLINE FOR HAMILTON'S FIVE-HOUR SPEECH: "PROPOSITIONS OF COLONEL HAMILTON, OF NEW YORK, IN THE CONVENTION FOR ESTABLISHING A CONSTITUTIONAL GOVERNMENT FOR THE UNITED STATES."

By most accounts, our man played only a minor role during the gathering, which finally reached a quorum to do business on May 25. Hamilton participated in the discussions for a little over a month, making one exceedingly long speech on June 18. No draft or transcript of the five- or six-hour oration survives, but we have Hamilton's outline and notes taken by several delegates.

By June 18, the convention already had two plans before it. The New Jersey Plan, introduced by William Paterson, essentially repeated the government structure that existed under the Articles of Confederation but gave Congress the explicit rights to tax and regulate commerce. Congress also would elect an executive committee, which would appoint a supreme tribunal as its judicial branch. In the New Jersey plan, each state had one vote in the single house of Congress, meaning that small states had as much power as large ones.

The Virginia Plan, drafted by James Madison, called for executive, legislative, and judicial branches. The legislative branch would have upper and lower houses with state representation in each based on population, thereby giving large states more power than small ones in both houses. The people would elect the lower house directly, and the lower house would choose members of the upper house from candidates nominated by state legislatures. The legislative branch could veto state laws inconsistent with national ones, but a council of the executive and judicial branches could veto the actions of the legislative branch—unless an unspecified majority of the legislative branch overrode that decision. All of this reduced state power and built checks and balances into national government.

He prudently backed away from that shockingly radical idea.

Hamilton preferred the Virginia Plan, but both weakened the national government at the expense of state power, and both gave Congress too much control over the executive and judicial branches. He nearly suggested abolishing the states altogether but prudently backed away from that shockingly radical idea. Ultimately he wanted a stable, permanent, republican government to foster liberty by maintaining law and order—no easy task then as now. According to Madison's notes, Hamilton said:

> *In every community where industry is encouraged, there will be a division of it into the few & the many. Hence separate interests will arise. There will be debtors & creditors &c. Give all power to the many, they will oppress the few. Give all power to the few, they will oppress the many. Both therefore ought to have power, that each may defend itself agst. the other.*

To achieve the balance, Hamilton proposed that the lower house of the national legislature—which he called the Assembly—consist of representatives elected by the people to three-year terms and the senate or upper house consist of men elected to serve during "good behavior"—meaning life for the well-behaved, as had been the case in the Roman Republic. His executive would be a person, not a committee, and also would serve during good behavior, conceivably for life. "Electors chosen by electors chosen by the people in election districts . . . or by electors chosen for that purpose by the respective [state] legislatures" would elect the chief executive, who would have

The Hamilton Plan.

JOHN LANSING JR.
SERVED BESIDE
HAMILTON AS
A NEW YORK
DELEGATE TO THE
CONSTITUTIONAL
CONVENTION IN
PHILADELPHIA,
1787.

*Hamilton departs
the Convention.*

*Hamilton becomes
the voice of
New York.*

the presidential powers we recognize today. Hamilton's "Supreme Judicial authority" called for twelve judges nominated by the executive, subject to Senate approval, to hold office, again, during good behavior. Apart from the number of judges, this is exactly the U.S. Supreme Court today.

Hamilton's plan for life terms struck his fellow delegates, contemporaries, and later historians and biographers as borderline monarchical. He refuted that characterization, explaining that its main objective was to strengthen the national government by weakening the powers of state legislatures. He also wanted the executive and the judiciary to have more independence from Congress than the Virginia or New Jersey plans allowed. Some scholars suggest that Hamilton, a shrewd military strategist, staked out an extreme position to push the convention toward a new structure more to his liking. If so, the ruse ultimately worked.

At month's end—frustrated by slow progress and needing to attend to legal matters in New York—he left Philadelphia for a couple of weeks. Business delayed him, however, and he didn't return until early August. By then, his fellow New York delegates, John Lansing Jr. and Robert Yates, had stormed off for good. They and other Anti-Federalists didn't like the momentum propelling the convention toward a stronger national government.

Hamilton became the sole New York delegate, a position that made him reluctant to speak his mind or vote on anything because most of New York's political leaders didn't share his radical views. After a week in Philadelphia, he scuttled back to New York, returning only in the convention's last days. At that point, the delegates elected him to serve on the Committee of Style, which cleaned up and finalized the Constitution.

Shortly after the convention ended, Hamilton wrote out some "Conjectures about the New Constitution." The unpublished document reverberated between the lines of *The Federalist* essays that soon appeared, detailing the likely outcome:

> *The new constitution has in favour of its success these circumstances—a
> very great weight of influence of the persons who framed it, particularly
> in the universal popularity of General Washington—the good will of the
> commercial interest throughout the states . . . the good will of most men
> of property . . . the hopes of the Creditors of the United States . . . [and] a
> strong belief in the people at large of the insufficiency of the present con-
> federation.*

THE SIGNING OF THE CONSTITUTION. WASHINGTON STANDS ON THE DAIS WHILE FRANKLIN SITS AT THE CENTER OF THE ROOM WITH HAMILTON LEANING IN TOWARD HIM.

Hamilton thought the odds favored adoption. If adoption failed, civil war would dismember the union. If no civil war came, then several confederacies would form among different states. Assuming adoption, "it is probable general Washington will be the President of the United States. This will insure a wise choice of men to administer the government and a good administration." If Washington didn't become the new government's first leader, they

If adoption failed, civil war would dismember the union.

would face "contests about the boundaries of power between the particular governments and the general government," same as above.

★ ★ ★ ★ ★

Hamilton starts
The Federalist.

For the Constitution to take effect, the states had to ratify it in ad hoc conventions of popularly elected delegates, which conveniently bypassed the state legislatures that Hamilton so distrusted. Still, he knew that ratification would prove a tough sell in New York, where Anti-Federalist sentiments ran deep.

First he needed to sell the Constitution to the general public, who would elect the delegates to the state's ratifying convention. Then he had to sell it to the delegates themselves. His marketing campaign? A series of essays that explained why the new Constitution was necessary, how the new federal government solved the problems that prompted its creation, and how in the long run the Constitution promised to make Americans safer, freer, and richer. His efforts ultimately produced eighty-five newspaper essays, collectively *The Federalist*, signed by "Publius."* The ad campaign, addressed "To the People of the State of New-York," lasted from October 1787 to May 1788.

> *The Constitution promised to make Americans safer, freer, and richer.*

But Hamilton had a law practice to maintain and a growing family to feed. By late 1787, he and Betsy had three children, ages five, three, and one, with another on the way. He couldn't write all the essays himself, so he recruited John Jay, an expert on foreign affairs, and his friend James Madison.

In *Federalist* No. 1, he grandstanded that the Constitution had worldwide significance. Americans had "to decide the important question, whether societies of men are really capable or not, of establishing good government from reflection and choice, or whether they are forever destined to depend, for their political constitutions, on accident and force." A wrong decision would lead to "the general misfortune of mankind." Seven months later, after seven of the thirteen states had ratified the Constitution, Hamilton closed the campaign with doses of hope and fear:

....
* The pseudonym honored Publius Valerius Publicola, an ancient Roman leader who helped establish the Roman Republic.

THE FIRST PAGE OF THE U.S. CONSTITUTION.

THE COPY OF *THE FEDERALIST* THAT ELIZABETH SCHUYLER HAMILTON GAVE TO HER SISTER ANGELICA SCHUYLER CHURCH.

A NATION without a NATIONAL GOVERNMENT is, in my view, an awful spectacle. The establishment of a constitution, in time of profound peace, by the voluntary consent of a whole people, is a PRODIGY, to the completion of which I look forward with trembling anxiety.... POWERFUL INDIVIDUALS, in this and in other states, are enemies to a general national government, in every possible shape.

The Federalist campaign had tanked.

Why was Hamilton trembling with anxiety and banging the drum so loudly? Simply put, the Federalist campaign had tanked. By late May 1788, the popular vote had 16,000 against ratification and only 7,000 for it. Which meant that the New York ratification convention would have 46 Anti-Federalist delegates and just 19 Federalists. Publius had failed miserably to persuade the people that the Constitution served their best interests.

But history unfolds in mysterious ways. George Washington

grasped what New York voters had missed. Hamilton had sent him a copy of the book version of *The Federalist* essays. Washington replied that

> when the transient circumstances & fugitive performances which attended this crisis shall have disappeared, that work will merit the notice of Posterity; because in it are candidly discussed the principles of freedom & the topics of government, which will be always interesting to mankind so long as they shall be connected in Civil Society.

★ ★ ★ ★ ★

George Washington grasped what New York voters had missed.

April elections sent Hamilton to the New York ratification convention in Poughkeepsie in June. He, John Jay, and Robert Livingston led the delegates in favor of ratifying. But opponents, led by Melancton Smith and John Lansing Jr.—who had left the Philadelphia convention in a huff in July 1787—heavily outnumbered them. Governor George Clinton, another strong opponent, chaired the convention.

The New York ratification convention.

The Constitution needed the approval of nine states to go into effect. By the time the New York convention began on June 17, South Carolina had become the eighth state to ratify, and conventions were under way in New Hampshire and Virginia. New Hampshire voted for ratification on June 21 and Virginia on June 25. The Constitution as we know it took its first breath.

The Constitution as we know it took its first breath.

The question in Poughkeepsie then became: Would New York join the Union? Anti-Federalists argued that ratification should depend on the adoption of amendments. But convention rules banned conditional acceptance. States could *recommend* that Congress consider additional amendments, but it was all or nothing.* Nevertheless, New York Anti-Federalists spent a month framing amendments for conditional ratification. Hamilton vehemently opposed them, rallying for the Constitution as it stood, sometimes in several speeches a day. He may have persuaded some Antis to join his side, but the outcome still looked grim.

Late in the game, Hamilton and Jay decided to play hardball. They let it be known that New York City, which overwhelmingly favored the Constitution, might secede from

The threat of losing New York City.

*These additional amendments later became the Bill of Rights.

ROBERT LIVINGSTON JOINED HAMILTON
IN LEADING NEW YORK'S PRO-
RATIFICATION DELEGATES.

MELANCTON SMITH HELPED LEAD
THE DELEGATES WHO OPPOSED
RATIFYING THE CONSTITUTION.

the state and join the Union on its own if the state failed to ratify. The threat of losing the city toppled the Antis. They agreed to make their proposed amendments recommendations rather than conditions.

Constitutionalists held a celebratory parade a few days before the final vote took place. The parade's centerpiece: a float in the form of ship, named *Federal Ship Hamilton*. Some even spoke of renaming the city Hamiltoniana or something similar, but that never came to pass.*

....

* Instead, the city still bears the name of James, Duke of York, later King James II, whom Parliament had deposed in the Glorious Revolution.

GOVERNOR GEORGE CLINTON, AN ANTI-
FEDERALIST, CHAIRED THE NEW YORK
RATIFICATION CONVENTION.

Then, on July 26, New York State voted 30 to 27 to ratify the Constitution. Still in Poughkeepsie, Hamilton hadn't seen the parade or ship named for him, but hearing of it surely gave him enormous satisfaction. The thirty-one-year-old had achieved so much already, yet his most important work lay ahead of him.

NEW YORK CITY CELEBRATES THE STATE'S RATIFICATION OF THE COUNTRY'S NEW CONSTITUTION WITH A PARADE. ITS CENTERPIECE: THE *FEDERAL SHIP HAMILTON*.

"He smote the rock of the national resources, and abundant streams of revenue gushed forth. He touched the dead corpse of the public credit, and it sprang upon its feet."

—DANIEL WEBSTER

{VI}

SECRETARY OF THE TREASURY

1789-1795

Hamilton played significant roles in the struggle for independence and the adoption of the Constitution, but other leaders—Washington and Madison in particular—had equal and even greater parts in both. Hamilton's most important contribution to history was as the first secretary of the Treasury. When it came to finance, he had no equal among his contemporaries or most subsequent statesmen.

Only Robert Morris came close. But Morris's understanding of finance and its history lacked the breadth and depth of Hamilton's, and Morris hadn't found success in implementing his more limited program. Morris steered the country monetarily through the end of the war, true, but he couldn't persuade the states to give Congress the taxing power it needed to survive. The Bank of North America provided little more than token support to government finances for a brief period, and his needlessly complex plan for a national currency went nowhere. He also insisted on maintaining his private business while in public office.

> *When it came to finance, Hamilton had no equal.*

When Hamilton became Treasury secretary in 1789, America had none of the six pillars of a successful financial system. By the time he stepped down in 1795, it had all of them. During his time in office, he executed a financial revolution that he had been planning for a decade. That plan involved more than just righting the government's finances, founding the first central bank, and setting the dollar as the nation's currency.

ALEXANDER HAMILTON AS
SECRETARY OF THE TREASURY.

All of that was easy enough to do with the power of his office. He had no authority as Treasury secretary, however, to establish a banking system or securities markets or to create corporations. But Hamilton pointed the way toward them. He incentivized state governments, entrepreneurs, and others to enact those aims. State governments chartered more banks and corporations; entrepreneurs applied to state governments for more charters, and they established securities markets.

Equipped with these modern financial tools, the American economy—which lay in tatters on the periphery of a Eurocentric model—developed modern economic growth virtually overnight.* Economic historians are discovering that America likely ranks as the first nation to accomplish that feat. Propelled by this sustained economic growth, America had become the world's largest, richest, and most dynamic economy a century later. In the century after that, it became a superpower.

Hamilton's financial reforms truly changed the course of history. Few historians or biographers, however, have seen it that way. Perhaps they've failed to see that strong financial capabilities hold the key to unlocking a nation's growth and power. Hamilton also executed his grand plan so quickly and effectively that he made it look easy. All who followed couldn't remember a time when his arrangements didn't apply. But it was far from easy.

> *Propelled by this sustained economic growth, America became a superpower.*

★ ★ ★ ★ ★

* That is: sustained growth of 1 percent or more per year in per capita income.

A SEPTEMBER 1789 LETTER FROM HAMILTON AS THE NATION'S NEW SECRETARY OF THE TREASURY, TO JOHN SCOTT, COLLECTOR OF CUSTOMS FOR CHESTER, MARYLAND.

Washington appointed Hamilton secretary of the Department of the Treasury on September 11, 1789. From the old Confederation, the young man inherited an empty Treasury. Ten days later, the House of Representatives directed him to prepare a plan "for the support of the public credit, as a matter of high importance to the national honor and prosperity." He delivered his "Report on Public Credit" in January 1790.

Hamilton's "Report on Public Credit."

He estimated the country's debts at $54 million, a fifth of that owed to foreign governments and investors and the rest to domestic creditors. State debts, mostly incurred during the war, ran to about $25 million. Hamilton argued that the federal government should assume those state debts because those debts had supported independence and assumption would strengthen the Union. That put total government debt at roughly $79 million. This, Hamilton said, was "the price of liberty," and he proposed to pay it in

America's debts.

full over time as soon as Congress enacted the necessary legislation. For a finance minister with no cash in hand, that was a bold gamble.

If America paid the interest according to the original borrowing terms, annual interest would come to $4.5 million. How could a government with practically nonexistent revenues afford operating expenses—around $0.6 million by his calculation—as well as huge annual interest payments? Survival required "the extension of taxation to a degree, and to objects, which the true interest of public creditors forbids."

Americans hate paying taxes, then as now, so he recommended paying the interest on the foreign debt in full but asking domestic creditors to agree to having their debts funded by a new loan at a reduced rate. That plan would reduce annual interest on the domestic debt from $4 million to around $2.7 million. Much more manageable. In turn, future government revenues would go toward regular interest payments, a tactic never undertaken before Hamilton. It was the beginning of the modern American government debt market, now the largest in the world for the debt of a single issuer.

To convince domestic creditors, Hamilton offered them call protection, meaning that the government could retire only a small amount of the debt each year even if market interest rates declined, which he confidently predicted they would. He recommended that no more than 1 percent of the debt be "called" each year, but Congress doubled that to 2 percent in the approved legislation.

A sinking fund.

To give the creditors further assurances, Hamilton proposed a federally administered sinking fund to apply surplus revenues and money borrowed at home or abroad to open-market purchases of public debt "until the whole of the debt shall be discharged." That way, investors could count on the government not just to pay interest on its debt but to redeem it. In turn, the government gained the ability to conduct open-market purchases to support debt prices. That benefit proved more than useful when the market for U.S. debt tanked in 1791 and more seriously in the Panic of 1792, the first of many financial crises.

Hamilton wanted to establish public credit so that in the future the government could borrow money easily, say, in times of war. After all, that ability had propelled the Italian city-states, the Dutch Republic, and Britain to success in their various rivalries. But public credit, once established, might tempt governments to run up debts that eventually they couldn't pay. To avoid that end, Hamilton ardently wanted "to see incorporated, as a fundamental maxim, in the system of public credit in the United States, that the creation of debt should always be accompanied with the means of its extinguishment." In other words, a fiscally responsible government should match borrowing to taxation.

Half a year of protracted debates took place along with side deals to garner votes. One of the early debates in February took up the topic of discrimination. Hamilton opposed this tactic, which proposed to pay current debt holders, identified as speculators, only the highest value that their securities had obtained in the market and to pay the difference between that value and face value to the original parties. When the government had no money to pay what it owed during the 1780s, its debts declined in market value to fractions of face value, and many original creditors had sold their securities at those depressed market values. It seemed only fair to give the original holders a share in the rise of the value of securities.

Many southerners didn't like Hamilton's overall plan for a variety of reasons. Madison, Hamilton's old ally and *Federalist* coauthor, surprised him and many others by arguing *for* discrimination, apparently to please the Virginians who had elected him to Congress. The main problem with discrimination is that it violated the terms of the original debt, which made the securities negotiable and thus more attractive by giving the owner rights to all future payments. Discrimination essentially allowed Congress to rewrite its debt contracts after the fact, which would have destroyed all confidence in public credit. Common sense prevailed, however, and the House defeated discrimination later that month.

The most important side deal that happened at the time involved the federal assumption of state debts, a crucial move that was going nowhere. Thomas Jefferson, then secretary of State, wrote

CONGRESSMAN MADISON ARGUED FOR FINANCIAL DISCRIMINATION, WHICH WOULD HAVE SHATTERED INVESTOR CONFIDENCE IN PUBLIC CREDIT.

A fiscally responsible government should match borrowing to taxation.

THOMAS JEFFERSON
AS SECRETARY
OF STATE BY
CHARLES WILLSON
PEALE, 1791.

about a conversation he had on the subject with Hamilton, who stressed "the necessity of it in the general fiscal arrangements and it's indispensible necessity toward a preservation of the union: and particularly of the New England states." Most southern congressmen opposed assumption because their states had paid much of their debts—and assumption implied that they had to pay other states' debts—and because assumption increased the power and scope of the federal government.

The Dinner Table Bargain.

Jefferson agreed to host a dinner for Hamilton and Madison, at which Hamilton convinced the southerners of the wisdom of the plan. Madison agreed to twist the arms

NEW YORK'S CITY HALL, WHICH SERVED AS
THE NATION'S FIRST CAPITOL BUILDING.
TODAY THE ALEXANDER HAMILTON U.S.
CUSTOMS HOUSE STANDS IN ITS PLACE.

THIS POLITICAL CARTOON, "CON-G-SS EMBARK'D ON BOARD THE SHIP *CONSTITUTION OF AMERICA* BOUND TO CONOGOCHEQUE BY WAY OF PHILADELPHIA," OFFERS A CYNICAL TAKE ON MOVING THE CAPITAL FROM NEW YORK CITY THROUGH PHILADELPHIA AND TO THE POTOMAC.

> *America helped finance the French Revolution, just as the French had helped finance the American Revolution.*

of those congressmen in return for Hamilton's help moving the national capital from New York City, through Philadelphia for ten years (to secure Pennsylvania's support for the deal), to a new city on the Potomac River. Washington, D.C., stands as America's capital today because the federal government shouldered state debts.

The Dinner Table Bargain cleared the way for enacting the recommendations of Hamilton's "Report on Public Credit." New loans, secured primarily through Dutch bankers, allowed for rolling over and discharging the foreign debts—mostly to France—by 1795. The timing of those payments meant that America helped finance the French Revolution, just as the French had helped finance the American Revolution.

With Congress's approval, Hamilton restructured the country's domestic debt, which went smoothly. But even with interest payments falling from $4 million to $2.7 million, new interest plus

ALEXANDER HAMILTON

An ACT making Provision for the Debt of the United States.

SEC. 1. WHEREAS juftice and the fupport of public credit require, that provifion fhould be made for fulfilling the engagements of the United States, in refpect to their foreign debt, and for funding their domeftic debt upon equitable and fatisfactory terms:

Be it enacted by the Senate and Houfe of Reprefentatives of the United States of America, in Congrefs affembled, That referving out of the monies which have arifen fince the laft day of December laft paft, and which fhall hereafter arife from the duties on goods, wares and merchandize imported into the United States, and on the tonnage of fhips or veffels, the yearly fum of fix hundred thoufand dollars, or fo much thereof as may be appropriated from time to time, towards the fupport of the government of the United States, and their common defence, the refidue of the faid monies, or fo much thereof as may be neceffary, as the fame fhall be received in each year, next after the fum referved as aforefaid, fhall be, and is hereby appropriated to the payment of the intereft which fhall from time to time become due on the loans heretofore made by the United States in foreign countries; and alfo to the payment of intereft on fuch further loans as may be obtained for difcharging the arrears of intereft thereupon, and the whole or any part of the principal thereof; to continue fo appropriated until the faid loans, as well thofe already made as thofe which may be made in virtue of this act, fhall be fully fatisfied, purfuant to the contracts relating to the fame, any law to the contray notwithftanding. *And provided,* That nothing herein contained, fhall be conftrued to annul or alter any appropriation by law made prior to the paffing of this act.

SEC. 2. And as new loans are and will be neceffary for the payment of the aforefaid arrears of intereft, and the inftalments of the principal of the faid foreign debt due and growing due, and may alfo be found expedient for effecting an entire alteration in the ftate of the fame:

Be it further enacted, That the Prefident of the United States be, and he is hereby authorized, to caufe to be borrowed on behalf of the United States, a fum or fums, not exceeding in the whole twelve million of dollars; and that fo much of this fum as may be neceffary to the difcharge of the faid arrears and inftalments, and (if it can be effected upon terms advantageous to the United States) to the paying off the whole of the faid foreign debt be appropriated folely to thofe purpofes: And the Prefident is moreover further authorized to caufe to be made fuch other contracts refpecting the faid debt as fhall be found for the intereft of the faid States. *Provided neverthelefs,* That no engagement nor contract fhall be entered into, which fhall preclude the United States from reimburfing any fum or fums borrowed within fifteen years after the fame fhall have been lent or advanced.

SEC. 3. And whereas it is defirable to adapt the nature of the provifion to be made for the domeftic debt, to the prefent circumftances of the United States, as far as it fhall be found practicable confiftently with good faith and the rights of the creditors; which can only be done by a voluntary loan on their part:

Be it therefore further enacted, That a loan to the full amount of the faid domeftic debt be, and the fame is hereby propofed; and that books for receiving fubfcriptions to the faid loan be opened at the Treafury of the United States, and by a commiffioner to be appointed in each of the faid States, on the firft

THE FUNDING ACT OF 1790, "AN ACT MAKING PROVISION FOR THE DEBT OF THE UNITED STATES."

> *Hamilton's gamble relied on economic growth.*

operating expenses came to more than $4 million by 1792, when the plan went fully operational. Where was Congress going to find $4 million a year? Hamilton recommended tax increases and extensions, which Congress enacted along with a few new ones, notably one on distilled spirits. Rates of taxation remained low, however, because, again, Americans detested taxes. Import tariffs also stayed low, 10-20 percent on average in the early 1790s.*

Hamilton's gamble relied not on tax increases but on economic growth. Rising incomes drew more imports and swelled customs collections. They also allowed the government to borrow money to cover shortfalls. That's why Hamilton's plan also called for a central bank and securities markets. The bank would loan money to the government and also to the private sector to extend commerce and facilitate growth. Securities markets operated in a similar way. Their existence increased the power of the Treasury to borrow, provided corporations with a way of raising equity, and offered private investors liquidity and income. In Hamilton's visionary plan, power and growth went hand in hand. Each was necessary for the other to succeed.

★ ★ ★ ★ ★

The Bank of the United States.

In his January 1790 report, Hamilton asked Congress to ask him for a proposal for a national bank. Congress obliged. The bank report came in December. In it, Hamilton listed three principal advantages of the bank. The first emphasized its contributions to economic growth. Bank lending to businesses created bank money—notes and deposits—to augment the supply from the mint. The second and third advantages accrued to the government: The bank offered a loan source to the government, and it facilitated the payment of taxes by lending to people who owed taxes and by increasing the amount and speed of circulating money.

> *He didn't want Congress to have control of the bank.*

Hamilton proposed a private corporation, chartered by Congress, to avoid "a calamitous abuse" when temptation might lead to excess. In other words, he didn't want Congress to have control of

*The purpose of the import tariff was to generate revenue, not protection, despite contentions that Hamilton was a protectionist. A truly protective tariff would obstruct imports and therefore generate little revenue. Hamilton wanted the money.

the bank. However, he did call for the government to own a 20 percent minority stake in it. Private investors would own the rest, which they could buy in installments, a quarter in hard money and the rest in 6 percent Treasury bonds. The latter provision increased demand and signaled a restoration of public credit; it also ensured that American, not foreign, investors benefited most. His design for the bank cleverly supported the public debt, just as the debt supported the bank. In his bank report, Hamilton formalized these provisions and others into twenty-four articles of a proposed constitution, which formed the basis for the bank's charter.

THE BANK OF THE
UNITED STATES
ON THIRD STREET
IN PHILADELPHIA,
1799.

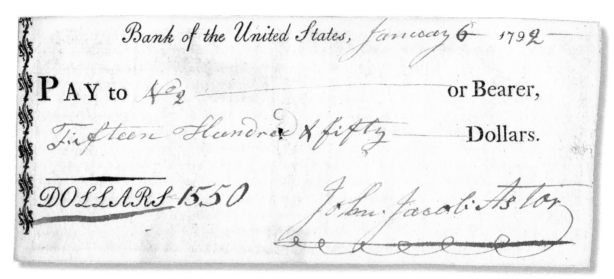

A CHECK DRAWN ON THE BANK OF THE UNITED STATES
AND SIGNED BY FINANCIER JOHN JACOB ASTOR, 1792.

The municipal government of Amsterdam entirely owned the Bank of Amsterdam, founded in 1609. Sweden's parliament entirely owned the Riksbank, founded in 1668 and the world's oldest central bank. On the other end of the spectrum, private stockholders entirely owned the Bank of England, founded in 1694.* So why did Hamilton construct a hybrid public-private corporation? Government investment in the bank would set the wheels in motion faster, but he also wanted an independent bank that could resist political control and the abuses that come with it, a principle we know today as central bank independence. He wanted the bank to meet government needs, including the right of inspection, and for the government to share in the profits. That last point, profit sharing, sent a clear message to the state legislatures: You, too, can charter banks and share in their profits.

But that wasn't the end of the story. The president had to approve the bank bill, and Washington hesitated when three trusted advisors—Secretary of State Jefferson, Attorney General Edmund Randolph, and Congressman Madison, all Virginians—argued that the Constitution didn't explicitly authorize the creation of the bank. Washington asked Hamilton to respond to their strict constructionist arguments.

Implied constitutional powers.

Hamilton countered with a sweeping defense that set forth the doctrine of implied constitutional powers, which the Constitution's "necessary and proper" clause supported. Legal scholars trace this doctrine, now an accepted principle of international

---

*The Bank of England remained in private hands for more than 250 years until Clement Attlee's Labour government nationalized it in 1946.

WASHINGTON AND HIS CABINET. FROM LEFT TO RIGHT: WASHINGTON, SECRETARY OF WAR HENRY KNOX, SECRETARY OF THE TREASURY ALEXANDER HAMILTON, SECRETARY OF STATE THOMAS JEFFERSON, ATTORNEY GENERAL EDMUND RANDOLPH.

constitutional law, to Hamilton's February 1791 essay, "Opinion on the Constitutionality of an Act to Establish a Bank." Two days after receiving Hamilton's opinion, Washington signed the bill into law. Perhaps the brief persuaded him, or maybe, as some scholars have suggested, Hamilton's victory came as part of a complex congressional deal to move the capital southward by 1800.

Either way, the bank publicly offered its stock in July 1791 to heavy oversubscription. Its doors opened in Philadelphia that December, and branches in Boston, New York, Baltimore, and Charleston did the same in 1792. It was the only corporation that Congress chartered, and obtaining that charter hadn't proved easy. In that sense, the bank also served a larger purpose. Its example urged the states to charter more banks of their own and, in turn, a growing number of nonbanking corporations.

The states heard the message. A month after Washington approved the bill, the New York Assembly finally chartered the Bank of New York, and it did so defensively. If they didn't charter a state bank, the federal bank's branch in New York City would dominate the state's banking market. Rhode Island chartered the Providence Bank in 1790 for exactly the opposite reason: It wanted to *attract* a branch of the federal bank. In 1792, Connecticut chartered three banks (Hartford, New London, New Haven),

State banks.

necessary as equivalent to requisite or needful or conducive to a particular end. Thus if it should be that it is necessary to France to maintain her connection with Spain this would only imply that the connection is... to Great Britain to maintain a good understanding with Holland this would only mean that the maintenance of that good understanding is useful to her or conducive to her interests. It would not imply that it is essentially or indispensable or absolutely requisite;

or a thing without which she could not exist or prosper as a nation.

Neither does such a signification accord with the popular use of the term. A man will say for instance "It is necessary I should breakfast before I go to business" this would not mean that he could not do business without having first breakfasted; but merely that his habits are such as to render it inconvenient to him to enter upon the business of the day before he has made that meal.

Considerations of political expediency do not favour such a construction; because it tends to create a disability in the government to pursue measures which though highly useful may not be absolutely essential; and of course abridges its power of doing good even in reference to the objects which are particularly confided to it.

It must ever be a matter of infinite uncertainty when a measure is necessary in the sense in which the word is understood by the Secretary of State. Many very intelligent men have contended that all regulations of trade are pernicious. There are many in this country who now maintain that all... extra burthens

HAMILTON'S DRAFT OF HIS REPORT ON THE CONSTITUTIONALITY
OF A NATIONAL BANK, FEBRUARY 23, 1791.

Virginia two (Alexandria and Richmond, although the latter never opened), and one each by New Hampshire (Portsmouth), New York (Albany), and Massachusetts (Boston). That same year, the Essex Bank opened for business in Salem, Massachusetts, and the Bank of South Carolina in Charleston—both without charters.

More charters followed. Three banks in 1790 became twenty-eight by 1800. They all did business with one another and with the five branches of the Bank of the United States. Hamilton jump-started an entire industry from a single corporation.

Hamilton jump-started an entire industry from a single corporation.

★ ★ ★ ★ ★

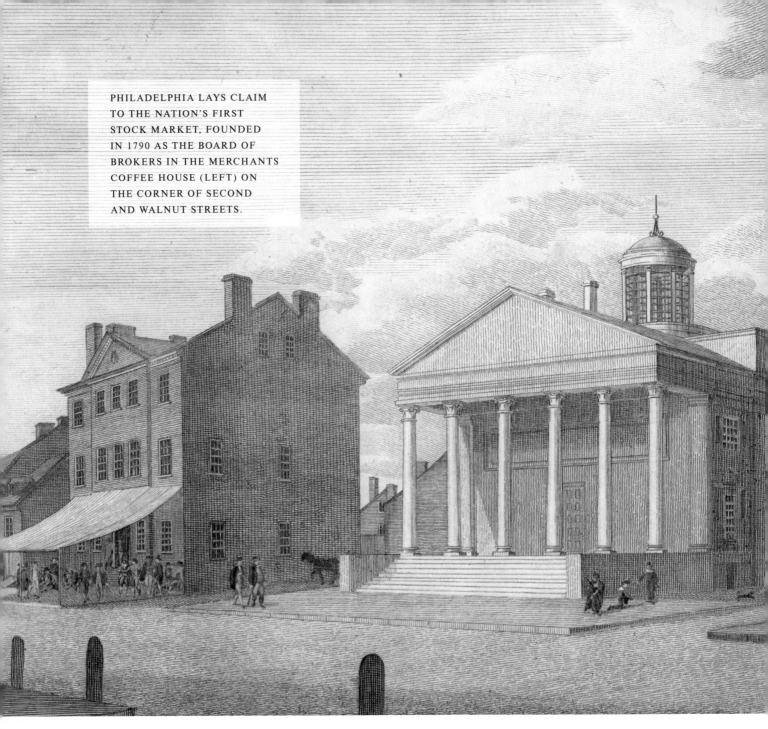

PHILADELPHIA LAYS CLAIM
TO THE NATION'S FIRST
STOCK MARKET, FOUNDED
IN 1790 AS THE BOARD OF
BROKERS IN THE MERCHANTS
COFFEE HOUSE (LEFT) ON
THE CORNER OF SECOND
AND WALNUT STREETS.

Securities markets.

Hamilton's financial program also jump-started the securities markets. As soon as these new securities reached private hands, markets actively traded them in several cities: Philadelphia, New York, and Boston in 1790, followed closely by Charleston and Baltimore. Philadelphia lays claim to the first stock exchange, established that year. In New York City, brokers met in May 1792 under a buttonwood tree on Wall Street and agreed

ALEXANDER HAMILTON

In 1794, Hamilton advocated amassing a huge force of federal troops to convince the Whiskey Rebellion insurgents to lay down their arms. Here Washington, Hamilton, and others lead those federal troops to suppress the rebellion.

Tontine Coffee House by Francis Guy, c. 1797 (building shown at left). Set in Lower Manhattan, the painting shows New York City's burgeoning industry. Diagonally opposite, on the far right, stands the Merchant's Coffee House, where the stockbrokers of the Buttonwood Agreement conducted business before the Tontine was built. To the center right, Wall Street leads down to the East River.

to trade with one another on preferential terms and with outsiders for higher fixed-commission rates. Thus began the New York Stock Exchange.

Newspapers printed the first price listings of actively traded securities in the 1790s. In New York, they reported on five: the three federal debt issues and the stocks of the Bank of the United States and the Bank of New York. Alexander Hamilton had created all five.

Thus began the New York Stock Exchange.

★ ★ ★ ★ ★

From Jamestown to independence, colonial legislatures had chartered just seven corporations. From 1781 to 1790, state legislatures approved another twenty-seven. Over the next decade, some three hundred corporations received charters. Of the nonbanking entities, the largest were insurance companies. Only two insurance companies had existed in America before 1791; states chartered thirty more from 1791 to 1800.

The rise of American corporations.

THE BUTTONWOOD AGREEMENT, WHICH TOOK PLACE OUTSIDE 68 WALL STREET, FOUNDED THE NEW YORK STOCK EXCHANGE.

They also established smaller corporations to handle infrastructure: inland navigation improvements, toll bridges, turnpikes, and water companies.

Most of these new corporations formed in the Northeast. The southern states—apart from South Carolina, a Federalist bastion—lagged in this area, but the northern states understood the hints that Hamilton dropped in his bank report. They generated revenues by charging fees for charters, by receiving interest and dividends from investments in corporate securities, and eventually by taxing corporations.

Several states also benefited from the settling of state accounts, which involved tallying up the costs of the war, each state's contributions to that cost, and each state's fair share based on population. Creditor states, which had paid more than their fair share, received the difference in federal securities that paid interest. Debtor states, which had paid less than their fair share, had the debts forgiven for political reasons.

Hamilton's financial policies greatly reduced state fiscal burdens. Several states saw increased revenues and reduced expenditures to the point where they could reduce and in some cases even eliminate state taxation. That helped cement the Union, one of the Washington administration's key goals. Hamilton received little credit for this achievement in his lifetime or from later historians, but it stands as one of his most important accomplishments.

★ ★ ★ ★ ★

The dollar. The least controversial element of Hamilton's reforms was setting the dollar as the nation's currency. Congress had requested him to issue a mint report, which came in January 1791. Until then, the country relied on foreign coins, especially the Spanish

THE TURBAN HEAD EAGLE GOLD COIN, 1795.

ALEXANDER HAMILTON

Congreſs of the United States:

AT THE THIRD SESSION,

Begun and held at the City of Philadelphia, on
Monday the ſixth of December, one thou-
ſand ſeven hundred and ninety.

———

RESOLVED *by the* SENATE *and* HOUSE *of* REPRESENTATIVES *of
the United States of America in Congreſs aſſembled,* That a mint
ſhall be eſtabliſhed under ſuch regulations as ſhall be directed by law.

Reſolved, That the Preſident of the United States be, and he is
hereby authorized to cauſe to be engaged, ſuch principal artiſts as
ſhall be neceſſary to carry the preceeding reſolution into effect, and to
ſtipulate the terms and conditions of their ſervice, and alſo to cauſe to
be procured ſuch apparatus as ſhall be requiſite for the ſame purpoſe.

FREDERICK AUGUSTUS MUHLENBERG,
Speaker of the Houſe of Repreſentatives.

JOHN ADAMS, *Vice-Preſident of the United States,
and Preſident of the Senate.*

APPROVED, March the third, 1791.

GEORGE WASHINGTON, *Preſident of the United States.*

"dollar"; paper money from the states, which gradually was withdrawn from circulation
to obey the Constitution; and the notes of the three banks of the time.

Hamilton's mint report defined the American dollar as certain weights of silver and
gold and called on Congress to establish a mint to make those coins as well as fractions
and multiples. Congress enacted the essence of the mint report in 1792.

The report defined the foundation of U.S. money as gold and silver dollars, which
Americans used in everyday transactions. More important, though, banks stockpiled

THE COPPER
PATTERN
DISME
(DIME), 1792.

THE
FLOWING
HAIR CENT,
1793.

those coins as reserves to support the deposits and notes they issued. Notes and deposits transferable by checks functioned as money because banks promised to convert them on demand into gold and silver coins, or specie.

Well-run banks could function with specie reserves that amounted to just a fraction

ALEXANDER HAMILTON

of their liabilities. People held and used bank money in most of their transactions because it was more convenient than gold or silver. In this arrangement, a poorly managed bank could even fail without threatening overall financial stability—although of course its liability holders would suffer losses. During financial panics, however, people lost confidence in banks and ran on them to convert notes and deposits into specie, which of course they lacked in sufficient amounts. Banks then had to suspend convertibility or find a way to borrow specie reserves from another source.* Hamilton's monetary system persisted until the 1930s. In many

Federal Reserve liabilities have replaced gold and silver.

respects, it looked a lot like our own today, with two key differences. Today the monetary base consists mostly of notes from the Federal Reserve, America's central bank, and from bank reserves held either as Federal Reserve notes or deposits. In other words, Federal Reserve liabilities have replaced gold and silver. The Federal Reserve also has an obligation to act as a bankers' bank to enhance financial stability by lending base money to banks during crises.†

★ ★ ★ ★ ★

America experienced its first financial crisis in March 1792, barely two years after Hamilton launched his program. It might have undone his plans just as they were getting off the ground. That's exactly what happened, as he well knew, in 1720 when John Law's French reform program collapsed along with the Mississippi Bubble.

Banking and securities markets represented new developments for many Americans in the early 1790s and appealed to their speculative instincts. For example, the Bank of the United States made its initial public offering of stock in July 1790. For $25, investors received a scrip giving them the right to a full share of $400 of stock by paying the remaining $375 in installments over the next couple of years. The value of the scrips themselves quickly escalated—to as much as $300—creating euphoria for those who had bought them at lower prices. Then they declined even more quickly to less than $200, creating misery for those who had bought them at higher prices, especially with

The Scrip Bubble.

....

* A central bank—or, if you like, a bankers' bank—eventually became that source, but it took a long time.

† The Bank of the United States sometimes functioned as a bankers' bank, but it had no obligation to do so.

borrowed money. "A bubble connected with my operations is of all the enemies I have to fear, in my judgment, the most formidable," Hamilton wrote to his friend Rufus King, a Federalist senator from New York.

The Panic of 1792.

An even larger bubble began inflating a few months later. A cabal of speculators led by William Duer, Hamilton's former assistant at the Treasury Department, hatched a plan to corner the market for 6 percent bonds, which could be used to make installment payments for bank shares. The cabal borrowed money right and left in early 1792 to procure the bonds. Some of that money may have come from the new Bank of the United States, which opened in December 1791, quickly expanded its lending business the following month, and just as quickly contracted it when faced with losing reserves. The 6 percents shot up to 125 percent of face value by March. Then Duer defaulted on his debts, triggering bankruptcies and the 6 percents to fall to 5 percent below face value in two weeks.

> *"A bubble connected with my operations is of all the enemies I have to fear ... the most formidable."*

Hamilton intervened to stanch the crisis. He urged banks—against their natural instincts—to continue lending to business borrowers who had to pay taxes to the government and promised the banks he wouldn't withdraw the tax money. He also orchestrated open-market purchases of government debt once again to calm investors' frayed nerves.

But most cleverly of all, he launched a plan for frightened investors to collateralize their securities at prices he named for bank loans, instead of selling them at fire-sale prices in the depressed markets. In crises, banks don't want to make loans, for fear of getting stuck with the collateral if prices keep falling, but Hamilton alleviated that concern by offering to take the collateral at prices he named. The plan worked: The markets calmed, and securities prices rebounded. Hamilton later repaid the bank loans that financed the open-market purchases with money borrowed from Dutch bankers. It was a brilliant piece of crisis management.

Little economic damage resulted, but the crisis had consider-

WILLIAM DUER, HAMILTON'S FORMER ASSISTANT, TRIGGERED THE PANIC OF 1792 BY TRYING TO CORNER THE MARKET ON 6 PERCENT GOVERNMENT BONDS.

ALEXANDER HAMILTON

able political fallout. Jefferson, Madison, and others already were organizing a Democratic-Republican Party to oppose Hamilton's Federalist Party. The Panic of 1792 fanned the fires that the Federalists were leading the country down the wrong path. They attacked and tried to topple Hamilton throughout the remainder of his time in office.

One of those attacks in 1794 concerned trade policy. From the time the new government had formed in 1789, Jefferson and Madison wanted to use trade policy as a lever to force Britain to ease the restrictions it had placed on American shipping and access to foreign markets, particularly those of the British Empire. The secretary of state and congressman also had pro-French, anti-British sympathies, a popular position given how the War of Independence played out.

The Democratic-Republican opposition may have painted them as such, but the Federalists were hardly pro-British. They pragmatically noted that most U.S. trade took place with Britain, not France, and that taxes on imports, mostly from Britain, generated most of the government's revenues. If America arched its back, the government of William Pitt the Younger understandably would retaliate. The resulting trade war would diminish American revenues and undercut everything Hamilton had done to restore public credit. On that basis, Hamilton and the Federalists stonewalled the Democratic-Republicans and prevented legislation that discriminated against Britain.

By the time Washington's second term began in 1793, France—now in the blood-drenched throes of the French Revolution—had gone to war with Britain. At Hamilton's behest, Washington announced a policy of neutrality toward the belligerents. That move rankled the pro-French Democratic-Republicans. Just before he stepped down as secretary of state at the end of 1793, Jefferson issued a report that documented Britain's restrictions on American shipping and trade, and he renewed the call for a get-tough policy. Meanwhile, Britain played into Jefferson's hands by increasing those restrictions.

It was a brilliant piece of crisis management.

Trade with Britain.

The Jay Treaty.

Hamilton explained to Congress and the president that Jefferson's plan would lead to a trade war and undermine the newly established public credit; it might even lead to a military showdown. To stop the wheels from rolling downhill, they sent John Jay to negotiate a formal treaty. Jay secured it early the following year, by which time Hamilton

TREATY

AMITY, COMMERCE,

AND

NAVIGATION,

BETWEEN

His Britannic Majesty

AND

The United States of America,

CONDITIONALLY RATIFIED
BY THE SENATE OF THE UNITED STATES,
AT PHILADELPHIA, JUNE 24, 1795.

———

TO WHICH IS ANNEXED,

A Copious Appendix.

———

PHILADELPHIA:

PRINTED BY HENRY TUCKNISS,
FOR MATHEW CAREY, NO. 118, MARKET STREET.

Aug. 12, 1795.

PROTESTERS IN CHARLESTON DENOUNCE THE JAY TREATY WITH BRITAIN, 1794.

had stepped down from office. Congress ratified the controversial treaty, which took effect in 1796 and lasted for a decade. It prevented a trade war and a shooting war and stands as another of Hamilton's triumphs over his enemies.

After the Jay Treaty expired, President Jefferson embargoed all British trade with America. That and subsequent measures by President Madison led to a steep drop in federal revenues, a decline of public credit, and ultimately the War of 1812—all pretty much as Hamilton had predicted. But of course Hamilton didn't live to see his predictions come true.

FARMERS IN WESTERN PENNSYLVANIA CONFRONT AN EXCISE MAN (TAX
COLLECTOR), THREATENING TO "TAR AND FEATHER THE RASCAL."

The Whiskey Rebellion. Hamilton had called for, and Congress subsequently enacted, a number of domestic taxes to increase and diversify government revenue. One of those taxes applied to distilled spirits. Larger distillers in coastal cities willingly complied, but smaller distillers on the western frontier resisted. In western Pennsylvania in mid-1794, those small distillers organized forceful opposition to the tax. They attacked federal agents appointed to collect it, burned down one agent's house, and threatened to kill any of their own who obeyed the federal law.

After peaceful negotiations failed, Washington called for 12,000 militiamen to march against the rebels. Hamilton had recommended such huge numbers of men on the grounds that the rebels, when confronted with such a large force, would lay down their arms and no one would get hurt. With Hamilton alongside, Washington commanded the troops for the first stage of the march before handing the reins to Governor Henry Lee III of Virginia, whose state had supplied some of the government's men. Lee and Hamilton confronted the rebels, who disbanded and fled. Some of the rebels were arrested and tried, and two were convicted. The president pardoned them, and his always-high popularity rose further. The Whiskey Rebellion ultimately increased respect for federal law by demonstrating that the government could and would enforce it. Hamilton's strategy had worked.

★ ★ ★ ★ ★

Hamilton's "Report on Manufactures," which he submitted in December 1791, was the longest of his official reports to Congress. It also had the least immediate impact because Congress didn't enact its recommendations right away, as it had done with his other reports. But its long-term impact was greater in both America and the world. It contained nothing less than a plan for how the government and private sector could cooperate to develop an underdeveloped economy.

Economic development plan.

It also offered one of the first extended commentaries on Adam Smith, the father of modern economics. Smith's magnum opus, *The Wealth of Nations*, appeared in 1776 and recommended that the best way for a government to encourage economic development was to confine itself to a limited agenda—defense, justice, and certain public works—and then simply stand aside (laissez-faire) to let the markets coordinate human instincts for, and interests in, self-betterment.

It contained nothing less than a plan for how the government and private sector could cooperate to develop an underdeveloped economy.

The Smith and Hamilton alternatives have dominated the conversation about government's role in economic development for more than two centuries. Smith has received more credit for his formulation, although in practice more governments have followed Hamilton's path.

What was that path? Hamilton liked free enterprise and free markets as much as anyone. But that's not the world in which he and the great Scot lived. In the mercantilist model, which prevailed then, European governments heavily regulated trade to promote exports and discourage imports. They wanted to increase their own power

ADAM SMITH,
AUTHOR OF
*THE WEALTH
OF NATIONS*.

A N

I N Q U I R Y

INTO THE

Nature and Caufes

OF THE

WEALTH OF NATIONS.

By ADAM SMITH, LL. D. and F. R. S.

Formerly Profeffor of Moral Philofophy in the Univerfity of GLASGOW.

IN TWO VOLUMES.

VOL. I.

———————————————

L O N D O N:

PRINTED FOR W. STRAHAN; AND T. CADELL, IN THE STRAND.

MDCCLXXVI.

TITLE PAGE OF *THE WEALTH OF NATIONS*, PUBLISHED 1776.

> *Hamilton liked free enterprise and free markets as much as anyone.*

and reduce that of their rivals. They wanted colonies to function as captive markets and sources of raw materials for home-country industries. They wanted their colonies to rely on the home country for financial services instead of developing their own—exactly why Britain banned banks and mints in America and insisted on regulating colonial currency from London. These policies had worked well and continued to work well for Britain. The kingdom had a rich economy, had won almost all of its wars, and was building a worldwide empire despite losing some of its North American colonies.

Hamilton wanted the same if not better for America. But that meant playing catch-up. In 1790, the House had asked him "to prepare and report . . . a proper plan . . . for the encouragement and promotion of such manufactories as will tend to render the United States independent of other nations for essential, particularly for military supplies." Hamilton replied that the country could achieve that aim by levying import taxes to give American industry an advantage until it grew strong enough to compete with Europe's. As a good economist, however, Hamilton preferred subsidies because they could accomplish the same result without making Americans pay higher prices. Moreover, the country could ban exports of strategic raw materials and exempt imports of raw materials from customs duties. It could encourage invention by granting patents and awarding prizes to inventors. It could lure skilled workers from Europe. It could improve internal transportation and thereby speed commerce.

Even before Hamilton delivered his report to Congress, he drew up a "Prospectus of the Society for Establishing Useful Manufactures," a model corporation to pool investor capital and demonstrate the promise of manufacturing. He proposed locating the society's factories in New Jersey, which could use waterpower generated by the falls of the Passaic River, not far from New York City. When New Jersey governor William Paterson eased the way for the society's charter, which Hamilton wrote, the state named the new factory town after Paterson.

The corporation had a successful initial public offering and opened for business. But after a promising start, it fell victim to poor management. Instead of building and operating its own factories, it turned itself into a company providing waterpower to factories built by others. It survived that way into the twentieth century, and Paterson ultimately did become a major center of American manufacturing.

THE FALLS OF THE PASSAIC RIVER THAT POWERED THE NEW NATION'S FACTORIES.

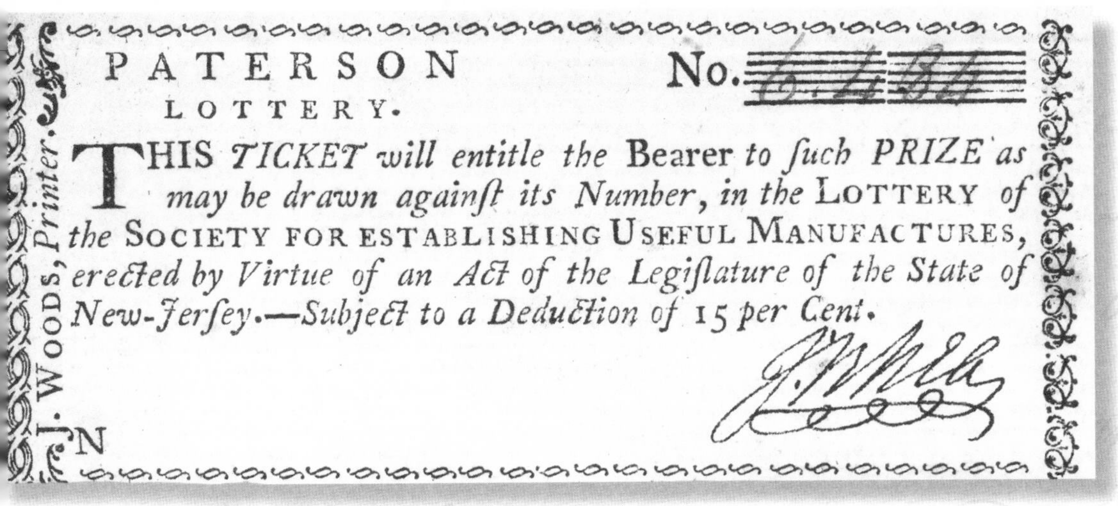

PATERSON No. 6.484

LOTTERY.

THIS *TICKET will entitle the* Bearer *to ſuch PRIZE as may be drawn againſt its Number, in the* LOTTERY *of the* SOCIETY FOR ESTABLISHING USEFUL MANUFACTURES, *erected by Virtue of an Act of the Legiſlature of the State of New-Jerſey.—Subject to a Deduction of* 15 *per Cent.*

J. WOODS, *Printer.*

N

LOTTERY TICKET SOLD TO RAISE MONEY FOR THE SOCIETY FOR ESTABLISHING USEFUL MANUFACTURES, BASED IN PATERSON, NEW JERSEY, 1791.

On December 1, 1794, shortly after returning from the campaign to suppress the Whiskey Rebellion, Hamilton wrote to President Washington and Frederick Muhlenberg, speaker of the House, to resign as secretary of the Treasury at the end of January, three weeks after his thirty-eighth birthday. Hamilton didn't say why, but we can glean the reasons from two letters he wrote to Angelica Schuyler Church, his sister-in-law, who had been living in England with her husband.

The first letter, dated December 8, 1794, came from Philadelphia:

> *My dear Eliza has been lately very ill. Thank God, she is now quite recovered, except that she continues somewhat weak. My absence on a certain expedition was the cause (with the army to suppress the whiskey insurrection in Pennsylvania)....*
>
> *Don't let Mr. Church be alarmed at my retreat—all is well with the public. Our insurrection is most happily terminated. Government has gained by it reputation and strength, and our finances are in a most flourishing condition. Having contributed to place those of the Nation on a good footing, I go to take a little care of my own; which need my care not a little.*

The second letter came from Albany and was dated March 6, 1795:

> *You know how much we all love you. 'Tis impossible you can be so well loved where you are. And what is there can be put in competition with the sweet affections of the heart?*
>
> *To indulge these the more freely is with me a principal motive for relinquishing an office in which 'tis said I have gained some glory and the difficulties of which had just been subdued.*
>
> *Eliza & our children are with me here at your father's house who is himself at New York attending the Legislature. We remain till June, when we become stationary at New York, where I will resume the practice of law. For My Dear Sister, I tell you without regret what I hope you anticipate, that I am poorer than when I went into office. I allot myself full five or six years of more work than will be pleasant though much less than I have had for the last five years.*

"I am poorer than when I went into office."

Hamilton had inherited an empty Treasury in 1789, but the nation's fortunes and finances had grown, exactly as he had planned. In the process, he had "gained some glory,"

ANGELICA SCHUYLER
CHURCH, HAMILTON'S
SISTER-IN-LAW.

which he also wanted. But his personal finances lay in shambles. As Treasury secretary, he received only $3,500 a year, much less than he could make as a lawyer and far less than the $25,000 that the president earned. Unlike Washington, Jefferson, Madison, and other peers in public service, he didn't have a plantation to generate outside income. He had to borrow money to make ends meet. He also regretted neglecting his wife and family in favor of the Treasury. Eliza (no longer Betsy) had a miscarriage while he was dealing with the whiskey rebels, and he blamed himself for it. Hamilton had more than enough reasons to return to private life.

"Once the federal government assumed control over domestic policy, slavery was doomed."

—JOSEPH J. ELLIS, *AMERICAN CREATION*

{VII}

ABOLITIONIST

1778–1800

As a boy in the West Indies, Hamilton developed a dislike of slavery that lasted throughout his life. Unlike most Americans, he grew up in a mostly black society. On Nevis and St. Croix, blacks outnumbered whites roughly 8 to 1, and his mother owned several slaves. But his distaste for slavery didn't prevent him from participating in transactions involving slaves. It started in the West Indies when he worked for Beekman and Cruger, and it occurred from time to time in New York City as a part of his legal practice and when he handled the business affairs of his brother-in-law and others.

Building a strong nation with a diverse and thriving economy was Hamilton's principal life goal. He and the other founders quickly learned that even talk of abolishing slavery in America could weaken the Union. They retreated from pressing the moral issue to attain what they considered a higher goal. Hamilton nonetheless positioned himself against slavery and in favor of abolition a number of times. Nearly every time he did, he faced rebuke and made enemies. As he marched from victory to victory as Treasury secretary, many of his slaveholding opponents—knowing he favored abolition and seeing that he was creating institutions that could threaten their interests in owning humans—came to see him as a dangerous man.

Without divulging their true motives, those politicians sought support from nonslaveholders to pull him from power. To force his resignation as Treasury secretary, they

> *Even talk of abolishing slavery in America could weaken the Union.*

THE SLAVE TRADE BY JOHN RAPHAEL SMITH, AFTER GEORGE MORLAND, 1791.

DANISH SUBJECTS
AND SLAVES ON A
PALM-LINED ROAD
ON ST. CROIX.

noisily branded him as corrupt, a monarchist, militarist, "consolidationist" (a pejorative term for a Federalist), an "Angloman" (pro-British), and an enemy of the people's rights and liberties.

He parried their thrusts, and the slavers failed to topple him—but they did pave the way for their own rise to power in 1801. They controlled the country for the next sixty years, not only preserving but extending the Peculiar Institution.

Did Hamilton own slaves?

"Mrs. H."

First, let's look at whether Hamilton himself owned slaves, as many prominent New Yorkers did during the late eighteenth century.

On May 22, 1781, Hamilton, a soldier not yet on his way to Yorktown, wrote to Governor Clinton that from his army pay he hoped "to receive a sufficient sum to pay the value of the woman Mrs. H had of Mrs. Clinton." Betsy Hamilton was pregnant, and neither she nor her husband knew how much longer he would be fighting the British. The couple may have decided that she needed help. If so, was it a hire or a purchase? We don't know for sure, but Hamilton biographer Forrest McDonald has said that Hamilton was writing about his back pay, which was "much less than enough to buy a slave," so "it is far more likely that Betsey, in keeping with common practice at the time, had merely hired a servant employed by or belonging to Mrs. Clinton."

Philip Schuyler, a slaveholder, wrote to his son-in-law on August 31, 1795: "The Negro boy & woman are engaged for you. I understand Mr. Witbeck has written you on the Subject and that he waits your answer finally to conclude the bargain." * Seven months later, on March 23, 1796, Hamilton's cash book contains an entry for $250 in favor of Philip Schuyler "for 2 Negro servants purchased by him for me."

"2 Negro servants."

PHILIP SCHUYLER, HAMILTON'S FATHER-IN-LAW, OWNED SLAVES AND BOUGHT TWO PEOPLE, A WOMAN AND BOY, ON HIS SON-IN-LAW'S BEHALF.

*Witbeck worked for Stephen van Rensselaer, a wealthy upstate New York landowner, as an estate manager.

Biographer Ron Chernow thinks Hamilton may have performed this transaction on behalf of John and Angelica Church, who in the mid-1790s were planning to move from London to New York. The Churches didn't return until May 1797, however, and, on Church's behalf, Hamilton did purchase a "Negro woman" for them then. The timing might raise doubts that Hamilton undertook the 1795–96 transaction for his in-laws, but the Churches also might have planned to return earlier than they did. He also could have been acting as an agent for someone else entirely.

In the end, it remains unclear whether Hamilton owned slaves. If he did, given his views, he no doubt felt intensely guilty about it, and the ownership was temporary. How do we know? Just before he died in 1804, Hamilton listed no slaves as assets in the modest estate he left to Eliza and their children.

★ ★ ★ ★ ★

On March 14, 1779, after the British had shifted their war efforts to the Southern Campaign, Hamilton wrote to John Jay, then president of Congress, to endorse a plan by John Laurens, a dear friend and another aide de camp to Washington. Laurens, also an abolitionist, wanted to raise several battalions of slaves from his native South Carolina to fight the British.

In the letter, Hamilton says

Slave battalions.

> *I frequently hear it objected to the scheme of embodying negroes that they are too stupid to make soldiers. This is so far from appearing to me to be a valid objection that I think their want of cultivation (for their natural faculties are probably as good as ours) joined to that habit of subordination which they acquire from a life of servitude, will make them sooner become soldiers than our White inhabitants....*
>
> *I foresee that this project will have to combat much opposition from prejudice and self-interest. The contempt we have been taught to entertain for the blacks, makes us fancy things that are founded neither in reason nor experience; and an unwillingness to part with property of so valuable a kind will furnish a thousand arguments to show the impracticality or pernicious tendency of a scheme which requires such a sacrifice. But it should be considered, that if we do not make use of them in this way, the enemy probably will.... An essential part of*

JOHN LAURENS BY CHARLES WILLSON PEALE, 1780. LAURENS, ANOTHER OF GENERAL WASHINGTON'S AIDES DE CAMP, WANTED TO RAISE BATTALIONS OF SLAVES TO FIGHT THE BRITISH. SOUTH CAROLINA REJECTED HIS PROPOSAL TWICE.

THE NEW YORK ANTI-SLAVERY OFFICE SOLD COPIES OF THIS 1837 BROADSIDE OF JOHN GREENLEAF WHITTIER'S "OUR COUNTRYMEN IN CHAINS," WHICH INCLUDES THE ILLUSTRATION "AM I NOT A MAN AND A BROTHER?"

ALEXANDER HAMILTON

the plan is to give them their freedom with their muskets. This will secure their fidelity, animate their courage, and I believe will have a good influence upon those who remain, by opening a door to their emancipation. This circumstance, I confess, has no small weight in inducing me to wish the success of the project; for the dictates of humanity and true policy equally interest me in favour of this unfortunate class of men.

Here he puts the natural faculties of blacks on par with whites—a provocative view that hardly anyone else in America, for or against slavery, shared then or for a long time. He also correctly predicted the plan's chances for success. South Carolina rejected Laurens's proposal twice. Hamilton's letter to Jay was private, so we can't say whether others knew of his association with the Laurens plan or his progressive views regarding slavery. But they did before long.

In 1785, Hamilton helped found the New York Society for Promoting the Manumission of Slaves and Protecting Such of Them as Have Been or May Be Liberated. Other members included Governor Clinton; Mayor James Duane; John Jay, the society's first president; and a number of Quakers, who stood at the forefront of the abolition movement. But abolishing slavery was a long-term goal. The immediate problem that prompted the formation of the society was the kidnapping of free blacks in the city to sell them into slavery. The 1790 census showed the city had a black population of 3,100, of whom two-thirds were slaves. All of New York State had 21,000 slaves and 4,600 free blacks.

Many members of the Manumission Society owned slaves. Hamilton and two other charter members comprised a committee tasked with how to handle this embarrassing situation. The committee proposed that its members immediately free slaves older than forty-five, and younger ones in seven years or on their thirty-fifth birthday. Many Society members found that prospect too liberal, so they tabled the report. But the group's continuing efforts met with success in 1799 when New York joined most of the other northeastern states in passing a gradual emancipation act to end slavery altogether by the 1820s.

If southern slaveholders hadn't heard of Hamilton's early abolitionist efforts, they certainly became aware of his stance on July 4, 1789. As part of the day's celebrations

"The contempt we have been taught to entertain for the blacks, makes us fancy things that are founded neither in reason nor experience."

The New York Society for Promoting the Manumission of Slaves.

The eulogy of General Greene.

ALEXANDER HAMILTON

THE NEW YORK CITY SLAVE MARKET ON WALL STREET, C. 1730.

IN THE SOUTHERN CAMPAIGN OF THE REVOLUTIONARY WAR, NATHANAEL GREENE (SHOWN HERE) SUCCESSFULLY EXPELLED CORNWALLIS FROM THE CAROLINAS, PAVING THE WAY FOR THE VICTORY AT YORKTOWN. HAMILTON'S CONTROVERSIAL EULOGY FOR HIM AT ST. PAUL'S CHAPEL IN MANHATTAN REVEALED HAMILTON'S ABOLITIONIST BELIEFS TO ALL ASSEMBLED.

Hamilton's oratory offended his audience not once but twice.

at St. Paul's Chapel, not far from Federal Hall, Hamilton delivered a eulogy on the life of General Nathanael Greene, who had died in Georgia three years earlier. Martha Washington, John and Abigail Adams, and many members of Congress attended.

Hamilton's oratory offended his audience not once but twice. He praised Greene for outwitting the Hessians early in the war. They "were baffled and almost beaten by a general without an army—aided or rather embarrassed by small fugitive bodies of vol-

ST. PAUL'S CHAPEL, C. 1812, WHERE HAMILTON RAILED AGAINST SLAVERY.

unteer militia, the mimicry of soldiership!" Washington and Hamilton disliked undisciplined militias, preferring a regular army of trained troops, but most Americans distrusted standing armies and took pride in their militias. Militiamen, after all, had played key roles in Greene's maneuvers that frustrated Cornwallis in the Southern Campaign. Hamilton had committed a serious faux pas.

Reflecting on the southern states' poor conditions when Greene took command there, Hamilton described Virginia as "debilitated by the excessive efforts of its early zeal and by the dissipation of its revenues and forces in Indian hostilities." So far so good, but then he described the state as being "incumbered by a numerous body of slaves bound by all the laws of *injured* humanity to hate their Masters." That line raised a red flag to the southern slaveholders in his audience. He had forewarned them—unwisely at best, dangerously at worst—that as head of the Treasury he was going to oppose their economic interests.

The Jay Treaty and "negroes or other property."

As secretary of the Treasury, Hamilton didn't say or write anything that offended slave interests, but he worked tirelessly to increase and consolidate federal power. Six months after stepping down, however, he returned to the subject when defending the controversial Jay Treaty. In 1794, Washington had sent Chief Justice John Jay to Britain, with instructions drawn up by Hamilton, to negotiate the treaty that maintained American neutrality between Britain and the French Republic. Part of Jay's mandate included resolving outstanding issues from the 1783 Treaty of Paris, by which Britain recognized American independence.

Article VII of the treaty stipulated that Britain withdraw its military forces from the United States "without causing any destruction, or carrying away any negroes or other property of the American inhabitants." The wording seemed to compel British forces not to destroy or take any American property *after* hostilities ceased. But that didn't apply to slaves seized during the fighting. American slaveholders, however, willfully interpreted the language to mean that Britain had to return any slaves that had been the property of Americans, and of course Britain hadn't returned any slaves. The Jay Treaty infuriated slaveholders by not dealing with this issue.

Writing as "Camillus," Hamilton supported the Jay Treaty by demonstrating that, under the laws of war as well as the laws of America, the British had no obligation to return slaves whom they had taken during the war. To do what the slaveholders wanted, Hamilton argued, would be both "odious and immoral."

> In the interpretation of Treaties things odious *or* immoral *are not to be* presumed. The abandonment of negroes, who had been induced to quit

DEFENCE

OF THE

TREATY

AMITY, COMMERCE, AND NAVIGATION,

ENTERED INTO BETWEEN

THE UNITED STATES OF AMERICA & GREAT BRITAIN

AS IT HAS APPEARED IN THE PAPERS UNDER THE

SIGNATURE OF

CAMILLUS.

A. Hamilton

NEW - YORK:

PRINTED AND SOLD BY FRANCIS CHILDS AND Co. AND SOLD BY
JAMES RIVINGTON, AT No. 156, Pearl-street; also, at the other Book
Stores of this City.——1795.

THE TITLE
PAGE OF
HAMILTON'S
DEFENSE
OF THE JAY
TREATY.

SEC. OF STATE

T. JEFFERSON.

their Masters on the faith of Official proclamations promising them liberty, to fall again under the yoke of their masters and into slavery is as odious and immoral a thing as can be conceived. It is odious not only as it imposes an act of perfidy on one of the contracting parties; but as it tends to bring back to servitude men once made free. The general interests of humanity conspire with the obligations which Great Britain had contracted towards the Negroes to repel this construction of the Treaty.

> *"To fall again . . . into slavery is as* odious *and* immoral *a thing as can be conceived."*

In other words, human rights trumped property rights. When Jefferson read "Camillus," he bristled. He knew "Camillus" was Hamilton and, as he so often did, pulled strings behind the scenes, goading Madison, who also owned many slaves, into action: "Hamilton is really a colossus to the anti-Republican party—without numbers, he is a host within himself. . . . We have had only middling performances to oppose to him—in truth, when he comes forward there is nobody but yourself who can meet him."

Madison wisely didn't respond publicly. Hamilton had bloodied him in previous wars of words—about financial discrimination and Washington's Neutrality Proclamation when Britain and France went to war—and the congressman no doubt saw the folly of trying to argue that re-enslaving blacks wasn't odious or immoral. Privately, however, he commented that "Camillus . . . will be betrayed by his anglomany into arguments as vicious and vulnerable as the Treaty itself."

With the consent of the Senate, Washington approved the Jay Treaty, and America remained at peace with both Britain and France for the next decade. For once Hamilton won a minor skirmish in the war of words over abolition.

★ ★ ★ ★ ★

In 1791 a slave revolt unfolded in the Caribbean in the French colony of Saint-Domingue, Haiti today. What eventually grew into the Haitian Revolution furnished the backdrop for Hamilton's last official efforts to promote emancipation.

The Haitian Revolution.

THOMAS JEFFERSON, A SLAVEHOLDER, VIEWED HAMILTON AS A THREAT TO THE POWER OF THE DEMOCRATIC-REPUBLICAN PARTY.

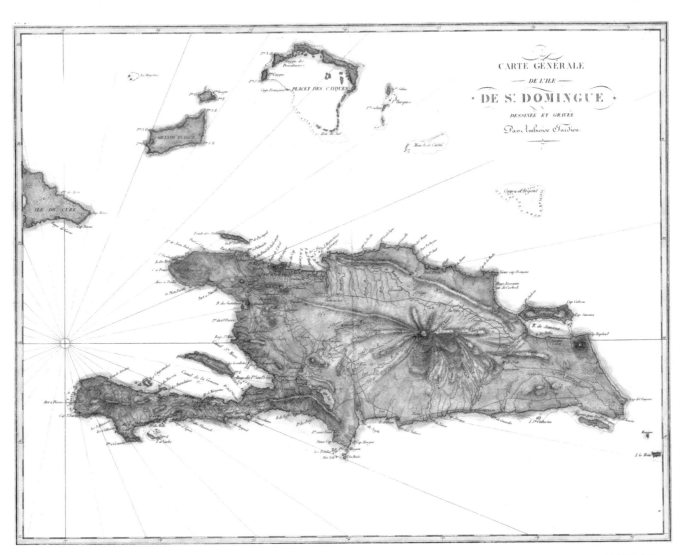

A MAP OF HISPANIOLA SHOWING THE FRENCH COLONY OF SAINT-DOMINGUE ON
THE WESTERN THIRD OF THE ISLAND, TODAY THE NATION OF HAITI.

The colony had half a million slaves—nearly the same number as all fourteen of
America's states—who took their inspiration for fighting inequality and injustice from
the French Revolution itself inspired by the American Revolution. Saint-Domingue produced about half the world's supply of sugar and coffee, so whoever controlled it could
secure enormous riches and wield great power. For a decade, that was Toussaint Louverture, a former slave with strong military and diplomatic skills. The insurrection began in
Saint-Domingue, but Louverture gradually extended his control over all of what became

A SLAVE UPRISING IN SAINT-DOMINGUE
BECAME THE HAITIAN REVOLUTION.

ALEXANDER HAMILTON

TOUSSAINT LOUVERTURE IN MILITARY UNIFORM.

Haiti. Among other goals, he wanted to establish a multiracial society of free people. France of course wanted to regain control of its lucrative colony.

The Jay Treaty had improved America's relations with Britain, which upset the French. In 1798, the Adams administration, led by Secretary of State Timothy Pickering, saw an opportunity to increase American trade with Haiti and to encourage Louverture to follow the U.S. example of declaring independence. Edward Stevens, Hamilton's childhood friend from St. Croix, became consul general to Saint-Domingue, which bordered on official recognition of Haitian independence, which infuriated the French.

With instructions from Pickering, Stevens went to open diplomatic relations with Louverture and to promote trade with America. Pickering asked Hamilton for advice on how Louverture ought to organize Haiti's government so that Stevens could share that advice. Hamilton complied, essentially recommending a military government with a strong executive, a judicial authority, and trial by jury in civilian cases.

As all of this was happening, President Adams hurled a wrench into Pickering's and Hamilton's plans. In early 1799, without consulting his advisors, Adams sent William Vans Murray to France to patch frayed relations

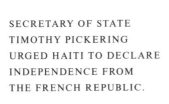

SECRETARY OF STATE
TIMOTHY PICKERING
URGED HAITI TO DECLARE
INDEPENDENCE FROM
THE FRENCH REPUBLIC.

WITHOUT CONSULTING HIS CABINET, PRESIDENT ADAMS SENT AN EMISSARY TO REPAIR RELATIONS WITH THE FRENCH REPUBLIC.

between the two republics.* "How is the sending an Agent to Toussaint to encourage the Independence of St. Domingo & a Minister to France to negotiate an accommodation reconcilable to consistency or good faith?" Hamilton tersely observed at the end of his letter to Pickering. France clearly wanted to reassert control over Haiti, so it was a good question, but one that apparently hadn't occurred to Adams.

An example of slaves rising up, rebelling against their masters, and establishing an independent nation didn't sit well with Jefferson and his fellow slaveholders. When he became president in 1801, he totally reversed America's policy toward Haiti, siding with the French. With Jefferson's rise to power, the abolitionist cause had lost yet another battle. The French managed to capture Louverture and shipped him off to prison in France, where he soon died, but they failed to retake the colony. Louverture's successors declared Haitian independence on January 1, 1804.

It was a good question, but one that apparently hadn't occurred to Adams.

WILLIAM VANS MURRAY TRIED TO SMOOTH DIPLOMATIC RELATIONS WITH THE FRENCH REPUBLIC AT THE SAME TIME THAT SECRETARY OF STATE PICKERING WAS ADVISING HAITI TO LIBERATE ITSELF FROM FRANCE.

....

*In sending Murray, Adams divided the Federalist Party, which contributed to his failure to win reelection in 1800.

"No man...contributed more to the birth of a peacetime military establishment...and no one posed a greater threat to the nation's emerging military traditions."

—RICHARD H. KOHN, *EAGLE AND SWORD*

{VIII}

MAJOR GENERAL

1795-1800

In 1795, after stepping down from the Treasury, Hamilton once again became a private citizen, returning to his law practice in New York City. Washington had counted him his most trusted advisor and hated to see him go. At Washington's request, Hamilton continued in that unofficial capacity. Most of Washington's cabinet also respected Hamilton's grasp of public issues and advocacy of sound policy measures, which rivaled the president's.

Hamilton returns to practicing the law.

As a minister without portfolio, Hamilton advised the president in 1795 to approve the Jay Treaty, and he defended it in a barrage of newspaper essays. Late that year, he drafted Washington's seventh annual message to Congress. In 1796, working with a draft that Madison had prepared in 1792, along with points furnished by the president, Hamilton wrote Washington's famous Farewell Address.

By a narrow margin of electoral votes, Adams beat Jefferson, who then became vice president. Jefferson's position quickly became a misery for Hamilton. Jefferson had opposed most of Hamilton's policies when the two had served in Washington's first cabinet. Their differences led to an acidic war of words in the papers, with Jefferson usually resorting to attacking Hamilton through surrogates. The Virginian lost nearly all his battles with Hamilton and resigned as secretary of state late in 1793, but his Democratic-Republican allies in Congress continued harassing Hamilton.

By the end of Washington's second term, France grew increasingly belligerent toward America. The French

> *Their differences led to an acidic war of words in the papers.*

PORTRAIT OF HAMILTON AS
A MAJOR GENERAL, C. 1800.

Friends & Fellow-citizens

The period for a new election of a citizen, to administer the Executive government of the United States, being not far distant, and the time actually arrived, when your thoughts must be employed in designating the person, who is to be cloathed with that important trust ~~for another~~ ~~term~~, it appears to me proper, especially as it may conduce to a more distinct expression of the public voice, that I should now apprise you of the resolution I have formed, to decline being considered among the number of those, out of whom a choice is to be made. —

I beg you, at the same time, to do me the justice to be assured that this resolution has not been taken, without a strict regard to all the considerations appertaining to the relation, which binds a dutiful citizen to his country — and that, in withdrawing the tender of service which silence in my situation might imply, I am influenced by no diminution of zeal for your future interest, no deficiency of grateful respect for your past kindness; but ~~am~~ ~~under~~ am supported by a full conviction

THE FINAL DRAFT OF WASHINGTON'S FAREWELL ADDRESS,
WHICH HAMILTON DRAFTED FOR THE PRESIDENT.

ALEXANDER HAMILTON

ADAMS AS PRESIDENT.

JEFFERSON AS VICE PRESIDENT.

ambassador even dabbled in the 1796 elections to secure Jefferson's rise to power. When the Virginian failed to win the presidency, France seized American ships. War loomed.

Hamilton's advice to Washington and then to Adams was the same as in 1794, when Britain had behaved similarly. Hamilton suggested that America undertake a diplomatic initiative, similar to Jay's mission, but with three diplomats, including one Democratic-Republican, to smooth the differences between the two

France seized American ships. War loomed.

THE

HISTORY

OF THE

UNITED STATES

FOR 1796;

INCLUDING A VARIETY OF

INTERESTING PARTICULARS

RELATIVE TO THE

FEDERAL GOVERNMENT

PREVIOUS TO THAT PERIOD.

PHILADELPHIA:

FROM THE PRESS OF *SNOWDEN & McCORKLE,*

NO. 47, NORTH FOURTH-STREET.

1797

JAMES CALLENDER'S SCURRILOUS COLLECTION OF PAMPHLETS ACCUSED HAMILTON OF SPECULATION AND NEARLY DESTROYED HIS REPUTATION.

The Reynolds affair.

countries. If the mission failed, Hamilton recommended strengthening America's defenses.

Adams more or less followed the path that Hamilton had recommended in the summer of 1797. The president dispatched John Marshall and Elbridge Gerry to join Ambassador Charles Cotesworth Pinckney in France. But the commissioners utterly failed. That failure catalyzed a series of events in 1798 that resulted in Hamilton's return to public service as a major general and inspector general of the U.S. Army, in charge of repelling a potential French invasion.

But before that happened, Hamilton had to deal with the second-worst decision of his entire life. Six years earlier, in the summer of 1791, he embarked on a torrid affair with a married woman named Maria Reynolds. Their liaison took many twists and turns. By 1793, Hamilton had learned some of life's harshest lessons. He also probably thought that he had put the whole nasty business behind him. If he did, the statesman was sadly mistaken.

★ ★ ★ ★ ★

In 1797, American readers devoured a series of pamphlets called *The History of the United States for the Year 1796; Including a Variety of Interesting Particulars Relative to the Federal Government Previous to That Period*. It sounds perfectly boring, yet the subject matter was anything but. The work, written by James Callender, a sensationalist journalist, sought to expose the machinations and intimate secrets of the rich and famous.

Numbers V and VI of the series, published midyear, contained allegations seemingly supported by documentary evidence that, while he served as Treasury secretary, Hamilton had engaged in private speculations with a shady character named James Reynolds and used his position for personal enrichment. Hamilton never cared much about making a lot of money. He cultivated his reputation for public service, which made these publications a grave threat to everything he held dear. His name appeared alongside that of James Reynolds, the husband of Maria Reynolds, Hamilton's mistress from 1791 to 1792.

Hamilton had a brilliant solution for this socially awkward problem. He wrote a full confession, amply documented, of his dealings with James and Maria Reynolds five to six years earlier, with all the lurid twists and turns. Why? Washington had stepped down from power; Adams was no Washington; and America verged on war with France. Hamilton knew the value of his powers and

OBSERVATIONS

ON

CERTAIN DOCUMENTS

CONTAINED IN NO. V & VI OF

" THE HISTORY OF THE UNITED STATES FOR THE YEAR 1796,"

IN WHICH THE

CHARGE OF SPECULATION

AGAINST

ALEXANDER HAMILTON,

LATE SECRETARY OF THE TREASURY,

IS FULLY REFUTED.

WRITTEN BY HIMSELF.

PHILADELPHIA:

PRINTED FOR JOHN FENNO, BY JOHN BIOREN.
1797.

*He wrote a full
confession, with
all the lurid twists
and turns.*

*"My real crime is an
amorous connection
with his wife, for a
considerable time
with his privity
and connivance."*

wanted to ensure he could fulfill his duty for further public service. To preserve his reputation, he risked the public embarrassment of himself, his wife, and his family.

In "Observations on Certain Documents," Hamilton bemoans the partisan spirit of the times, which had led to attacks on the integrity of public officials, including President Washington. Hamilton recounted political attacks by Democratic-Republican members of Congress on his management of the Treasury and alleged favors he had done for friends during his tenure as secretary. Each time, the ensuing investigations had exonerated him fully. But he knew what underpinned it all:

The charge against me is a connection with one James Reynolds for purposes of improper pecuniary speculations. My real crime is an amorous connection with his wife, for a considerable time with his privity and connivance, if not originally brought on by a combination between the husband and wife with the design to extort money from me.

The "connection" began in July 1791, after Eliza Hamilton and their children left Philadelphia to escape from the threat of yellow fever that often wrought havoc there in July and August. The family went to stay with Eliza's Schuyler family. Hamilton stayed in Philadelphia, too busy to join them.*

According to Hamilton, Maria Reynolds came to his house that July and asked to see him. When he appeared, she recounted her family connections in New York and told him a tale of woe about being abandoned by her husband without enough money to get back to her friends in New York. She asked him to help her. Hamilton indicated that it wasn't convenient, but he intended to send or bring money to her at a boardinghouse that evening.

I inquired for Mrs. Reynolds and was shewn up stairs, at the head of which she met me and conducted me into a bed room. I took the bill out of my pocket and gave it to her. Some conversation ensued from which it was

---

* Nearly half of the twenty-seven volumes of *The Papers of Alexander Hamilton* cover the five or so years of his time at Treasury.

quickly apparent that other than pecuniary consolation would be acceptable.

After this, I had frequent meetings with her, most of them at my own house. . . . In the course of a short time, she mentioned to me that her husband had solicited a reconciliation. . . . She told me besides that her husband had been engaged in speculation, and she believed could give information respecting the conduct of some persons in the department which would be useful. I sent for Reynolds. . . .

He confessed that he had obtained a list of claims from a person in my department which he had made use of in his speculations. . . .

Mr. Reynolds told me he was going to Virginia, and on his return would point out something in which I could serve him. I do not know but he said something about employment in a public office.

> *"She met me and conducted me into a bed room. . . . It was quickly apparent that other than pecuniary consolation would be acceptable."*

At some point, Hamilton realized that he was being set up, but he did nothing to evade the trap being set. Handsome and famous, he had a military bearing and a flirtatiousness that made him attractive to many women. Maria Reynolds, an attractive woman, was twenty-three when their affair began. Over and over, she convinced Hamilton that she found him incredibly attractive. Totally smitten, he let his judgment slip.

> *Totally smitten, he let his judgment slip.*

When Reynolds returned to Philadelphia in 1791, he asked Hamilton for a job in the Treasury Department. Hamilton did his due diligence and refused. Reynolds showed his true colors, arched his back, and demanded satisfaction. According to Hamilton, "It was easy to understand that he wanted money, and to prevent an explosion, I resolved to gratify him." Hamilton paid Reynolds a thousand dollars at the end of the year.

Hamilton pays blackmail to James Reynolds.

Then, in January 1792, events turned bizarre. Hamilton received a letter from Reynolds inviting him to "*renew my visits to his wife.*" Hamilton briefly had suspended those visits, and his absence, Maria said, was breaking her heart. So her supposedly noble husband swallowed his pride and grief to gull Hamilton again: "If I recollect rightly, I did not immediately accept the invitation, nor 'till after I had received several very importunate letters from Mrs. Reynolds."

Reynolds encourages the affair.

The blackmail continued; so did the affair. Hamilton was paying hush money.

Around this time, another character enters the story: Jacob Clingman, a friend of

The blackmail continued; so did the affair.

James Reynolds and a former clerk of Speaker of the House of Representatives Frederick Muhlenberg. On a couple of visits to the Reynolds house, Clingman encountered Hamilton going and coming. He asked about these unusual arrangements, and Maria told him that Hamilton had given her husband large sums of money. Reynolds himself boasted that he and Hamilton had engaged in speculative activities.

Hamilton made a few more payments that spring, sometimes disguised as loans, and then it appears he ended the affair with Maria and contact with Reynolds. Later that year, Treasury comptroller Oliver Wolcott Jr. charged Reynolds and Clingman with fraudulently obtaining a four-hundred-dollar payment owed to a former soldier by posing as executors of his estate. Wolcott had them both arrested. The fraudsters had obtained the soldier's name from a document given

to them illegally by a Treasury employee. Clingman asked Muhlenberg, his old boss, to intercede on his behalf, and the Speaker of the House brokered a deal in which the charges against Clingman and potentially Reynolds would be dropped if the money and the purloined document were returned.

In the process, Clingman told Muhlenberg that Reynolds had damaging information concerning Hamilton and his speculations with Reynolds. Muhlenberg shared this allegation with Senator James Monroe and Congressman Abraham Venable, who visited Reynolds in jail. Reynolds implied, without naming Hamilton, that he had such damaging information. They also visited Maria, who lied that her husband's story was correct. In his

FORMER SPEAKER OF THE HOUSE
FREDERICK MUHLENBERG LEARNED FROM
A CONFESSED FRAUDSTER THAT HAMILTON
MIGHT HAVE ENGAGED IN ILLEGAL
ACTIVITIES WHILE TREASURY SECRETARY.

OLIVER WOLCOTT JR., HAMILTON'S SUCCESSOR IN THE TREASURY DEPARTMENT, HAD
APPREHENDED JAMES REYNOLDS TRYING TO STEAL MONEY FROM A FORMER SOLDIER.

confessional pamphlet, Hamilton remarked of her: "The variety of shapes which this woman could assume was endless."

Officials investigate Hamilton's side of the story.

Armed with the accounts of Maria Reynolds and James Reynolds, and other information, Muhlenberg, Monroe, and Venable sought Hamilton's side of the story. He vehemently denied any speculation, showed them his correspondence with James and Maria Reynolds, and admitted to the affair. Satisfied that his sins were personal and not governmental, Muhlenberg, Monroe, and Venable agreed to drop the matter and promised confidentiality. Relieved, Hamilton even let them take the damning documents for further study, to be returned to him later—a common practice in the eighteenth century, when copies of letters and documents were harder to obtain than now.

> *"The variety of shapes which this woman could assume was endless."*

Callender's speculations, bolstered by some of these documents, appeared in mid-1797. Copies had been made. Hamilton asked his three visitors to confirm their assurances of their lack of involvement in Callender's revelations. Muhlenberg and Venable denied any involvement, but Monroe, a Democratic-Republican and a bitter Anti-Federalist, waffled. Hamilton voiced his suspicion that Monroe had betrayed him; Monroe denied it. But apparently the senator had given the documents to John Beckley, clerk of the House. Beckley, also an Anti-Federalist, had retained the copies for future use. Beckley probably had given them to Callender.

Hamilton triumphs.

Hamilton might have embarrassed himself publicly, but he proved his integrity as Treasury secretary. Eliza also forgave him. Their fifth child, John Church Hamilton, was born as the Reynolds affair played out in 1792, and William Stephen Hamilton came along in August 1797 when Hamilton was preparing his public confession of adultery.

Hamilton's character flaws.

The Reynolds affair reveals three major flaws in Hamilton's character. Succumbing to the temptations of infidelity doesn't seem as unusual or surprising as it once might have. But Hamilton placed excessive trust in others and took them at their word. Such generous belief in others wounded him throughout his life. The third flaw is the rarest: his willingness to reveal his most embarrassing actions at great length and with full documentation. A few years later, James Callender tried to expose Jefferson by reporting that the Virginian had fathered several children with Sally Hemings. Jefferson reacted with studied silence, and sympathetic scholars and biographers staunchly defended him for two centuries—until DNA testing proved Callender's allegations.

> *Hamilton placed excessive trust in others and took them at their word.*

ALEXANDER HAMILTON

From a Painting by JVanderlyn.

Eng'd by H. B. Hall N. Y. 1877.

JAMES MONROE, AN ARDENT ANTI-FEDERALIST, HELPED INVESTIGATE
THE ALLEGATIONS OF FINANCIAL IMPROPRIETY AGAINST HAMILTON.

MAJOR GENERAL

★ ★ ★ ★ ★

The XYZ Affair.

Early in 1798, news arrived that President Adams's diplomatic mission to France had failed. The commissioners—Gerry, Marshall, and Pinckney—reported that they hadn't even received the courtesy of meeting French officials. Instead, three agents of the French government, dubbed X, Y, and Z in the reports of the commission, asked them to pay a large bribe to French officials, particularly Talleyrand, the foreign minister. The American negotiators refused to submit to this indignity.

When news of the XYZ Affair spread through America, it sparked a wave of anti-French sentiment, suggestions that war with France was coming, and condemnations of the pro-French Democratic-Republican Party led by Vice President Jefferson. Suddenly Jefferson's party looked less like the loyal opposition that favored France and more like a threat to American security.

The Alien and Sedition Acts.

The Adams administration and Congress reacted to the war fever by passing the Alien and Sedition Acts and by calling for expanded military and naval forces. At the time, the country had state militias and the "Old Army," which was dealing with Native American threats on the western frontier. Proposed legislation called for a "New Army" of some 12,500 men and an even larger "Provisional Army" that existed mostly on paper but could be mobilized when needed.

Hamilton had misgivings about the Alien and Sedition Acts, seen then as now as an overreaction to French incursions against American commerce and the insult of the XYZ Affair. In June 1798, he wrote to Oliver Wolcott Jr., his successor as Treasury secretary, about the Sedition Act:

> *I have this moment seen a Bill brought into the Senate intitled a Bill to define more particularly the crime of Treason &c. There are provisions in this Bill which according to a cursory view appear to me highly exceptionable & such as more than any thing else may endanger civil War. . . . I hope sincerely the thing may not be hurried through. Let us not establish a tyranny. Energy is a very different thing from violence. If we make no false step we shall be essentially united; but if we push things to an extreme we shall then give to faction body & solidarity.*

With regard to the Alien Act, Hamilton wrote to Senator Theodore Sedgwick that the act seemed "deficient in precautions against abuse and for the security of Citizens. This should not be."

FIFTH *CONGRESS* OF THE UNITED STATES:

At the Second Session,

Begun and held at the city of *Philadelphia*, in the state of PENNSYLVANIA, on *Monday*, the thirteenth of *November*, one thousand seven hundred and ninety-seven.

An ACT *concerning aliens.*

BE it enacted by the Senate and House of Representatives of the United States of America, in Congress assembled, *That it shall be lawful for the President of the United States at any time during the continuance of this act, to order all such aliens as he shall judge dangerous to the peace and safety of the United States, or shall have reasonable grounds to suspect are concerned in any treasonable or secret machinations against the government thereof, to depart out of the territory of the United States, within such time as shall be expressed in such order, which order shall be served on such alien by delivering him a copy thereof, or leaving the same at his usual abode, and returned to the office of the Secretary of State, by the Marshal or other person to whom the same shall be directed. And in case any alien so ordered to depart, shall be found at large within the United States after the time limited in such order for his departure, and not having obtained a license from the President to reside therein, or having obtained such license shall not have conformed thereto, every such alien shall on conviction thereof, be imprisoned for a term not exceeding three years and shall never after be admitted to become a citizen of the United States. Provided always, and be it further enacted, That if any alien so ordered to depart shall prove to the satisfaction of the President, by evidence to be taken before such person or persons as the President shall direct, who are for that purpose hereby authorized to administer oaths, that no injury or danger to the United States will arise from suffering such alien to reside therein, the President may grant a license to such alien to remain within the United States for such time as he shall judge proper, and at such place as he may designate. And the President may also require of such alien to enter into a bond to the United States, in such penal sum as he may direct, with one or more sufficient sureties to the satisfaction of the person authorized by the President to take the same, conditioned for the good behaviour of such alien during his residence in the United States, and not violating his license, which license the President may revoke whenever he shall think proper.*

Sec. 2. And be it further enacted, That it shall be lawful for the President of the United States, whenever he may deem it necessary for the public safety, to order to be removed out of the territory thereof, any alien who may or shall be in prison in pursuance of this act; and to cause to be arrested and sent out of the United States such of those aliens as shall have been ordered to depart therefrom and shall not have obtained a license as aforesaid, in all cases where in the opinion of the President the public safety requires a speedy removal. And if any alien so removed or sent out of the United States by the President shall voluntarily return thereto, unless by permission of the President of the United States, such alien on conviction thereof, shall be imprisoned so long as in the opinion of the President, the public safety may require.

Sec. 3. And be it further enacted, That every master or commander of any ship or vessel which shall come into any port of the United States after the first day of July next, shall immediately on his arrival make report in writing to the collector or other chief officer of the customs of such port, of all aliens, if any, on board his vessel, specifying their names, age, the place of nativity, the country from which they shall have come, the nation to which they belong and owe allegiance, their occupation and a description of their persons, as far as he shall be informed thereof, and on failure every such master and commander shall forfeit and pay three hundred dollars, for the payment whereof on default of such master or commander, such vessel shall also be holden, and may by such collector or other officer of the customs be detained. And it shall be the duty of such collector or other officer of the customs, forthwith to transmit to the office of the department of State true copies of all such returns.

Sec. 4. And be it further enacted, That the circuit and district courts of the United States, shall respectively have cognizance of all crimes and offences against this act. And all marshals and other officers of the United States are required to execute all precepts and orders of the President of the United States issued in pursuance or by virtue of this act.

Sec. 5. And be it further enacted, That it shall be lawful for any alien who may be ordered to be removed from the United States, by virtue of this act, to take with him such part of his goods, chattels, or other property, as he may find convenient; and all property left in the United States, by any alien, who may be removed, as aforesaid, shall be, and remain subject to his order and disposal, in the same manner, as if this act had not been passed.

Sec. 6. And be it further enacted, That this act shall continue and be in force for and during the term of two years from the passing thereof.

Jonathan Dayton Speaker of the House of Representatives.

Vice President of the United States and President of the Senate.

Approved June 25, 1798.
John Adams
President of the United States.

I certify that this act did originate in the Senate.

Attest,
Samuel A. Otis Secretary

you be' vet pretty Woman and we should like to give you
the hug Fraternale, Begar we do not want to quarrel
with you, as a proof, my Brother the
grand Directeur's are at this moment
take all de Care possible of your
Baggage - derefore if you vill go back
and bring litel more of de S.t Argent
ou shall be admit to de honor of
e sitting, we only ask de favor
e never sieze on properly

infringed on

By gar
oit took i
Legislate

PRIVATE PLUNDER
FOR THE
DIRECTORS

NA

THIS POLITICAL CARTOON COMMENTING
ON THE XYZ AFFAIR SHOWS FIVE
FRENCHMEN PLUNDERING AMERICA
WHILE THE NATIONS OF EUROPE WATCH.

HAMILTON SHARED HIS RESERVATIONS ABOUT THE THE ALIEN ACT WITH SENATOR THEODORE SEDGWICK (LEFT), WITH WHOM HE LATER LAID OUT A PLAN TO ADDRESS THE POSSIBILITY OF VIRGINIA AND KENTUCKY SECEDING FROM THE UNION.

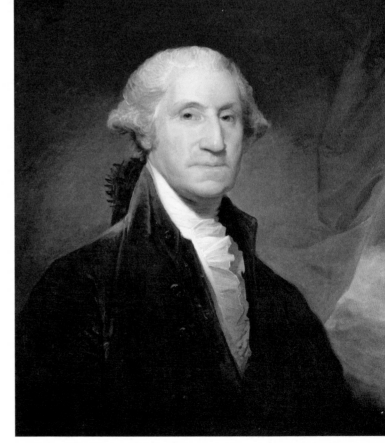

IN 1798, PRESIDENT ADAMS CALLED ON FORMER PRESIDENT WASHINGTON TO LEAD THE COUNTRY'S NEW ARMY TO COUNTER FRENCH HOSTILITIES. WASHINGTON REQUESTED THAT HAMILTON BE GIVEN THE RANK OF MAJOR GENERAL AND THE POSITION OF INSPECTOR GENERAL.

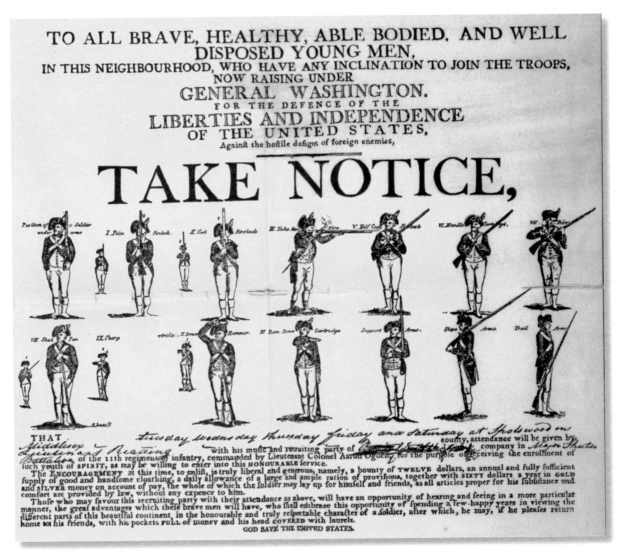

A BROADSIDE RECRUITING MEN TO JOIN AMERICA'S NEW ARMY
UNDER WASHINGTON DURING THE QUASI WAR.

Adams called on Washington to serve as the titular head of the new forces. The former president, now sixty-six years old and living on his Mount Vernon plantation in Virginia, didn't relish the idea of leaving home to prepare for a war that might not happen, though. He agreed to assume command only if Adams gave him the authority to appoint the generals who would organize, train, and lead the new army and to take the field only if war actually came.

Adams agreed to these stipulations—until Washington wanted Hamilton to head the new army with the rank of major general and to serve as inspector general of all army forces, roughly equivalent to today's army chief of staff. Hamilton wielded great power among the Federalist Party, which threatened Adams's position, and the president

Congress establishes a new U.S. Army.

resented that members of his own cabinet still consulted the former Treasury secretary. Adams had developed a deep dislike for Hamilton. He also noted that other, older army officers had outranked Hamilton in the War of Independence and therefore deserved the top appointment more.

Hamilton becomes major general and inspector general.

Adams argued with Washington, but the father of the country stood his ground, threatening to resign if Adams refused to agree to his terms. Washington greatly respected his most trusted advisor's military prowess and leadership skills, as did much of Adams's cabinet—many of them holdovers from Washington's administration. The old general and the president's cabinet rightly valued ability above seniority for choosing the head of the army. Washington prevailed, and Adams complied, but the showdown delayed organizing the new army for several months.

Having to swallow the bitter pill of Hamilton's appointment left a bitter taste in Adams's mouth, so he barely lifted a finger to get the army up and running. In early 1799, he undercut the entire buildup, which required unpopular new taxes to fund. Again without consulting anyone, he sent a new peace mission to France, not long after the ignominious XYZ Affair, but the mission had to wait until the French explicitly assured that they would receive the ambassadors. Commissioners Oliver Ellsworth and

Adams had developed a deep dislike for Hamilton.

IN THE COUP OF 18 BRUMAIRE, NOVEMBER 1799, GENERAL BONAPARTE SEIZED CONTROL OF FRANCE AS FIRST CONSUL.

ALEXANDER HAMILTON

DURING THE QUASI WAR (1798–1800), FRENCH SHIPS HARASSED AMERICAN SHIPS AND TRADE. HERE THE U.S.S. *CONSTELLATION* (LEFT) CAPTURES THE FRENCH FRIGATE *L'INSURGENTE* ON FEBRUARY 9, 1799.

William Davie didn't sail for Europe until late in 1799, where they joined the third commissioner, William Vans Murray, now the ambassador to the Netherlands.

The commission's negotiations with the French didn't start until the spring of 1800. By that time, General Napoléon Bonaparte had staged the coup that launched him to power as first consul. Negotiations lasted six months and resulted in the Convention of 1800, which achieved a weak peace that ended the Quasi War. The Convention also ended the alliance between France and America that had enabled the colonists to win the War of Independence. Adams considered it his proudest achievement.

The Convention of 1800.

Meanwhile, General Hamilton was doing his best to organize the new army. He doubted that Adams's second peace mission would work after the first had failed, and

*France was
in turmoil.*

*Hamilton's
military plans.*

he advised the president as much—to no effect. Hamilton rightly saw that France was in turmoil. It served America's best interests, he believed, to see what happened across the Atlantic before taking on the risk of being outwitted by French diplomacy. Again.

General Hamilton also was shaping plans to seize Florida and Louisiana, then in Spanish hands, in part because he perceived that the French Republic probably would seize them from the weak Spanish crown. France indeed took back the Louisiana Territory in 1800—the day after signing the convention with America—which posed a new threat to the United States that ended only when Bonaparte agreed to the Louisiana Purchase in 1803. Hamilton, ever the military planner, also considered using U.S. forces, perhaps with British naval aid, to liberate Spain's colonies in Latin America in favor of American interests in the Western Hemisphere.*

In subsequent years, Hamilton has faced scrutiny as a militarist, that he wanted to use military force to subdue domestic as well as foreign enemies. As a former soldier

* Twenty years later, revolutions against Spanish rule in Latin America achieved those objectives.

and member of the Confederation Congress, he certainly sympathized with the pleas of the army to be paid during the Newburgh Conspiracy in 1783. But he didn't participate in the tensions, and he kept Washington apprised so he could nip the threat in the bud. Nor do we have solid evidence that Hamilton endorsed the army menacing Congress with military force. The Massachusetts militia put down the Shays Rebellion in 1787. Hamilton, like most national leaders, approved of the action but otherwise had no involvement in it. As Treasury secretary, on the other hand, he had a heavy hand in planning and executing the government's response to the Whiskey Rebellion in 1794. President Washington assembled and led the massive force that Hamilton had recommended, ending the rebellion and upholding the rule of law with minimal loss of life.

In reaction to the Alien and Sedition Acts, Vice President Jefferson and Madison had drafted and introduced resolutions in the legislatures of Kentucky and Virginia holding that states had a right to secede from the Union if they disagreed with federal laws. Kentucky and Virginia adopted the resolutions, and Hamilton received reports that the Virginia legislature had passed measures to raise a military force to resist federal authority. Hamilton wrote to Senator Sedgwick:

> *The first thing in all great operations of such a Government as ours is to secure the opinion of the people. To this end, the proceedings of Virginia and Kentucke with the two laws complained of should be referred to a special Committee. That Committee should make a report exhibiting... the tendency of the doctrines advanced by Virginia and Kentucke to destroy the Constitution of the UStates–and ... the full evidence they afford of a regular conspiracy to overturn the government.... No pains or expence should be spared to disseminate this Report. A little pamphlet containing it should find its way into every house in Virginia.... In the mean time the measures for raising a Military force should proceed with activity.... When a clever force has been collected let them be drawn towards Virginia for which there is an obvious pretext–& then let measures be taken to act upon the laws & put Virginia to the test of resistance.*

Hamilton's response contained a backup plan to move federal forces toward Virginia, much the same as in the Whiskey Rebellion, but these are hardly the machinations of a battle-hungry fighter.

A month after Hamilton wrote Sedgwick, the Fries Rebellion—a taxpayer uprising similar to the Shays and Whiskey rebellions—broke out in eastern Pennsylvania.

The Fries Rebellion.

AS WITH THE SHAYS REBELLION AND THE WHISKEY REBELLION, IN THE FRIES REBELLION AMERICANS ROSE UP AGAINST WHAT THEY FELT WAS UNFAIR TAXATION POLICY. THE FEDERAL GOVERNMENT INTERVENED AND PREVAILED AGAINST THE REVOLT.

WITH THE RESOLUTION OF THE QUASI WAR BETWEEN FRANCE AND AMERICA IN 1800,
MAJOR GENERAL HAMILTON RESIGNED HIS COMMISSION AND DISBANDED HIS MEN.

ALEXANDER HAMILTON

Hamilton once again authorized a "shock and awe" strategy. Writing to Secretary of War James McHenry, who had reported the rebellion, Hamilton said:

> *Beware, my Dear Sir, of magnifying a riot into an insurrection, by employing in the first instance an inadequate force. Tis better far to err on the other side. Whenever the Government appears in arms it ought to appear like a Hercules, and inspire respect by the display of strength. The consideration of expence is of no moment compared with the advantages of energy.... Will it be inexpedient to put under marching Orders a large force provisionally, as in eventual support of the corps to be employed—to awe the disaffected?*

"Beware ... of magnifying a riot into an insurrection."

Here as elsewhere, General Hamilton employed a strategy of using military force as a last resort after exhausting political and diplomatic channels of conflict resolution. But if and when such force had to be employed, it ought to impress and overwhelm so as to minimize death and destruction.*

But the crowning piece of evidence that Hamilton was no militarist came when the American people grew tired of paying taxes to support the military buildup of 1798 and 1799. As Adams's second peace mission to France got under way, Congress decided the new army was no longer necessary and ordered it to be disbanded. General Hamilton—called the American Bonaparte by some—didn't stage a coup and seize power as the Corsican general had done. Instead, he followed the orders of his civilian superiors and disbanded his men in an orderly manner.

Hamilton resigns from the army.

---

* In our time, this strategy is called the Powell Doctrine, after General Colin Powell.

"Hamilton and Jefferson slowly and reluctantly switched roles."

—KARL-FRIEDRICH WALLING, *REPUBLICAN EMPIRE*

ver at the head of a company of Artille
ofed for the particular defence of this St
had better pretentions to the allowance
than to whom it was actually made —
it has it not been extended to me

{IX}

LAST YEARS

1800-1804

❧

In 1800, after ten years in Philadelphia, the seat of the federal government moved to the District of Columbia. That year Jefferson went head-to-head with Adams for the presidency and ultimately defeated the Federalist incumbent—but only after the House resolved a tie between Jefferson and Burr that made Burr vice president. Hamilton ironically helped his old nemesis attain the top spot, but in the process his actions damaged both the Federalist Party and his ability to lead it.

Hamilton critically opposed the Jefferson administration, frequently corresponded with other Federalist leaders, founded his own newspaper to air his views, and increasingly focused on his law practice. He also devoted significant time to his family, which his extensive career in public service had prevented. He bought land in upper Manhattan and built a country house, the Grange, for his growing brood. It was the only house he ever owned. Then, while politicking in the New York gubernatorial election of 1804, Hamilton allegedly said something that prompted Burr, who lost the race, to challenge Hamilton to their now-infamous duel.

★ ★ ★ ★ ★

President Adams resented that Washington had forced his hand to put Hamilton in charge of the new army. The president also started behaving even more erratically. France and Britain were at war, but neutral America was enjoying prosperous trade. Why risk English animosity by sending a mission to France? Adams persisted and told

President Adams grows paranoid.

SCENE FROM THE INFAMOUS DUEL
BETWEEN HAMILTON (RIGHT)
AND VICE PRESIDENT BURR.

ADAMS GREW INCREASINGLY
PARANOID AND IRASCIBLE
AS PRESIDENT.

others that Hamilton was leading a pro-British faction in America. In the spring of 1800, as Adams's chances of reelection dissolved, the president blew his top and summarily fired Secretary of War James McHenry and Secretary of State Timothy Pickering.

McHenry described Adams's behavior not long after he and Pickering had been sacked in a letter to his nephew that he shared with Hamilton:

> The President disregarding these considerations [the advice not to send the mission to France], from a different view of the subject, or looking only to his own election, and measuring the operation of the mission upon it, could be well with nobody who did not think well of the mission.... From that moment, I began to perceive a new set of principles were to be introduced, and that the acts of the administration were, as far as practicable to be made subservient to electioneering purposes. Every day increased his alarm on this subject, and distrust of those gentlemen near him, who did not constantly feed him with news or hopes flattering to his election. At times he would speak in such a manner of certain men and things, as to persuade one that he was actually insane....
>
> He requested to see me on the 5th instant [May 5, 1800].... He took up other subjects, became indecorous and at times outrageous. General Washington had saddled him with three Secretaries, Wolcott, Pickering, and myself. I had not appointed a gentleman in N. Carolina, the only elector who had given him a vote in that State.... I had biased General Washington to place Hamilton in his list of Major Generals before Knox. I had Eulogized General Washington, in my report to Congress, and had attempted in the same report, to praise Hamilton. In short there was no bounds to his jealousy. I had done nothing right. I had advised a suspension of the mission. Every body blamed me for my official conduct and I must resign. I resigned the next morning. Mr. Pickering was thrown out a few days later.

"He would speak in such a manner of certain men and things, as to persuade one that he was actually insane."

Adams was falling victim to paranoia, and he grew obsessed with General Hamilton's role in his perceived tribulations. The president's mania, in turn, seems to have pushed Hamilton just as hard to deny his Federalist rival reelection. Still smarting from having to resign his military commission, he wrote Adams to demand an explanation of reports of what the president had been saying about him:

It has been repeatedly mentioned to me that you have, on different occasions, asserted the existence of a British Faction *in the Country, embracing a number of leading or influential characters of the* Federal Party ... *and that you have sometimes named me, at other times plainly alluded to me, as one of this description of persons....*

I must, Sir, take it for granted, that you cannot have made such assertions or insinuations without being willing to avow them, and to assign the reasons to a party who may conceive himself injured by them.

Adams ignored the letter. Two months later, Hamilton wrote again: "by whomsoever a charge of the kind in my former letter may, at any time, have been made or insinuated against me, it is a base wicked and cruel calumny; destitute even of a plausible pretext to excuse the folly or mask the depravity which must have dictated it."

Hamilton attacks Adams.

Hamilton fumed and then made a bold move. He circulated a long letter exposing the president's defects: "Letter from Alexander Hamilton, Concerning the Public Conduct and Character of John Adams, Esq., President of the United States." The letter appeared just as the 1800 elections were starting and revealed a deep rift in the Federalist ranks that had been growing for a couple of years. Hamilton's Federalist friends recoiled, and their Republican enemies rejoiced.

The Democratic-Republicans defeat the Federalists.

Two months later, Jefferson and Burr on the Republican ticket defeated the Federalist ticket of Adams and Pinckney. Jefferson received 73 electoral votes, Adams 65, and the popular vote skewed even more in Jefferson's favor. But Hamilton's diatribe against Adams probably made no difference.

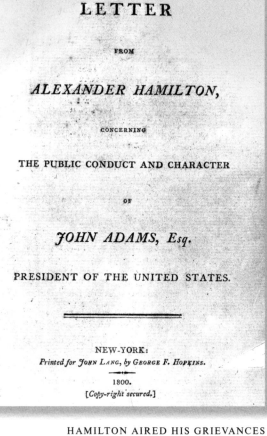

LETTER

FROM

ALEXANDER HAMILTON,

CONCERNING

THE PUBLIC CONDUCT AND CHARACTER

OF

JOHN ADAMS, Esq.

PRESIDENT OF THE UNITED STATES.

NEW-YORK:
Printed for John Lang, by George F. Hopkins.
1800.
[*Copy-right secured.*]

HAMILTON AIRED HIS GRIEVANCES AGAINST ADAMS IN PUBLIC AND SPLIT THE FEDERALIST PARTY, WHICH ALLOWED JEFFERSON TO BECOME PRESIDENT.

Burr had conquered New York City, a Federalist stronghold, which undercut their power base in the New York legislature. It was the New York legislature that picked the state's presidential electors, so Burr's cunning political tactics had guaranteed the election's outcome in the spring.

Another factor also decided the 1800 election before it began. In 1787, a compromise allowed the Constitution to count a slave, who of course couldn't vote, as three-fifths of a man for the purposes of determining a state's electoral votes. Jefferson received almost all of the South's electoral votes and became the only president in U.S. history whose election depended on the Constitution's three-fifths clause. A little more than 15 percent of his electoral votes came from that clause. Without them, Adams would have won.

There was, however, a problem. All the Republican electors in 1800 cast their votes for both Jefferson and Burr, meaning the two men tied. By the rules that applied then, the House of Representatives had to have a runoff election in which each state had one

Jefferson became the only president in U.S. history whose election depended on the Constitution's three-fifths clause.

Hamilton helps Jefferson defeat Burr.

	Thomas Jefferson of Virginia	Aaron Burr of New York	John Adams of Massachusetts	Charles Cotesworth Pinckney of South Carolina	John Jay of New York
New Hampshire			6	6	
Massachusetts			16	16	
Rhode Island			4	3	1
Connecticut			9	9	
Vermont			4	4	
New York	12	12			
New Jersey			7	7	
Pennsylvania	8	8	7	7	
Delaware			3	3	
Maryland	5	5	5	5	
Virginia	21	21			
Kentucky	4	4			
North Carolina	8	8	4	4	
Tennessee	3	3			
South Carolina	8	8			
Georgia	4	4			
	73	73	65	64	1

THE TALLY OF ELECTORAL VOTES FOR THE PRESIDENTIAL ELECTION OF 1800. JEFFERSON AND BURR EACH RECEIVED 73, TRIGGERING A RUNOFF ELECTION IN THE HOUSE; ADAMS 65; PINCKNEY 64; AND JOHN JAY 1.

vote. Hamilton wanted Pinckney to win but favored Jefferson over Adams. For the run-off, the House voted an astounding thirty-five times, each resulting in a tie. Behind the scenes, however, Hamilton had embarked on a vigorous letter-writing campaign to encourage Federalists to vote for Jefferson. He worked particularly hard on James Bayard Sr., Delaware's lone congressman, who therefore controlled his state's vote. Like many Federalists, Bayard supported Burr for 35 ballots. On the 36th, he abstained, which made Jefferson president. Jefferson had benefited from having Hamilton on his side.

★ ★ ★ ★ ★

Hamilton founds the New-York Evening Post.

Philip Hamilton dies in a duel.

In November 1801, Hamilton cofounded the *New-York Evening Post*, which quickly became his primary vehicle for airing his views in public. Eight days later, tragedy struck.

Philip, the Hamiltons' eldest child, had gone to the theater one evening with a friend and sat near a New York lawyer, George Eacker, a Republican who earlier that year had criticized the Federalists and the elder Hamilton's financial and military policies publically. The young Hamilton and his friend apparently insulted Eacker in the theater, and mutual insults continued outside. Despite attempts at reconciliation, Eacker

NEW-YORK EVENING POST.

MONDAY, NOVEMBER 16, 1801. *No.* 40, *Pine-stre*

PROSPECTUS

OF

V-YORK EVENING POST.

tor will endeavor that this Paper pear in a dress worthy of the liberal pa- is already promised.

derive its principal support from the our City, particular attention will be whatever relates to that large and re- s of our fellow-citizens. The earliest nformation will be industriously col- ithfully presented; and we hope that g department may, for convenience, accuracy, vie with any in the city. of this paper, is to diffuse among the t information on all interesting sub- alcate just principles in religion, mor- ics; and to cultivate a taste for sound

e openly profess our attachment to that litics denominated FEDERAL, because the most conducive to the welfare of ty, and the best calculated to ensure to our present form of government, prove of that spirit of dogmatism which e claim to infallibility; and willingly honest and virtuous men are to be found . Persuaded that the great body of the is country only want correct informa- ble them to judge of what is really best; g that nothing will so directly conduce ble end, as candid and liberal discus- aper shall be equally free to all parties. nications, therefore, shall be inserted mpartiality, and equal secrecy as it re- ame of the author; reserving, however, subjoining a reply whenever we shall ecessary or proper. But it would be in- ith the rules which we have prescribed not to declare explicitly that we never irrency to any thing scurrilous, indecent, r profane, or which may contravene the inciples of social order.

e shall be duly studious of Originality, ail ourselves of the contents of the vari- papers, Pamphlets, Magazines and Re- ed in our own country, or elsewhere; not be of any moment, as it respects the ether an interesting piece of information, ritten essay, which they have probably , has appeared in any other paper or not. d, as our great design is to disseminate principles, which are the best and indeed support of good Government, we shall ady eye upon this our primary object, neglect no means by which we may think best promoted.

thus given a general outline of our Plan, it needless to make an elaborate display ons: We rely for support on what shall insic merit of the paper itself.

necessary that the Editor should exer- wn judgement on determining on the pro- nserting any Original Communication, it ve him from an unpleasant embarrassment of his duty, to have them transmitted to out the names of the Authors.

WILLIAM COLEMAN, *Editor.*

POSTSCRIPT.

will be attached to the above daily paper,

FOR LONDON,

The staunch regular trading ship JULIANA, R. Roath, master, will be dispatched in 10 or 12 days, having half her cargo on board. For freight or passage, having superior accommodations, apply on board at Old-slip, or to

COIT & WOOLSEY,
98 Murray's wharf.

Who have received per ship Mercury from Liverpool,
A consignment of DRY GOODS, which will be sold at a moderate advance, consisting of 2 bales Coatings, 4 do. Rose Blankets, 10 cases Hats, 4 do. Hosiery, and 20 trunks Calicoes, Chintzes, Quilting, Muslins, Velverets, Corduroys, Thicksets, &c. &c. Nov. 16

FOR CALCUTTA,

The well known ship CITIZEN, C. Blakeman, master, burthen 285 tons, was built in Philadelphia of live oak and red cedar, and coppered in Liverpool about 11 months since, and in every respect is well fitted for the voyage, and is intended to be dispatched with all convenient speed. She will take on board merchandize or specie out, and will return direct to this port with goods, the manufacture of that country, to which effect she will be provided with a Supercargo, competent to the business of the voyage; and it is probable she may touch on her outward passage at Teneriffe, 150 or 200 pipes of wine will there be received on freight, if a contract for the same is made before sailing from here. For terms of which, or freight, or passage direct to Calcutta, apply to HOYT & TOM.

WHO HAVE FOR SALE,
600 boxes Havannah Sugars assorted
150,000 Spanish Segars, 30 crates Earthenware
2 hhds. and 3 bbls. St. Croix Sugars.
Nov. 16

FOR HULL,

The British brig MINERVA, captain M'Bride. Said brig lays at Bowne's wharf, and will sail about the first of December. For freight of 600 barrels, apply to the captain on board, or to

JOHN KNOX;
Nov. 16. No. 97 Water street.

FOR GREENOCK,

The good and substantial British Brig RECOVERY, D. Campbell, master; will sail with all convenient dispatch, having a considerable part of her freight now engaged. For the remainder, or Passage, apply to the master on board, at the wharf adjoining the new Bath, north river, or to

SMITH and WYCKOFF,
Nov. 16. No. 211 Pearl-street.

FOR AMSTERDAM,

The ship MAGNET, Thomas Marsh, master, a substantial good vessel, burthen about 300 tons, and will be ready to take on board in a few days. If immediate application is made, the freight will be taken on very moderate terms; for which, or passage, having good accommodations, apply to

SMITH & WYCKOFF,
Nov. 16 No. 211 Pearl-street.

FOR BORDEAUX,

The brig HUNTER, lying at White's wharf, North-river, is now ready to take in, and can be dispatched in ten days. For freight or passage apply to
Nov. 16 W. M. SETON.

FOR MARTINIQUE,

Five Hundred Barrels will be taken on freight in a good vessel, for Martinique, if immediate application is made to SUYDAM & WYCKOFF,
Nov. 16. No. 21 South-street.

For Norfolk and Richmond,

The remarkable fine new Schooner LION, William Clark, Master, a regular trader, will sail in the course of ten days. For freight or passage, having elegant accommodations, apply on board, at Jones' wharf, coffee house slip, or to

BETHUNE & SMITH,
Nov. 16. Murray's Wharf.

FOR SALE or CHARTER,

The schooner NEW-YORK, burthen 135 tons, built of live oak and cedar, and in every respect a staunch good vessel. For terms of sale apply to

JOHN OZUILE, 9 Beekman-street, or
RICHD. I. TUCKER, 103 Water-street.

14 boxes Havanna brown sugars, and 2 tierces arrow root, are offered for sale on liberal terms, by RICHARD I. TUCKER. Nov. 16. 2w

For Sale, Freight or Charter,

The remarkable fast sailing ship SALLY, burthen about 265 tons—stows well, and in every respect a complete vessel. For terms apply to

ROBERT I. THURSTON,
Nov. 16. tf. No. 297 Water-street.

For FREIGHT or CHARTER,

The ship HIRAM, Captain Jocelin, burthen 142 tons; a fine vessel, sails fast, and is well found; will be ready to receive a cargo in 12 days. For terms apply to JAMES & SAMUEL WATSON,
No. 111 Front, or 44 Broad-street.

Who will land from said ship in a day or two,

63 hhds. Jamaica Rum of high proof,	18 bales Natchez Cotton,
650 Cherry and Walnut Plank & Scantling,	2 bbls. Beaver Fur,
	41 hhds. good Sugar for retailing.

THEY HAVE ALSO FOR SALE,

250 boxes Brown Soap	260 firkins Butter, of
60 do. Mould Candles	the best quality,
50 bbls. Boston Beef,	for shipping,
1000 sides Soal Leather.	Nov. 16

For FREIGHT or CHARTER,

The Ship VENUS, Lemuel Bunce, master, burthen 199 tons.—Apply to
Nov. 16. WILLIAM NEILSON & Co.

For FREIGHT or CHARTER
for the West-Indies,

The brig GENIUS, burthen 90 tons, Daniel Cornwall, master—a remarkable fast sailer. Apply to the captain on board at Old slip, or to

JOHN MURRAY & SON,
Nov. 17. No. 269 Pearl street.

For FREIGHT or CHARTER,

The new and substantial British ship CHARLES, James Moyes, master, burthen per register 250 tons (will carry 450 tons.) She is on her first voyage. Please apply to

JOHN MAC GREGOR,
Nov. 16. 84 Broad-way.

For FREIGHT or CHARTER,

The ship NEPTUNE, burthen about 200 tons, stows well and is in complete order for sea. For terms, Apply to MINTURN & BARKER.
Nov. 16.

FREIGHT
For Copenhagen or Hamburgh,

The bark BERKKESKOW, Capt. Gubriel Tallhammer, is ready to receive freight for either of the above places. If application is made to the Captain on board, at Gouverneur's wharf.
Nov. 16 GOUVERNEUR & KEMBLE.

WANTED TO CHARTER,

Three or four vessels, drawing under 10 feet water, to load with lumber at Newbern, N. Carolina, for Jamaica, By
Nov. 16. DICKSON & STOCKHOLM.

For FREIGHT or CHARTER
to a port in Europe or the West-Indies,

The ship NANCY, burthen about 220 tons. For terms apply to

JOHN MURRAY & SON,
Nov. 16. No. 269 Pearl street.

FOR CHARTER,
To any of the West-India Islands,

The brig FRANCIS NIXON, burthen 150 tons—sails fast. Apply

TROY, LANSINGBURGH AND WATERFORD
NAVIGATION LOTTERY.

SCHEME.

1	Prize of	20,000 Dollars, is	20,000
1		10,000	10,000
1		5,000	5,000
1		2,000	2,000
3		1,000	3,000
20		500	10,000
60		200	12,000
150		100	15,000
340		50	17,000
600		20	12,000
9,600		10	96,000
1	First drawn number		1,000
1	do. on the 5th day		1,000
1	do.	10th day	1,000
1	do.	15th	2,000
1	do.	20th	2,000
1	do.	25th	2,000
1	do.	30th	2,000
1	do.	35th	3,000
1	do.	40th	3,000
1	do.	45th	5,000
1	do.	50th	4,000
10,788	*Prizes.*	*Dollars*	225,000
26,712	*Blanks.*		
37,500	Tickets at 6 Dollars, is	*Dlls.*	225,000

Subject to a Deduction of 15 *per cent.*

☞ Less than two and an half Blanks to a Prize.

The Managers will certainly commence drawing in the City of New-York, *on the first Tuesday in May next*, and will continue to draw 750 Tickets each day until completed, as they have disposed of the LOTTERY to a Company of Gentlemen in this city, who are to sell the Tickets at the original price of *Six Dollars*, until the first of December.

This Lottery is for the purpose of raising *Thirty Thousand Dollars*, to improve the Navigation of Hudson's River, between the City of Albany and the Villages of Troy, Lansingburgh, and Waterford—Agreeably to Three several Acts of the Legislature of this State.

DAVID GELSTON,
PHILIP TEN EYCK, } *Managers.*
JOHN BORDMAN,

The Tickets in the above Lottery are for sale at GAIN & TEN EYCK'S Book-store, No. 148 Pearl-street.——Prize-Tickets in the New-York State Road Lottery taken in payment. Nov. 16 tf

THE *COUNCIL of APPOINTMENT* having thought proper to displace the subscribers from their former business as Auctioneers, they have (from the recommendation of many of their friends) commenced the Wholesale and Retail Grocery business, at their old *Auction Store*, No. 145, Pearl-Street, where they will be happy to receive the orders of their friends and public in general. They have selected a choice assortment of the following articles, which they will dispose of on the lowest terms—

70 hhds. 3d and 4th proof St. Croix Rum,
3 do. Country Rum,
5 pipes Gin, 100 cases old Claret,
11 pipes }
15 hhds. and } superior quality Port Wine,
64 qr. casks }
15 qr. casks old Sherry Wine,
18 pipes old Lisbon do.
4 do. London particular Madeira,
150 casks Hibbert's first qual. Brown Stout,
20 boxes superior quality Mustard,
100 boxes & 50 jars fresh Raisins,
100 boxes Havannah Sugars assorted
4 pipes Old Cogniac Brandy, 4th proof
30 boxes playing Cards assorted, Boston Manufactory.
50 chests Hyson }
60 do. Hyson Skin } TEAS of superior quality.
30 do. Souchong }
together with a general assortment of GROCERIES.
Nov. 16 H. G. RUTGERS & Co.

BETHUNE & SMITH, *Murray's wharf,*

HAVE FOR SALE,

EIGHTY-FIVE hogsheads Richmond and Petersburg Tobacco,
13 kegs Richmond manufactured do,
850 bbls kiln dried Indian Meal, of a superior quality—500 bushels southern Corn,
5 casks bottled Scotch Ale, very fine,
One pipe London particular Madeira Wine,
One hundred boxes Tin Plates

M'CREADY AND REID
No. 97 William-Street,

HAVE received, by the late arriva Europe, a general assortment of DRY G which will be sold on reasonable terms, w and retail—Among which are the following viz.—
2 bales superfine Rose Blankets,
1 do. red, white and yellow flannel
3 cases Cambric Muslins, from 1/8 to 5 ling pr yard,
3 do. Nuns Thread, from No. 3 to 44,
3 do. purple Shawls,
1 do. fancy do.
1 do. three threaded Cotton Yarn,
1 do. Women's Hose, from 1 to 18s pr
2 do. Scotch damask Table Cloths, el patterns, from 5-4ths to 8 by 10.
Nov. 16.

JOHN & Wm. TABELE,
260, *Pearl-street,*

HAVE received by the late arriv London, a large and general assortmen and 9-8 fancy calicoes & chintzes, do. furni 9-8, 5-4 and 6-4 camel hairshawls in cases Book and jaconet muslin, 9-4 and 6-4 cam Dimities, Irish linens, womens white, b coloured silk gloves and mitts, mens and cotton and worsted stockings, mens black loured silk stockings, broadcloths, cassimer ings and duffels, thicksetts, callimancoes, and tabborets, black India sattins, sewin twist, &c.

And by the Hope, from Amsterdam,
White and brown platillas, britannias, blue and black cloths, bed-ticks, white line bordered, tapes and bobbins, hair ribbon, ve bon, black lace, &c.
Also on hand, about 15 ton pig lead. N

JOHN & WILLIAM TABEL
No. 260 *Pearl-Street,*

HAVE imported in the snow Anna Koper, from Bremen, the following viz.—
White and brown Platillas, Britannias, Sheelings, Brown and white Hessians, Brown Rolls, Tickienburghs and Osna Best Raven Duck. Nov.

THE SUBSCRIBER has for sale, fr from the cargo of the ship Sansom, fr cutta, an assortment of WHITE PIECE GO

ALSO,

50 tierces Rice.	60 hhds. Jamai
15 bales Sea-Island Cotton,	10,000 Pieces Nankeens,
29 tierces and 34 bls Jamaica Coffee,	A quantity o Bottles in case
	And as usual, O

DEIRA WINE, fit for immediate use.
Nov. 16 ROBERT LE

RICHARD & JOHN THORN
No. 141 *Pearl-street,*

HAVE just imported by the Fact London, and Liverpool Packet fro pool, a fashionable assortment of GOODS
3 bales London superfine blue, black, ionable mixt Cloths.
4 ditto do. blue, black, and fa mixt Cassimeres,
3 trunks fashionable Swansdowns, a nets Vest Patterns,
10 bales Rose Blankets, 1 do. Duffel do.
6 do. Blue Strouds, 2 trunks pat. worst
6 do. coarse Cloths,
3 trunks mens and womens cotton Hose
2 do. fashionable fancy Cords,
2 boxes Dimities,
6 do. mens fine fashionable Hats,
4 bales fashionable Coating.
Imported in the ship Caledonia from Liverpo
4 bales blue Duffels, and
3 trunks silk Umbrellas.
Imported in the General Mercer from Liver
6 bales mixed Coatings, 3 do. Swanski
4 do. white, red, and yellow Flannels
3 do. green and red Baize. N

AR HIBALD GRACIE has r his Counting-Room from his dwellin No. 110 Broadway, to his new Fire Proof S

THE FIRST ISSUE OF THE *NEW-YORK EVENING POST,* WHICH HAMILTON COFOUNDED AS A VEHICLE TO SPREAD HIS POLITICAL VIEWS.

PHILIP HAMILTON,
THE ELDEST CHILD
OF ALEXANDER AND
ELIZA HAMILTON,
DIED IN A DUEL AT
WEEHAWKEN IN
NOVEMBER 1801.

refused to accept offers of mutual apologies. Both young Hamilton and his friend then challenged Eacker to duels. Philip's friend and Eacker met on the field of honor first, and neither suffered injury. Philip Hamilton didn't prove so lucky. Alexander Hamilton advised his son not to fire until Eacker had fired and then to shoot in the air.

The two young men met at Weehawken, New Jersey, just across the Hudson from what is now Hell's Kitchen in Manhattan. Eacker fired first, and the bullet mortally pierced Philip's hip and arm. With his parents at his bedside, Philip died of infection that night. He was nineteen years old. Hamilton's friend Robert Troup remarked, "Never did I see a man so completely overwhelmed with grief as Hamilton has been."

With his parents at his bedside, Philip died of infection that night. He was nineteen years old.

But even family catastrophe didn't still Hamilton's pen for long. In the winter of 1801–1802, the *Post* published a series of his essays called *The Examination*, in which Hamilton responded to Jefferson's first annual message to Congress.* Jefferson had called for eliminating all internal taxes, reducing defense expenditures, leaving enterprise to handle itself, reducing the federal court system, and granting nearly immediate citizenship to immigrants.

Hamilton attacks Jefferson.

Writing as "Lucius Crassus"—a famous orator in ancient Rome—Hamilton argued against Jefferson's policies in *The Examination* essays. Instead of laissez-faire economics, he recommended infrastructure investments to foster faster growth. He also needled Jefferson's style of governing:

> *Industry will succeed and prosper in proportion as it is left to the exertions of individual enterprise. This favorite dogma, when taken as a general*

----

* Now called the State of the Union address.

rule, is true; but as an exclusive one, it is false, and leads to error in the administration of public affairs. In matters of industry, human enterprise ought, doubtless, to be left free in the main, not fettered by too much regulation; but practical politicians know that it may be beneficially stimulated by prudent aids and encouragements on the part of the Government. This is proved by numerous examples too tedious to be cited; examples which will be neglected only by indolent and temporizing rulers, who love to loll in the lap of epicurean ease, and seem to imagine that to govern well, is to amuse the wondering multitude with sagacious aphorisms and oracular sayings.

Setting aside the dig at Jefferson's navel-gazing cult of personality, Hamilton proves himself a pragmatic realist here. A laissez-faire policy—which Jefferson probably picked up from Adam Smith—was good "in the main" but hardly an "exclusive" rule. Government had a role in the economy. Even two centuries ago, examples were "numerous."

In private letters, Hamilton offered an equal lack of optimism in Jefferson's policies. In June 1802 he wrote to Rufus King, his friend and the American ambassador to Britain:

Truly, My dear Sir, the prospects of our Country are not brilliant. The mass is far from sound. At headquarters a most visionary theory presides. Depend upon it this is the fact to a great extreme. No army, no navy no active commerce—national defence, not by arms but by embargoes, prohibition of trade &c.—as little government as possible within—these are the pernicious dreams which as far and as fast as possible will be attempted to be realized. Mr. Jefferson is distressed at the codfish having latterly emigrated to Southern Coast lest the people there should be tempted to catch them, and commerce of which we have already too much receive an accession. Be assured this is no pleasantry, but a very sober anecdote.

> *"The prospects of our Country are not brilliant. The mass is far from sound."*

★ ★ ★ ★ ★

BONAPARTE'S OFFICIAL AUTHORIZATION FOR THE SALE OF THE
LOUISIANA TERRITORY TO AMERICA, APRIL 1803.

The Louisiana Purchase. France had ceded the territory of Louisiana to Spain during the Seven Years' War in 1762. In 1800, Bonaparte reclaimed it. Jefferson and Hamilton agreed on few points, but one of them was that French control of Louisiana—more specifically the port of New Orleans—represented a grave threat to American power.

In 1802, Bonaparte equipped a large French force to cross the Atlantic, suppress the revolt in Haiti (temporarily), reinstitute slavery, and proceed to Louisiana. Hamilton recommended that U.S. forces seize Louisiana first, and then negotiate. Jefferson decided to negotiate first.

Hamilton objected to Jefferson's strategy, of course. "There is not the most remote probability that the ambitious and aggrandizing views of Bonaparte will commute the

A MAP OF THE LOUISANA
TERRITORY IN 1804.

ALEXANDER HAMILTON

territory for money. Its acquisition is of immense importance to France, and has long been an object of her extreme solicitude." What Hamilton probably didn't know was that the French invasion force was succumbing to yellow fever and Haiti's black forces. That double setback caused Bonaparte to change his mind about establishing French control over Louisiana and to sell the whole territory to America.

News of the deal reached the United States at the end of June. Most northern Federalists opposed it because they feared it would reduce their national influence while increasing that of the South and extending the reach of slavery. But Hamilton immediately saw it as benefiting the national interest. He wrote in the *Evening Post* on July 5,

> *This purchase has been made during the period of Mr. Jefferson's presidency, and, will, doubtless, give éclat to his administration. Every man, however, possessed of the least candour and reflection will readily acknowledge that the acquisition has been solely owing to a fortuitous concurrence of unforeseen and unexpected circumstances, and not to any wise or vigorous measures on the part of the American government....*
>
> *To the deadly climate of St. Domingo, and to the courage and obstinate resistance made by its black inhabitants are we indebted for the obstacles which delayed the colonization of Louisiana.*

★ ★ ★ ★ ★

People v. Croswell *and the truth of libel.*

Jefferson called the Federalists' time in power "the reign of witches," and he and Madison suggested that states had a right to leave the Union if they disagreed with federal law. The Democratic-Republicans detested the Alien and Sedition Acts, which the Federalists had enacted during the war fever of 1798, but after 1800 the Democratic-Republicans prosecuted newspaper editors for libeling national leaders just as the Federalists had done earlier.

One such instance began in September 1802 when Harry Croswell, an upstate New York editor, published the following in his newspaper: "The charge is explicitly this:— Jefferson paid Callender for calling Washington a traitor, a robber, and a perjurer—For calling Adams, a hoary headed incendiary; and for most grossly slandering the private characters of men, who, he well knew were virtuous." This is the same James Callender who made allegations of financial impropriety against Hamilton, pushing our man to

write his Reynolds pamphlet, and the same who later charged Jefferson with fathering children by Sally Hemings, one of his slaves.

Under English common law, still New York law at the time, the truth of a statement offered no defense against libel. Printing the truth about a public figure or private individual could have malicious intent. Croswell was charged with libeling Jefferson and convicted in 1803—even though the statement he published was substantially true. Croswell appealed his conviction, and Hamilton joined the defense team. In February 1804, he appeared before New York's Supreme Court in Albany to defend his client. Hamilton reviewed the history of libel in English common law, challenged its appropriateness in a republic, and argued that the truth mattered in a libel case, provided the intent of an alleged libel wasn't malicious but to provide the public with information.

Hamilton lost the case, but his eloquent plea had a deep impact on the judges, lawyers, and state legislators in the audience. In 1805, New York changed its libel law

Hamilton's jurisprudence spread across the country.

to read in part, "in every prosecution for writing or publishing any libel, it shall be lawful for the defendant, upon the trial of the cause, to give in evidence in his defence, the truth of the matter contained in the publication charged as libelous: Provided always . . . that the matter charged as libelous, was published with good motives and for justifiable ends."

With slight modifications, the 1805 law was written into New York's revised constitution of 1821, and there it remains. As America moved west, the New York Constitution became a model for those of other, newer states, and Hamilton's jurisprudence spread across the country.

Burr demands satisfaction.

On June 18, 1804, Aaron Burr wrote a terse letter to Hamilton, enclosing a copy of another, earlier letter by one Charles Cooper that an Albany newspaper had published. The earlier letter said that during Burr's campaign for New York governor, Hamilton had expressed the opinion that Burr was "a dangerous man, and one who ought not to be trusted with the reins of government." Further: "I could detail to you a still more despicable opinion which General Hamilton has expressed of Mr. Burr."

Vice President Burr knew that Jefferson and the Democratic-Republicans were going to drop him from their ticket in the national elections later that year, so he had decided to run for governor of New York. Morgan Lewis, the candidate whom Hamilton backed, soundly defeated him. With those two setbacks before him, Burr was not a happy man in June 1804. He demanded of Hamilton "a prompt and unqualified acknowledgment or denial of the use of any expressions which could warrant the assertions of Dr. Cooper" and seethed particularly at the "still more despicable" part of Cooper's letter.

On June 20, Hamilton responded to the vice president:

Burr was not a happy man in June 1804.

I stand ready to avow or disavow promptly and explicitly any precise or definite opinion, which I may be charged with having declared of any Gentleman. . . . It cannot reasonably be expected, that I shall enter into any explanation upon a basis so vague as that which you have adopted. I trust,

*on more reflection, you will see the matter in the same light with me.
If not, I can only regret the circumstance, and must abide the
consequences.*

Hamilton's dismissive response didn't satisfy Burr at all.
Over the following week, they exchanged several more letters,
usually by agents who left their own accounts of the events.
The outcome: Burr challenged Hamilton to a duel.

Hamilton wrote out a statement that began with why
he shouldn't accept the challenge. His religious and moral
principles opposed dueling; he had a dear wife and seven
children who needed him; he had creditors who might suffer if his assets didn't cover the debts of his estate; and he
bore Burr no ill will. But the statement concluded with why
he felt he had to accept the challenge:

> *To those, who with me abhorring the practice of Duelling
> may think that I ought on no account to have added to the
> number of bad examples—I answer that my relative situ-
> ation, as well in public and private aspects, enforcing all
> the considerations which constitute what men of the world
> denominate honor, impressed on me (as I thought) a pecu-
> liar necessity not to decline the call. The ability to be in
> future useful, whether in resisting mischief or effecting good,
> in those crises of our public affairs, which seem likely to
> happen, would probably be inseparable from a conformity
> with public prejudice in this particular.*

Once again—and for the last time—Hamilton put his interest in
public service above all else.

The duel took place early in the morning on July 11, 1804, at
Weehawken, in the same place where his son Philip had died at the
hands of a dueling pistol. In separate boats, Burr and Hamilton
were rowed across the Hudson at sunrise, around 5 a.m., accompanied by their seconds and physicians. Dueling was illegal in both
New York and New Jersey at the time. Both men were residents of

BURR KNEW THE DEMOCRATIC-
REPUBLICAN PARTY WAS GOING
TO DROP HIM, SO HE RAN FOR
GOVERNOR OF NEW YORK. HAMILTON
BACKED ANOTHER CANDIDATE.

*Burr challenged
Hamilton to a duel.*

BURR (LEFT) AND HAMILTON
FACE OFF AT WEEHAWKEN.

HAMILTON THREW AWAY HIS
SHOT BY FIRING INTO THE AIR.
BURR DIDN'T EXTEND THE SAME
COURTESY TO HIS OPPONENT.

Hamilton aimed his pistol in the air and threw away his shot. Burr aimed at Hamilton and fired.

and lawyers in New York, and New Jersey enforced its laws against dueling more leniently. So they, like many other New York duelists, selected New Jersey's isolated dueling ground just below the Palisades.

The duel took place around 7 a.m. As he had promised, Hamilton "reserved" his first shot. He aimed his pistol in the air and threw away his shot. The weight of evidence provided by the seconds is that Hamilton fired into a tree well above and to the right of Burr. A few seconds later, Burr aimed at Hamilton and fired,

wounding his antagonist mortally. Burr appeared somewhat stunned when Hamilton
fell and twice tried to approach and speak to him. For legal reasons, Burr's second
advised him against doing so and turned Burr away and toward his boat.

Hamilton's physician, Dr. David Hosack, came forward to tend to the wounds. Hamilton was carried unconscious to his boat. The crew rowed him back to New York City,
and along the way Hamilton regained consciousness. He was taken from the dock in
Greenwich Village to the nearby home of William Bayard. Hamilton twice asked Benjamin Moore, the Episcopal bishop of New York, to give him communion. Bishop Moore
balked because he and the Church were against dueling. After Hamilton repented his

Hamilton dies.

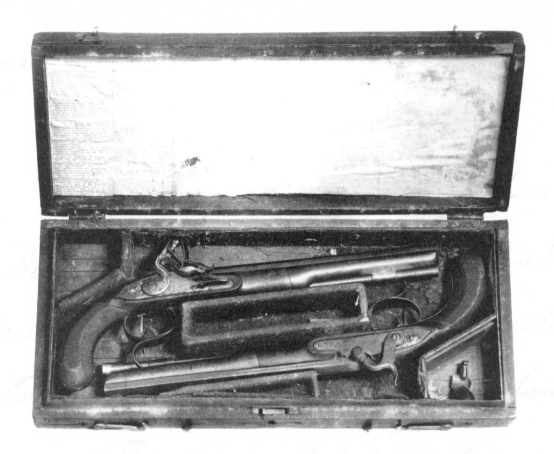

sins, renounced dueling, and forgave everyone involved in the duel, the bishop relented. Surrounded by grieving family and friends, Hamilton died the next afternoon, July 12, around 2 p.m.

New York City soon fell into shock over the death of its most prominent citizen, as did many parts of the nation. Two days after his death, the city organized something like a state funeral, complete with military honors, for a private citizen. Hamilton's longtime friend Gouverneur Morris gave the funeral oration. Four of Hamilton's sons— Alexander, James Alexander, John Church, and William Stephen—sat weeping on the platform near him. Eliza Hamilton, overcome with grief, didn't attend. She, her two daughters—Angelica and Elizabeth—and her youngest son, two-year old Philip, remained at home. Hamilton's body was laid to rest in the cemetery of Trinity Church on Broadway, fittingly at the start of Wall Street.

Those are the facts of the infamous duel, but larger questions remain. First, why did Hamilton accept the challenge in the first place? The showdown had its roots in hearsay that any good lawyer—much less a great lawyer like Hamilton—could have

HAMILTON DIED AT THE BAYARD HOUSE IN LOWER MANHATTAN ON WHAT IS NOW HORATIO STREET.

dismissed easily, accompanied perhaps with mollifying words to assuage Burr's wounded ego. Hamilton's note on why he accepted contains the germ of an answer. He went to the duel to retain the honor that the times demanded for future public service. But how could he undertake that service if he died first? Hamilton was betting that Burr *wouldn't* kill him, as had happened in many other duels of the day. Accepting Burr's challenge turned out to be the biggest misjudgment of Hamilton's life.

But why did Burr kill Hamilton? An ambitious man, Burr knew that killing his rival—a national figure admired for his accomplishments—would destroy or at least damage his own political career. Which of course it did. Burr had compelling reasons *not* to kill Hamilton. If neither man had an interest in or at least scruples against

> *Hamilton was betting that Burr wouldn't kill him.*

killing the other, then what happened? Joseph Ellis notes that a duelist often aimed to graze his opponent and speculates: "What is possible, but beyond the reach of available evidence, is that Burr really missed his target, too, that his own fatal shot, in fact, was accidental."

If we follow Ellis's supposition, the most famous duel in American history had an outcome that neither man intended. Only Burr could have confirmed it, but Burr never seemed to think he had to explain his actions in life to anyone. His strategy for getting ahead was to talk less and smile more.

That's one of the reasons that Hamilton opposed him throughout their political careers. To Hamilton, Burr had no principles and never wrote or said much to explain himself. Burr seemed to think that people should choose him to lead them merely because of his good breeding and genteel manners.* Burr fancied himself an American

....

*His father and grandfather both served as presidents of the College of New Jersey, today Princeton University.

HAMILTON'S TOMB
AS IT APPEARED IN
THE NINETEENTH
CENTURY.

aristocrat. Hamilton, the exact opposite, had come from nothing and risen by virtue of his brains and hard work. He was a meritocrat. He was also open—perhaps too open—to voicing his thoughts and opinions. Two politicians couldn't have been more different, yet each had a common interest in making sure the other man survived the duel. But Hamilton died at the age of forty-seven. His tomb stands in Lower Manhattan, not far from where, as an artillery officer, he fought to transform America from a ragtag assortment of British colonies to a federal union of states.

Eliza Hamilton survived her husband for half a century, dying in 1854 at age ninety-seven. In addition to caring for her elder daughter, Angelica, who suffered from mental illness after Philip died in the 1801 duel, Eliza devoted the remainder of her

ELIZA HAMILTON
BY·HENRY INMAN,
1825.

long life to a private orphanage and the preservation of Alexander Hamilton's role in
American history and our memory of it.

In 1806, she cofounded the Orphan Asylum Society of New York City, called
Graham Windham today. She served as one of its officers for 42 years, including
its leader from 1821 to 1848. After failing to find a suitable biographer for her late
husband, she gave the task to her son John Church Hamilton, who compiled multi-

volume studies of his father's career based on Hamilton's voluminous records and other documents. Eliza moved to Washington, D.C., in 1848 to spend the last six years of her life at the home of her younger daughter, Elizabeth Hamilton Holly. She is buried next to her husband in the Trinity Church cemetery.

The five sons who survived Hamilton followed their father's legacy by pursuing legal and military careers that, in the words of a grandson, Allan McLane Hamilton, "were, in a measure, commonplace. Little remains to show that they ever distinguished themselves.... It cannot be said that any one, in a conspicuous way, resembled his father." James Alexander Hamilton (1788–1878), a possible exception, served briefly as acting secretary of state under President Andrew Jackson.

After killing Hamilton, Burr served out his term as vice president, avoiding New York and New Jersey, which had indicted him for murder. The indictments later were dropped. Burr headed west and involved himself in what many regarded as treasonous schemes to break off the trans-Appalachian west from America. Burr was arrested, tried for treason, and acquitted in 1807—to the chagrin of Jefferson, whose administration pursued and indicted him. Burr lived in Europe from 1808 to 1812 and returned to New York, where he led an undistinguished life and career until his death in 1836.

Hamilton's old political antagonists—Presidents Adams, Jefferson, Madison, and Monroe—lived for decades after Hamilton died and used the time to burnish their own historical images. Despite Eliza Hamilton's best efforts, no one was telling Hamilton's story during those decades.

{ PART TWO }

★

LEGACIES

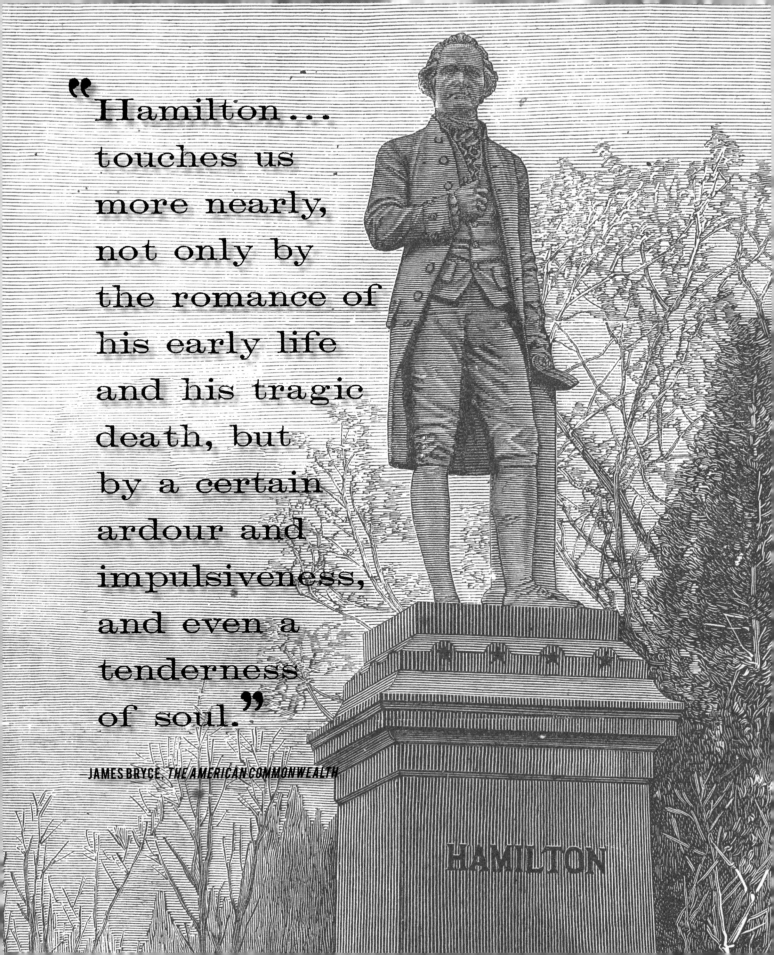

"Hamilton... touches us more nearly, not only by the romance of his early life and his tragic death, but by a certain ardour and impulsiveness, and even a tenderness of soul."

—JAMES BRYCE, *THE AMERICAN COMMONWEALTH*

HAMILTON

{X}

HAMILTON AND THE DEVELOPMENT OF AMERICA

In 1782, Hamilton described America as "a number of petty states, with the appearance only of union, jarring, jealous and perverse, without any determined direction, fluctuating and unhappy at home, weak and insignificant by their dissensions, in the eyes of other nations." Yet in 1910, when Lord Bryce, Britain's ambassador to America, crafted a revised edition of his classic book, *The American Commonwealth*, America's position in the world had changed vastly. The nation had grown, in the words of Hamilton's visionary hope, "noble and magnificent," becoming "a great Federal Republic, tranquil and prosperous at home, respectable abroad." Washington and Hamilton had provided the "determined direction" that led to America's maturation. Hamilton in particular achieved this end by establishing a constitutional government, reforming the nation's finances, promoting military preparedness, and advocating for liberating the country from the stain of slavery.

★ ★ ★ ★ ★

During the 1780s, Hamilton strove for a stronger government and union of the states as the receiver of continental taxes for New York, a member of the Confederation Congress, a delegate to the Annapolis Convention, a member of the New York Assembly, and one of the delegates to the Constitutional Convention. He signed the Constitution

JOHN CHURCH HAMILTON COMMISSIONED
THIS STATUE OF HIS FATHER IN
1880, WHICH STANDS IN CENTRAL
PARK, IN NEW YORK CITY.

on behalf of New York State and organized *The Federalist Papers* project to explain the new Constitution and promote its ratification. He led the pro-Constitution forces at the New York ratifying convention to victory against long odds.

The legacy of the Constitution.

More than anyone else, Hamilton breathed life into the Constitution's words and created a living, working plan of government. He advised Washington to take an expansive view of presidential powers, guiding and supporting the president as he did so. His reports on public credit, the national bank, and a mint laid the groundwork for a fiscally responsible federal government and stimulated private-sector development. His visionary report on manufactures received little support from Congress—although Congress sanctioned its recommended tax increases months later—but in the next century many of its recommendations became federal policy.

Judicial review.

Hamilton paved the way for judicial review, the principle that an independent judiciary has the right and obligation to review actions of the executive branch and laws passed by legislative bodies and to declare them void if they conflict with the Constitution. In *Federalist* No. 78, Hamilton argued:

> *More than anyone else, Hamilton created a living, working plan of government.*

The interpretation of laws is the proper and peculiar province of the courts. A constitution is in fact, and must be, regarded by the judges as a fundamental law. It therefore belongs to them to ascertain its meaning as well as the meaning of any particular act proceeding from the legislative body. If there should happen to be an irreconcilable variance between the two,... the constitution ought to be preferred to the statute, the intention of the people to the intention of their agents.

In 1803, Chief Justice John Marshall, a friend and disciple of Hamilton, adopted his mentor's position in *Marbury v. Madison*, the landmark Supreme Court decision that firmly entrenched the standard of judicial review, which emerged as a pillar of the checks and balances that the Constitution had created among the branches of government.

The Constitution that Thomas Jefferson inherited when he became president in 1801, in a peaceful transition from a Federalist to a Democratic-Republican administration, owed as much to Hamilton as any other founder. Hamilton had established what constitutional government meant in practice, as opposed to just words on paper.

★ ★ ★ ★ ★

CHIEF JUSTICE JOHN MARSHALL, ONE OF HAMILTON'S FRIENDS AND FOLLOWERS, ENSHRINED THE DOCTRINE OF JUDICIAL REVIEW IN THE U.S. SUPREME COURT'S DECISION IN *MARBURY V. MADISON*.

The legacy of reforming America's finances.

As General Washington's right-hand man during the War of Independence, Hamilton found it scandalous how ineffectively the Continental Army was supplied and paid, and he watched as the paper currency issued by Congress and the states lost value. His studies of financial history—especially the Dutch Republic, Britain, and France—pointed him to the conclusion that not only did a strong financial system enable a government to govern, maintain sovereignty, and wage war effectively against its enemies but also that a diversified, credit-based economy fostered investment and allowed for modern economic growth.

History recognizes Hamilton as a skillful modernizer. As Treasury secretary, he established the new federal government's credit, defined the dollar as the nation's monetary base, and founded the first central bank. He also induced state governments to charter more banks and other corporations and persuaded private entrepreneurs to establish securities markets to give liquidity to all the new financial instruments of his grand plan.

America's financial revolution in the early 1790s stands as Hamilton's greatest contribution to history.

America's financial revolution in the early 1790s stands as Hamilton's greatest contribution to history. He fought in the Revolutionary War, helped write and implement the Constitution, and established the workings of the new federal government, but all of those developments might have happened without him. Hamilton alone recognized the importance of finance for both the government and the economy, and Hamilton alone had the competency to formulate and execute a grand plan that propelled the country to enormous power and influence over the course of the twentieth century.

Historians used to contend, and some still do, that America rose because people settled the West, harnessed natural resources for use in the Industrial Revolution, and effected a transportation revolution. But that view tells only part of the story.

Expansion and growth through fiscal stability.

The nation's borders expanded to encompass all that western land because of strong public credit. When Bonaparte offered to sell the Louisiana Territory, Jefferson's government didn't have the cash to buy it. But the U.S. government's credit stood in such outstanding quality that U.S. Treasury bonds—which found a ready market in the financial centers of Europe—bankrolled most of the purchase price. The rest of the money came from the American government's agreement to take over and pay claims that Americans had against France for seizing their property during the Quasi War. Fifteen years earlier, when the federal government had no revenue powers beyond looking to the states, a massive international financial transaction—the largest in history to that point—

would have been impossible. Jefferson owed the greatest achievement of his presidency to Hamilton's financial system.

The ability to borrow helped the government maintain its territory and sustain its sovereignty in the otherwise unremarkable War of 1812. Military and naval preparedness, Hamilton's goals when antagonists branded him a militarist in the 1790s, allowed America to resolve border disputes with British-controlled Canada in the 1840s. Borrowing also underwrote the Mexican-American War of 1846–48, in which the United States seized and paid for the large territory now known as the Southwest. At war's end, Mexico ceded half of its territory to America in return for $15 million and the U.S. government's agreement to pay claims that its citizens had against Mexico. For another $10 million, America made the Gadsden Purchase, acquiring more land from Mexico in 1853 and forming the continental borders that persist today. Before pioneers "won" the West, the U.S. government triumphed over it through military strength and borrowing power—both legacies of Hamilton.

Jefferson owed the greatest achievement of his presidency to Hamilton's financial system.

From the 1790s to the 1820s, the sale of turnpike stock to private investors familiar with equity markets led to financing better roads throughout the northeastern states. When New York State decided to build the Erie Canal in 1817, it issued state bonds purchased by American and foreign investors. New York employed Hamiltonian principles by levying new auction and salt taxes to service the bonds. Other states borrowed rashly and defaulted on their debts in 1841 and 1842.

The rise of American industry.

A steamboat cost less than a turnpike road or a canal, but it still proved too pricey for most individual operators. An increasing number of state banks financed them, however: 100 by 1810, 300 by 1820, 700 by the mid-1830s, and almost 1,600 by 1860. Banks also funded the construction and operation of the first American factories, which trailed fast behind Britain's Industrial Revolution. New England industrialists applied to state legislatures for bank charters to ensure their access to bank credit. Equity investors eagerly snapped up bank shares, which became—along with insurance company stocks and government bonds—the chief listings on early U.S. securities markets.

Railroads appeared in the late 1820s. Invariably organized as corporations to pool the capital of many investors, railroads devoured capital, requiring substantial investments before earning a return. Selling shares financed most of the early, smaller ones, while later, larger ones relied heavily on bond financing. By mid-century, America was becoming a world power, ready to open Japan to trade, to rid itself of slavery, and to

AMERICA'S FINANCIAL STRENGTH ALLOWED IT TO SURVIVE
THE WAR OF 1812. HERE THE U.S.S. *CONSTITUTION* CAPTURES
THE H.M.S. *CYANE* AND H.M.S. *LEVANT* IN FEBRUARY 1815.

FEDERAL BORROWING UNDERWROTE THE MEXICAN-AMERICAN WAR, INCLUDING THE BATTLE OF CHAPULTEPEC, AND ALLOWED THE U.S. TO PURCHASE HALF OF MEXICO'S TERRITORY.

NEW YORK STATE USED HAMILTON'S FINANCIAL STRATEGIES
TO FUND THE CONSTRUCTION OF THE ERIE CANAL.

lead the world economy. Hamilton's policies created the underpinnings of all these developments, and the expansion that began with him moved ever onward. By the eve of World War I, America had amassed the largest banking system in the world, nearly 40 percent of the world's bank deposits, which represented more than the next three leading countries—Britain, France, and Germany—combined.

Business historians indicate that around 1910 the world had some 450,000 corporations; some 270,000, or 60 percent of the pie, were American. Most remained small, but a good number of them—the Pennsylvania and New York Central Railroads, United States Steel, General Electric, Standard Oil, the Bell Telephone Company—

THE DISTRICT GOVERNORS OF THE FEDERAL RESERVE IN 1914, A SYSTEM
THAT HAMILTON HAD ADVOCATED MORE THAN A CENTURY EARLIER.

expanded into world leaders in both assets and profits. Today, U.S. corporations number in the millions, more than any other country. The country still boasts the world's largest banking system and has featured, for more than a century, a central bank (the Federal Reserve) to restore Hamilton's original financial architecture. The wheels that Hamilton set in motion more than two centuries ago continue to turn.

★ ★ ★ ★ ★

The wheels that Hamilton set in motion more than two centuries ago continue to turn.

As Hamilton moved through his military ranks—captain, lieutenant colonel, colonel, major general—he always espoused military preparedness. The eighteenth century was a dangerous time. The European powers fought one another mercilessly at home and abroad. America stood on the periphery with around 4 million people, nearly 20 percent of them owned by others. In contrast, France had about 28 million people, Britain roughly 11 million, and Spain perhaps 10 million, and all three nations ruled over vast empires. America won its independence by the skin of its teeth, with French help, but remained highly vulnerable with a small population spread over a large territory.

Hamilton advocated a standing army, a navy and coast guard to protect the country's ports and overseas commerce, coastal and interior fortifications, and a military academy to train officers and engineers. For these stances, his opponents vilified him as a militarist. Their argument: Hamilton exaggerated the foreign threats that they believed militias could handle. Hamilton's detractors didn't want to bear the costs or responsibilities of a permanent military establishment. As a point of history, Hamilton won. Jefferson signed the law creating the U.S. Military Academy at West Point, New York, in 1802. As America grew stronger, foreign threats diminished.

As a point of history, Hamilton won.

The globe changed with World Wars I and II. America became the leading military and economic power. Then the Cold War divided the world into communist powers, the so-called free world, and developing nations. The United States countered the threat of communist expansion by maintaining large military forces, forming alliances, and establishing military bases across the globe.

The 1990s witnessed the collapse of the Soviet Union and the thawing of the Cold War. By then, America had taken up lesser wars in the Middle East and Afghanistan, first to counter the aggression of Saddam Hussein, who threatened to disrupt the flow of oil, and then against Islamic terrorists in Iraq, Afghanistan, and most recently Syria.

The world once again mirrors the hostile, threatening place that existed in Hamilton's time.

The world once again mirrors the hostile, threatening place that existed in Hamilton's time. To protect its interests, America has implemented policies recommended by Washington and Hamilton at the beginning. The military establishment now includes a technologically advanced U.S. Army, Navy, Marine Corps, Air Force, and Coast Guard, several service academies to train officers, and numerous training facilities—all at great cost. America spends more on its military establishments than the combined expenditures of the next nine or ten largest spenders.

★ ★ ★ ★ ★

Hamilton detested slavery. But he and others realized that pressing for abolition would fracture the Union and reduce North America into another bloody patchwork of warring states with conflicting objectives. Slavery took a backseat to the interests of national unity. With Hamilton's untimely death, the country lost the one mind best equipped to execute a financial plan to end slavery gradually and perhaps peacefully. But again it was his financial policies that paved the way for its eventual dissolution by building up a diversified economy in the free states of the North.

The legacy of slavery and abolition.

With Hamilton's untimely death, the country lost the one mind best equipped to execute a financial plan to end slavery.

From 1801 to 1861, slaveholders and their acolytes controlled the federal government, protecting the Peculiar Institution that provided them with wealth and power. They represented a minority in their home states, which presented the problem of maintaining that power as more and more non-slave-owning white citizens gained voting rights. Southern slaveholders solved the problem by demonizing blacks as inferior, dangerous unless enslaved, and claimed that all hell would break loose if slavery ended unless free blacks were "colonized" to some far-off place. They argued self-servingly that whites and blacks couldn't possibly live together in harmony. Jefferson himself made most of these points in his book, *Notes on the State of Virginia*. The slave-owning oligarchs of the South only had to dust them off and use them for their own purposes.

Southern whites swallowed these racist arguments, along with the additional arguments that compensated emancipation would prove costly and the expense to taxpayers would rise even more when adding the costs of colonization. Unfortunately, northern whites also heeded these dubious positions. Even Abraham Lincoln—a rising politician opposed to slavery and any extension of it beyond the states where it already existed—at first thought that colonization would be necessary.

Despite the proliferation and prevalence of these self-interested assertions, more and more Americans recognized slavery as a stain on the land of the free, where all men supposedly were created equal. After Lincoln became president in the election of 1860, most of the southern states seceded from the Union, founding the Confederate States of America and launching their own war of independence. Under Lincoln's leadership and four blood-soaked years of combat, the Union defeated the Confederacy and abolished slavery by exercising the strong federal power that Hamilton had advocated almost a century earlier.

ALEXANDER HAMILTON

"I consider Napoleon, Pitt and Hamilton to be the three greatest men of our epoch, and if I had to choose among the three, I would without hesitation give the premier place to Hamilton."

—C. M. DE TALLEYRAND

ALEXANDER·HAMILTON

{XI}

HAMILTON'S IMPACT ON WORLD HISTORY

T alleyrand, a French statesman and diplomat, served as a foreign minister or ambassador in a series of France's governments from the outbreak of the French Revolution in 1789 to the reign of King Louis-Philippe in the 1830s. His vaunted status allowed him to observe and, in many cases, meet the leading politicians and statesmen of his era, including Hamilton.

Talleyrand's opinion of Hamilton.

On a diplomatic mission in England in 1792, Talleyrand avoided the worst excesses of the French Revolution, including the overthrow of King Louis XVI. After Britain and France went to war, the British told him to leave or face repatriation to France. So in 1794 Talleyrand went to America. During his two-year hiatus in the States, the French minister met Hamilton and scrutinized his work, both as Treasury secretary in Philadelphia and as a private citizen and lawyer in New York.

Talleyrand considered Hamilton the greatest statesman of his era. He believed Hamilton understood Europe with all of its machinations, rivalries, and threats better than any other American. Talleyrand also associated America's booming economy with Hamilton's reforms. On his way to a party one night in New York, he strolled by Hamilton's law office and saw him toiling by candlelight. The Frenchman remarked: "I have just come from viewing a man who had made the fortune of his country, but now is working all night in order to support his family."

Hamilton understood Europe with all of its machinations, rivalries, and threats better than any other American.

THIS STATUE OF HAMILTON
STANDS OUTSIDE THE MUSEUM
OF THE CITY OF NEW YORK.

> *"I have just come from viewing a man who had made the fortune of his country, but now is working all night in order to support his family."*

Later, as France's foreign minister, Talleyrand allegedly sent agents to demand a bribe from President Adams's first peace commissioners. In 1803, he told Robert Livingston, who had just negotiated the Louisiana Purchase, "You have made a noble bargain for yourselves, and I suppose you will make the most of it." He knew that, thanks to Hamilton, the American government's excellent credit would finance the purchase. The Treasury bonds sold easily to European investors, providing Bonaparte with more financing for his European conquests.

★ ★ ★ ★ ★

Adam Smith, the Scottish economist, once wrote:

> *Were the Americans, either by a combination or by any other sort of violence, to stop the importation of European manufactures, and, by thus giving a monopoly to such of their own countrymen as could manufacture the like goods, divert any considerable part of their capital into this employment, they would retard instead of accelerating the further increase in the value of their annual produce, and would obstruct instead of promoting the progress of their country towards real wealth and greatness.*

Incentives to bolster industry.

Hamilton dismissed Smith's advice, but in the short run Smith was right. If Americans could buy goods cheaper from Europe than they could make themselves, they should. Jefferson agreed. America's comparative economic advantage lay in agriculture, and exports of its agricultural products could finance the purchase of manufactures.

Hamilton, however, reasoned more dynamically about economic policy and national security. With encouragement from government—preferably by subsidies but also by tariffs on imported manufactures and other aids—Americans could grow industries to compete with and perhaps even dominate the trades of England and Europe. This overarching theme pervaded Hamilton's "Report on Manufactures" of 1791, which transformed into policy when America exceeded Britain and all other nations in industrial production in the nineteenth century.

C. M. DE TALLEYRAND SERVED AS A
STATESMAN ON THE INTERNATIONAL
STAGE FOR MORE THAN FORTY
YEARS AND COUNTED HAMILTON
THE GREATEST MAN OF HIS AGE.

Friedrich List and German economics.

In 1825, Friedrich List, a German professor of politics and administration, migrated to America in order to avoid a prison sentence for his liberal views. He settled in eastern Pennsylvania, where he noted the prosperity and economic dynamism of the young country and partook in a variety of business ventures and investments. He came under the influence of Matthew Carey and his son Henry Charles Carey, political economists and advocates of Hamilton. They urged List to read Hamilton's writings, which shaped his views.

In the early 1830s, List returned to Europe and advocated building railways. He advocated the Zollverein, a customs union or free-trade area for the various German states. In 1841, he wrote a book called *The National System of Political Economy*, based on Hamilton's policies in America, which later influenced other parts of the world. Using Hamilton as his guide, List advocated an industrial policy of aiding infant industries, mostly through tariffs, until they grew strong enough to compete with those in England. He viewed England as hypocritical for favoring its home industries with a variety of mercantilist regulations and advocating univer-

THROUGH FRIEDRICH LIST, A LEADING NINETEENTH-CENTURY GERMAN ECONOMIST, HAMILTON'S ECONOMIC PRINCIPLES SHAPED THE MODERN WORLD.

sal free trade once those industries became the most technologically advanced in the world. List encouraged Germany and similar countries that lagged behind Britain in economic development to follow Hamilton's policies.

Germany followed List like the Bible, particularly after the economic unification of the Zollverein led to political unification under the leadership of Prussia's "iron chancellor," Otto von Bismarck, from the 1860s to the 1890s. By following List's policy prescriptions, Germany's economy soon rivaled Britain's.

Russian economics and industrialization.

List's prescriptions also migrated to Russia, where finance minister Sergei Witte adopted them wholesale in the 1890s. Russia began a rapid industrialization and on the eve of World War I ranked fifth in industrial production, behind America,

Britain, Germany, and France. But the United States still stood miles ahead of the others.*

★ ★ ★ ★ ★

European explorers reached Japan in the sixteenth century and established trading and cultural contacts. While the English were busy colonizing and populating North America at the beginning of the seventeenth century, in Japan the ruling Tokugawa shogun ceased contact with the rest of the world, except for a minor concession to Dutch traders, Japan's sole point of contact with the outside world for the next two centuries.

Japanese financial modernization.

In the early 1850s, President Millard Fillmore dispatched Commodore Matthew Perry and a fleet of U.S. Navy ships to Japan to open the country—with gunboat diplomacy—and establish trading relationships. America had long traded with China, but the switch from wind and sail to coal and steam required refueling stations along routes to Asia. Intimidated by Western naval power, the Japanese signed unequal treaties with America and the European powers, granting them concessions such as minimal import tariffs.

In 1868, a group of modernizers returned the emperor to power, replacing the shogun, in the Meiji Restoration. The Meiji leaders embarked on a program of rapid political, economic, financial, military, and educational modernization and determined to restore the sovereignty lost in the unequal treaties. They used a systematic approach that entailed sending delegations to Western countries to study the secrets of their success.

The Iwakura Embassy (1871–73) visited America for some seven months, studying American institutions and meeting with, among others, President Ulysses S. Grant and his cabinet members, most of whom were Republicans and disciples of Hamilton, whose star was rising in the post–Civil War decades. The Iwakura mission then trekked to Britain and the European continent. Germany—a recently unified nation lagging behind Britain and France but making rapid strides to catch up—particularly interested them. They met Bismarck and learned of Friedrich List, whose book they translated into Japanese.

The Iwakura Embassy.

The Iwakura mission tried without success to renegotiate the unequal treaties. As

....

* American production in 1914 exceeded the output of Britain, Germany, and France combined.

IN THE EARLY 1870S,
THE IWAKURA MISSION
SOUGHT TO RENEGOTIATE
JAPAN'S UNEQUAL
WESTERN TREATIES AND
TO STUDY HOW WESTERN
SOCIETIES FUNCTIONED.

such, Japan couldn't follow List's leading prescription for modernization: establishing tariffs to protect infant industries. They did learn, however, about Hamilton's leading prescription for strengthening a national government and promoting economic development: financial modernization. Unequal treaties imposed no barriers to Japan's financial modernization.

The Japanese quickly undertook financial modernization similar to Hamilton's. They superseded the old system of taxes on the peasantry, paid in rice, with taxes paid in money based on estimated land values. They also introduced a new yen currency to replace older forms of money. The old system used the rice to pay the samurai warrior class. They converted rice payments into long-term government bonds, which were used to pay off the samurai, who thenceforward received annual interest on their bonds instead of rice. The government also allocated revenue to establish modern industrial plants designed to demonstrate to Japanese entrepreneurs the latest Western industrial technologies—similar to the Society for Establishing Useful Manufactures.

The new government bonds provided capital, which entrepreneurial samurai used to invest in banks and other enterprises. The bonds, as they had in America in the 1790s, also led to the emergence of securities trading markets. Tokyo and Osaka created stock exchanges in 1878. These markets then traded the equity shares of a growing number of corporate enterprises.

Japanese modernizers observed the workings of America's fairly recent system of national banks introduced by the Lincoln administration during the Civil War. The Japanese copied that system and within three years founded more than 150 national banks in their own country—but the new system floundered. The new banks flooded the country with banknotes, causing rampant inflation.

Japan looked outside for answers. Europe seemed not to have this problem because the countries there had central banks, as had the United States under Hamilton's tenure in the Treasury Department. (In the 1830s, President Andrew Jackson had vetoed Congress's bill to recharter the Bank of the United States, which left America without a central bank until the Federal Reserve System restored that crucial piece of Hamilton's financial architecture.)

Japan needed a central bank. Japan's finance minister, Masayoshi Matsukata, founded the Bank of Japan in 1882 as a central bank akin to the Belgian model. He introduced policies to control Japan's inflation and within a few years achieved success by converting yen into silver. To stabilize government finances further, Matsukata sold the government's model factories to private entrepreneurs. He also launched other currency and banking reforms, centralizing currency production and converting national banks into ordinary banks. Japan used an indemnity paid in gold by China after Japan's victory in the first Sino-Japanese War (1894–95) to back the yen with gold and go on the gold standard in 1897. That move allowed Japan to borrow on good terms in the world's leading capital markets. By century's end, Japan had more than 1,500 commercial banks with

The Japanese quickly undertook financial modernization similar to Hamilton's.

By employing Hamiltonian policies, Japan shot far ahead of its Asian neighbors.

more than 1,000 branches. Observing Japan's rapid economic growth, the American ambassador called Matsukata the Alexander Hamilton of Japan. By employing Hamiltonian policies, Japan shot far ahead of its Asian neighbors economically and militarily and in time became the one non-Western nation to equal the nations of the West in just about every aspect of development.

Asian economics.

After decades marred by global war and the Great Depression, more nations of the world—many the former colonies of the great powers—adopted Hamiltonian policies in the second half of the twentieth century. South Korea and Taiwan in particular stand as notable examples. But those policies have spread to other entities, such as the city-state of Singapore and the special administrative region of Hong Kong. Hamilton designed his policies to improve a nation in a world of nation-states. With more nation-states than ever before, Hamiltonian policies will continue to appeal in the decades ahead.

Hamilton versus laissez-faire.

The alternative, which attracts many economists and policy makers, especially in rich countries, is market fundamentalism, the idea that free markets will guide nations to prosperity if governments simply cut taxes and spending and deregulate economic life. To Smith, Jefferson, Madison, and others, it made sense: America excelled at farming, and the whole world needed food and clothing, so America's agricultural products would find a ready and growing market. But that approach too easily leads to dangers to sovereignty, political vulnerabilities, and second-class economic status.

Wonders don't always or even often unfold.

Good arguments abound on each side, but Hamilton's approach more often prevails. Why? Simple realism. The nations in a world of nation-states actually practice Hamilton's approach, despite being advised by market fundamentalists to follow Smith's laissez-faire prescriptions and watch wonders unfold. Wonders don't always or even often unfold. The tax cuts and deregulation of recent decades were supposed to lead to economic marvels in America but instead they led to the Great Recession. At that point, market fundamentalists appealed for massive governmental intervention. They didn't practice what they had preached.

Some nations in Europe followed a more market-fundamentalist path, cutting taxes and spending to implement austerity policies. They practiced what they preached, but the results weren't encouraging: New crises emerged along with a slower recovery than the one that took place in America. A more Hamiltonian approach might have worked better. We'll have to see whether pragmatism eventually overcomes ideology.

MASAYOSHI MATSUKATA FOLLOWED HAMILTONIAN PRINCIPLES TO REFORM HIS COUNTRY'S
FINANCES, WHICH SET JAPAN ON A COURSE FOR ENORMOUS ECONOMIC PROSPERITY.

The legacy of
The Federalist.

As we just saw, Hamilton's impact on the world deals mostly with the economic policies of nations, but effective economic and financial policies depend on governments strong enough to implement them. Hamilton realized that as he pondered what he and others called the "imbecility" of the government of America under the Articles of Confederation.

But a government capable of carrying out policies to produce economic development and growth should be more than just strong. It also ought to be free and democratic. Unfortunately our era has many examples of authoritarian governments that executed Hamiltonian policies, compromising both the political and human rights that the founders cherished.

So even more than economic policies, we should look to Hamilton and his brethren for their insights on the purposes of government. Governments should work not only to make people rich economically, safe from domestic threats to lives and property, and foreign threats to sovereignty; they also should work to make people free.

The Federalist began as a propagandistic ad campaign in 1787 to persuade the people of New York to support the U.S. Constitution by electing its supporters as delegates to the state ratification convention. It flopped because anti-Constitution delegates outnumbered supporters by more than two to one. Despite the flop, however, *The Federalist* became a primary source for understanding what the Constitution meant to its framers.

The reputation and importance of *The Federalist* continues to grow. U.S. Supreme Court justices often cite it in their decisions. When the Soviet Union imploded and shattered back into independent countries, statesmen and pundits advised their leaders to read *The Federalist* to learn how to set up viable governments. In the summer of 2016, the United Kingdom voted to leave the European Union, threatening the survival of both unions. Both Britons and Europeans might find guidance on how to maintain a union of states in the pages of *The Federalist*—assuming it's not already too late.

> *We should look to Hamilton and his brethren for their insights on the purposes of government.*

> *The reputation and importance of* The Federalist *continue to grow.*

That failed ad campaign of 1787–88 has become the most important American contribution to political science. Hamilton and his collaborators publicized a plan of government to help people become safe and rich. By looking back at *The Federalist*, people can move forward from the age-old problem of government oppression and become free.

"The state which Alexander Hamilton had planned and inaugurated Abraham Lincoln completed and confirmed."

—F. S. OLIVER, *ALEXANDER HAMILTON: AN ESSAY ON AMERICAN UNION*

GOALS AND ACHIEVEMENTS

⸻ ◆ ⸻

The partnership between Washington and Hamilton began in 1777 and lasted for twenty-three years, until Washington's death at Mount Vernon on December 14, 1799. In late November of that year, Hamilton had sent Washington a detailed plan for a military academy that he had submitted to Secretary of War James McHenry. Hamilton asked for Washington's suggestions. The two men had often discussed the need for a national military academy, and Washington as president had recommended on several occasions that Congress establish it. Congress didn't act.

On December 12, Washington wrote Hamilton to express his agreement with Hamilton's plan and his sincere "hope that the subject will meet with due attention, and the reasons for its establishment, which you have so clearly pointed out in your letter to the Secretary, will prevail upon the Legislature to place it upon a permanent and respectable footing." Two days later, Washington lay dead—felled by an illness he contracted while riding his estate in a freezing storm and by the common medical practice of bloodletting.

Washington's secretary, Tobias Lear, wrote Hamilton the next day to inform him of Washington's death, saying that "all the aid of medicine had not the desired effect. Bearing his distressed situation with the fortitude of an Hero, he retained his composure and reason to the last moment, and died, as he had lived, a truly great man." Hamilton replied that the sad news "filled my heart with bitterness. Perhaps no man in this community has equal cause with myself to

The death of Washington.

Two days later, Washington lay dead.

THE STATUE OF HAMILTON
THAT STANDS OUTSIDE THE U.S.
TREASURY DEPARTMENT, 2014.

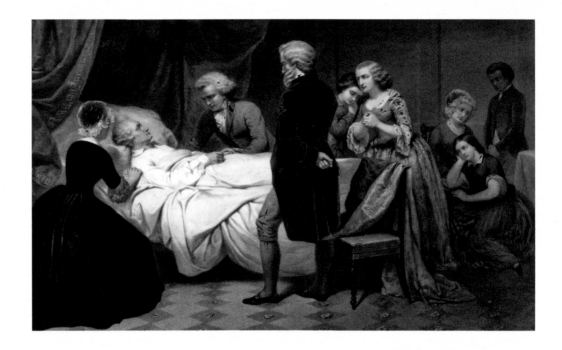

deplore the loss. I have been much indebted to the kindness of the General, and he was an Aegis very essential to me.... If virtue can secure happiness in another world he is happy. In this the Seal is now put upon his Glory." With the death of his old friend and mentor, Hamilton had lost the greatest, most consistent supporter of his entire public life.

Hamilton in summary.

While fighting under the general's command, Hamilton was an unusual soldier. In 1777, between battles and his duties as Washington's principal aide de camp, he found time to read and take notes on Plutarch's *Lives*, Malachy Postlethwayt's *Universal Dictionary of Trade and Commerce*, and the orations of the ancient Athenian statesman Demosthenes. From the *First Philippic* of Demosthenes, Hamilton copied two passages:

> *As a general marches at the head of his troops, so ought wise politicians, if I dare to use the expression, to march at the head of affairs; insomuch that they ought not to wait for the event, to know what measures to take; but the measures which they have taken, ought to produce the event.*

and

> *Where attack him it will be said? Ah Athenians war, war itself will discover to you his weak sides, if you seek them.*

adding two words of commentary on these passages: "Sublimely simple." We can look at Hamilton's entire life as putting the insights of Demosthenes into practice. Hamilton was a man of action, a doer. He made things happen. But he also was a thinker. He based his actions on thoughtful analysis, on "reflection and choice," as he put it in *Federalist* No. 1, rather than on "accident and force," which for too long had ruled human affairs.

As a thinker, he persuaded others of what he thought they needed to do; then as a practicing soldier, politician, statesman, and financier, he led them toward the goal. Most of history's leading characters are either deep thinkers or people of action. Hamilton was both. In his teenage essays of 1774 and 1775, he made the case for American independence and the military strategy that achieved it. As a soldier and officer, he participated at a high level in the war planning, culminating in a key role in the decisive victory at Yorktown. He analyzed the defects of the government under the Articles of Confederation and called for a convention to remedy them. As a congressman, legislator, and delegate, he continued working toward constitutional ratification and reform. As the nation's first Treasury secretary, he did as much as anyone to organize the workings of the new federal government, setting it on a course to make the American economy the world's richest and largest. As an officer, congressman, and inspector general, he also did as much as anyone to create America's military establishment. Doing so proved unpopular in his time both because of the cost and Americans' aversion to taxation and a standing army. But Hamilton stuck to his guns because he knew from experience that the only thing costlier than spending too much on military preparedness was not spending enough.

Most of history's leading characters are either deep thinkers or people of action. Hamilton was both.

Hamilton subordinated his detestation of slavery to what he perceived as the greater goal of national unity. His untimely death removed the one man in a position of power to implement a national financial plan that could have ended slavery without bloodshed. Yet the policies he effected ensured its end. By the 1860s, the northern states had a sophisticated, agile economy that Lincoln mobilized to support warfare on a scale never before seen in history.

Hamilton's goals and achievements soon became the goals and achievements of the country. We live today in a Hamiltonian nation. But few outside the scholarly world have realized it. The musical *Hamilton*, a work of genius by Lin-Manuel Miranda about a genius, has brought and is bringing Hamilton's story to a wide range of people of all ages and interests. It has become a part of Hamilton's long-reaching legacy.

The musical.

LIN-MANUEL
MIRANDA AS
HAMILTON
IN THE HIT
MUSICAL.

ALEXANDER HAMILTON

One of the first triumphs of *Hamilton*—apart from its critical and box-office triumph—is preserving Hamilton's likeness on the ten-dollar bill. A tin-eared, bureaucratic Treasury Department decided early in 2015 that it was high time for a woman to appear on American currency and that the ten-dollar note fit the bill. Thanks to *Hamilton* and the cries of those who understood his signal contributions to financial history, public opinion mobilized to force the Treasury to halt its senseless plan. Hamilton will remain the ten-dollar founding father, as he should.

The ten-dollar-bill controversy.

His name graces counties in New York, Florida, Tennessee, Ohio, Indiana, Illinois, Nebraska, and Kansas. The U.S. Customs House in New York City bears his name. Both Columbia University and the Coast Guard Academy named their main buildings

Hamilton among us.

THE U.S. COAST GUARD CUTTER *ALEXANDER HAMILTON*, HOMEPORTED IN CHARLESTON, SOUTH CAROLINA, ARRIVES IN MIAMI IN NOVEMBER 2014.

THE GRANGE,
HAMILTON'S HOME.
TODAY IT FORMS PART
OF HAMILTON GRANGE
NATIONAL MEMORIAL
IN UPPER MANHATTAN.

for him. Three U.S. Coast Guard cutters and two U.S. Navy ships (a cutter and a submarine) have borne his name. Statues of him stand in Central Park, Manhattan, and before the Treasury Department in Washington, D.C. You can visit his birthplace in Nevis, his home in Upper Manhattan, and his tomb in Lower Manhattan.

Hamilton once again is emerging from the shadows of American history, as he should. His story is the story of what America has become—a safe, free, wealthy country—and what it still strives to be: a place where all citizens have equal rights and are equal before the law.

HAMILTON'S TOMB AS
IT APPEARS TODAY IN
LOWER MANHATTAN.

{ ACKNOWLEDGMENTS }

An author has many debts that giving credit can offset partially. For about a quarter of a century, three scholars have had continuing discussions with me about Hamilton, his work, and his place in history: David J. Cowen, now president and CEO of the Museum of American Finance; my New York University colleague George David Smith, and my former NYU colleague, now at Augustana College in South Dakota, Robert E. Wright. Close behind come Douglas A. Irwin of Dartmouth and the late Thomas K. McCraw of Harvard Business School, with whom I have had or had numerous exchanges. These five gentleman scholars did much to shape my thinking about Hamilton and the early history of America.

Louise Mirrer, president of the New-York Historical Society, deserves my thanks for inviting me in 2004 to give a series of six lectures on Hamilton's financial policies and their impact, in connection with the Society's major exhibition *Alexander Hamilton: The Man Who Made Modern America*. The NYHS's knowledgeable audiences gave me valuable feedback.

The Museum of American Finance, to which this book is dedicated and with which I have been associated in one way or another since 1990, has been a source of continuing inspiration. Its founder and first chairman, John E. Herzog, performed a notable service to his country and the world by establishing an institution that educates us about finance and its history. David Cowen now leads the museum with the incredibly dedicated and able assistance of Kristin Aguilera, Tony Critelli, Robert Dinkelmann, Jeanne Baker Driscoll, Maura Ferguson, Alan Hurley, Chris Meyers, Sarah Poole, Linda Rapacki, Mindy Ross, and Ben Urizar. I have learned from all of them.

John Herzog's interest in financial history began decades ago when he began collecting historical financial instruments and documents. John introduced me to the scripophily community, two members of which, Ned Downing and Ira Unschuld, shared with me items from their collections that increased my appreciation of what Hamilton did.

The Alexander Hamilton Awareness Society, founded and led since 2011 by Rand Scholet, is doing much to bring Hamilton from the shadows through its website and by organizing annual events that keep alive our memory of the man and his contributions to the founding of America. I have participated in these events and learned at them from meeting other Hamiltonians. Through the AHA Society, I met Michael E. Newton, a scholar engaged in careful and meticulous

THE ISLAND OF NEVIS, WHERE
HAMILTON WAS BORN.

researches of Hamilton's life that are clearing up errors and misunderstandings in the extant literature about him.

I always wondered why Hamilton had such a facility with numbers, accounts, and mathematics, obviously valuable traits for a financier and treasurer. Douglas Hamilton, a friend and descendant of Hamilton, offered a possible explanation. He shared some genealogical work showing that Alexander descended from the Scottish mathematician John Napier, inventor of natural or Napierian logarithms.

The following institutions (and individuals) supported my research on early U.S. financial development and the impact of Hamilton's policies: the Alfred P. Sloan Foundation (Jesse H. Ausubel, Ralph E. Gomory); NYU Stern's Berkley Center for Entrepreneurial Studies (William J. Baumol, Alexander Ljungqvist); the National Bureau of Economic Research (Claudia D. Goldin); and the National Science Foundation. Skilled co-investigators on sponsored research projects include the late John B. Legler, John J. Wallis, the late Jack W. Wilson, and Robert E. Wright.

To Henry Kaufman, one of the few statesmen of Wall Street, I owe a huge debt of gratitude. Henry founded NYU Stern School of Business's chair in financial history, of which I became the initial occupant from 1990 to 2015. Henry has been a great friend and source of inspiration. We share a surprisingly minority opinion that all MBAs and business leaders ought to have some knowledge of economic and financial history. To the MBA and other students who enrolled in my Development of Financial Institutions and Markets course, I appreciate your help in sharpening my thoughts and presentations over twenty-five years.

I also have to thank Richard R. West, former dean of NYU Stern, who hired me in 1990 for the best job a financial historian could have: the Henry Kaufman professorship of the history of financial institutions and markets. Dick West brought me to New York City, where my first office overlooked Trinity Church, Hamilton's resting place, and the start of Wall Street. To my lifelong interest in Hamilton, this added inspiration.

I thank James Jayo, my editor at Sterling Publishing, who had the initial idea for this illustrated biography of Hamilton, and my friend Leah Spiro of Riverside Creative Management, who brought James's idea to me and persuaded me of its merits. I also salute Lorie Pagnozzi for her interior design that breathes life into my words on the page and photo editor Stacey Stambaugh for her good eye, resourcefulness, and comprehensive visual knowledge of the period.

Finally, I express gratitude to my family for their encouragement and support: wife Edith, daughters Anne and Peggy, sons-in-law Bob and Percy, and grandchildren Sunny, Leo, Meryl, Charlotte, Matthew, and Fenno.

{ NOTES }

For complete bibliographical information, see pages 263-266.

Introduction: Emerging from the Shadows

viii   "Hamilton is perhaps the least loved founding father." Staloff, op. cit., 125?26.

xiii   "the ruling passion of the noblest minds" *Federalist No. 72. Papers of Alexander Hamilton* (hereafter *PAH*), Harold Syrett et al. eds., IV, 613.

I. Immigrant

2   "I wish there was a War" *PAH*, I, 4.

6   "my ambition is prevalent" *PAH*, I, 4.

7   "natural faculties" H to John Jay, March 24, 1779, *PAH*, II, 17-19, at 18.

16   "The sacred rights of mankind" *PAH*, I, 122.

II. Soldier

24   "That he is ambitious" *Washington: Writings*, Library of America, 1997, 1013.

32   "It was a model of discipline" Michael E. Newton, *Alexander Hamilton: The Formative Years*, 2015, 177.

32   "a mere stripling" Newton, *Alexander Hamilton*, 177-78.

40   "I believe it is never practiced" Newton, *Alexander Hamilton*, 223.

41   "I approve entirely of all the steps you have taken" Newton, *Alexander Hamilton*, 226.

42   "nothing less than America's first great state paper" Fleming, *Washington's Secret War*, 178.

47   "Do you soberly relish" *PAH*, II, 398.

47   "Next fall Completes my doom" *PAH*, II, 348.

48   "opportunities, as the principal and most confidential aid" *Washington: Writings*, Library of America, 1997, 1013.

51   "I am not conscious of it, sir" *PAH*, II, 564.

III. Reformer

54   "Our whole system is in disorder" Hamilton, *The Continentalist No. III*, *PAH* II, 661.

60   "The only plan that can preserve the currency" *PAH*, II, 244-45.

63   "Political writers on the affairs of France" Steuart, op. cit., in the modern edition, A. S. Skinner, ed. (1998) 3, 262-63.

63   "We may therefore by means of this establishment" *PAH*, II, 248.

66   "The confederation . . . gives the power of the purse" *PAH*, II, 404

66   "too timid and indecisive" *PAH*, II, 401.

66   "immediately a convention of all the states" *PAH*, II, 407.

66   "Congress should have complete sovereignty" *PAH*, II, 408.

67   " 'Tis by introducing order into our finances" *PAH*, II, 606.

67   "The tendency of a national bank" *PAH*, II, 618.

69   "A national debt if it is not excessive" *PAH*, II, 635.

74   "There is something noble and magnificent" *PAH*, III, 106.

IV. Legislator

72   "The two most extraordinarily statesmanlike intellects" Zane, op. cit., 363.

73   "I have been employed for the last ten months" *PAH*, III, 192.

74   "Judge [Robert] Yates" *PAH*, III, 140.

74   "[John] Lansing is a good young fellow" *PAH*, III, 140.

76   [Abraham] Yates . . . is a man" *PAH*, III, 139.

76   "The present governor" *PAH*, III, 137-38.

V. Constitutionalist

92   "We live today" Rossiter, op. cit., 11.

95   "future Convention with more enlarged powers" *PAH*, III, 689.

95   procure the concurrence" *PAH*, III, 689.

100   "In every community where industry is encouraged" *PAH*, IV, 192.

101   "good behavior . . . by electors" *PAH*, IV, 207-08.

101   "Electors chosen by electors" *PAH*, IV, 208.

102   "Supreme Judicial authority" *PAH*, IV, 208.

102   "The new constitution has in its favour" *PAH*, IV, 275-76.

103   "it is probable general Washington" *PAH*, IV, 276.

104   "contests about the boundaries of power" *PAH*, IV, 277.

104   "to decide the important question" *PAH*, IV, 301-02.

106   "A NATION without a NATIONAL GOVERNMENT" *PAH*, IV, 721.

107   "when the transient circumstances" *PAH*, V, 207.

VI. Secretary of the Treasury

112   "He smote the rock" Daniel Webster, *The Papers of Daniel Webster: Speeches and Formal Writings 1800-1837* (1980), 1, 452.

115   "for the support of the public credit" *PAH*, VI, 66, fn. 99.

115 "the price of liberty.' *PAH*, VI, 69.

116 "the extension of taxation" *PAH*, VI, 87.

116 "until the whole of the debt shall be discharged" *PAH*, VI, 107.

109 "ardently wanted 'to see incorporated' " *PAH*, VI, 106.

118 " 'the necessity of it in the general fiscal arrangements" As cited by S. Elkins and E. McKittrick, *The Age of Federalism* (1993), 155.

122 "calamitous abuse" *PAH*, VII, 331.

134 "a bubble connected with my operations" *PAH*, IX, 76.

142 "prepare and report . . . a proper plan or plans" *PAH*, X, 230 fn. 125.

142 "Prospectus of the Society for Establishing Useful Manufactures" *PAH*, IX, 144-53.

144 "My dear Eliza has been lately very ill" *PAH*, XVII, 429.

144 "You know how much we all love you" *PAH*, XVIII, 288.

VII. Abolitionist

146 "Once the federal government" Ellis, op. cit., 175.

148 "to receive a sufficient sum" *PAH*, II, 642.

149 "much less than enough to buy a slave" Forrest McDonald, Alexander Hamilton (1979), 373, n. 12.

149 "The Negro boy & woman" *PAH*, XIX, 204.

149 "for 2 Negro servants" *The Law Practice of Alexander Hamilton*, J. Goebel, Jr. and J. H. Smith, eds., V, 409.

151 "I frequently hear it objected" *PAH*, II, 17-18.

158 "were baffled and almost beaten" *PAH*, V, 350.

158 "debilitated by the excessive efforts" *PAH*, V, 351.

161 "In the interpretation of treaties" *PAH*, XVIII, 519.

161 "Hamilton is really a colossus" *PAH*, XVIII, 478.

161 "Camillus . . . will be betrayed" *PAH*, XVIII, 478.

167 "How is the sending an agent" *PAH*, XXII, 493.

VIII. Major General

168 "No man . . . contributed more" Kohn, op. cit., 286.

174 "The charge against me" *PAH*, XXI, 243.

174 "I inquired for Mrs. Reynolds" *PAH*, XXI, 250-51.

175 "It was easy to understand" *PAH*, XXI, 253.

175 "If I recollect rightly" *PAH*, XXI, 254.

178 "The variety of shapes" *PAH*, XXI, 262.

180 "I have this moment" *PAH*, XXI, 522.

180 "deficient in precautions" *PAH*, XXII, 453.

189 "The first thing in all great operations" *PAH*, XXII, 452-53.

193 "Beware, my Dear Sir." *PAH*, XXII, 552-53.

IX. Last Years

194 "Hamilton and Jefferson slowly and reluctantly" Walling, op. cit., 286. [change wording to reflect editing of epigraph]

197 "The President disregarding these considerations" *PAH*, XXIV, 508-10.

198 "It has been repeatedly mentioned to me" *PAH*, XXV, 51.

198 "by whomsoever a charge" *PAH*, XXV, 125-26.

202 "Never did I see a man" *PAH*, 25, 437.

202 "Industry will succeed" *PAH*, XXV, 467.

203 "Truly, my Dear sir" *PAH*, XXVI 14-15.

204 "There is not the most remote probability" *PAH*, XXVI, 83.

206 "This purchase has been made" *PAH*, XXVI, 129-30.

206 "The charge is explicitly this" *The Law Practice of Alexander Hamilton*, J. Goebel, Jr., ed., I, 777.

208 "in every prosecution for writing" *The Law Practice of Alexander Hamilton*, J. Goebel, ed., I, 846, n.124.

208 "a dangerous man" *PAH*, XXVI, 244.

208 "I could detail to you" *PAH*, XXVI, 246.

208 "a prompt and unqualified acknowledgment" *PAH*, XXVI, 243.

208 "I stand ready to avow or disavow" *PAH*, XXVI, 248-49.

209 "To those, who with me abhorring" *PAH*, XXVI, 280.

216 "What is possible, but beyond the reach" Joseph J. Ellis, *Founding Brothers: The Revolutionary Generation* (2000), 31.

X. Hamilton and the Development of America

222 "Hamilton . . . touches us more nearly" Bryce, op. cit., 687.

223 "noble and magnificent" *PAH*, III, 106.

224 "The interpretation of laws" *PAH*, IV, 658.

XI. Hamilton's Impact on World History

238 "I consider Napoleon, Pitt and Hamilton" Talleyrand, ETUDE SUR LA REPUBLIQUE DES ETATS-UNIS D'AMERIQUE (1876), as cited by Gottfried Dietze, *The Federalist: A Classis on Federalism and Free Government* (1960), 11, n. 39 (author's translation).

239 "I have just come from viewing" Richard B. Morris, *Alexander Hamilton and the Founding of the Nation* (1957), 587.

240 "You have made yourselves a noble bargain" Joseph J. Ellis, *American Sphinx: The Character of Thomas Jefferson* (1996), 247.

240 "Were the Americans" Adam Smith, *An Inquiry into the Nature and Causes of the Wealth of Nations* (New York: Modern Library, 1937 [1776]), Bk. II, Ch. V, 347-48.

Epilogue

250 "The state which Alexander Hamilton had planned" Oliver, op. cit., 412.

252 "As a general marches at the head of his troops" *PAH*, I, 390.

{ BIBLIOGRAPHY }

Primary Sources

Goebel, Julius Jr., et al., eds. *The Law Practice of Alexander Hamilton: Documents and Commentary.* 5 vols. (New York: Columbia University Press, 1964–1981.

Postlethwayt, Malachy. *Universal Dictionary of Trade and Commerce.* London, 1751.

Smith, Adam. *An Inquiry into the Nature and Causes of the Wealth of Nations.* New York: Modern Library, 1937 [1776].

Steuart, Sir James. *An Inquiry into the Principles of Political Oeconomy: Being an Essay on the Science of Domestic Policy in Free Nations.* Andrew S. Skinner, ed. 4 vols. London: Pickering & Chatto, 1998 [1767].

Syrett, Harold C., et al., eds. *The Papers of Alexander Hamilton* (PAH herein). 27 vols. New York: Columbia University Press, 1961–87.

Washington, George. *Washington: Writings.* New York: Library of America, 1997.

Secondary Sources

Books

Adair, Douglass. *Fame and the Founding Fathers.* Indianapolis: Liberty Fund, 1998 [1974].

Anderson, William G. *The Price of Liberty: The Public Debt of the American Revolution.* Charlottesville: University Press of Virginia, 1983.

Appleby, Joyce. *Inheriting the Revolution: The First Generation of Americans.* Cambridge: Harvard University Press, 2000.

Austin, Ian Patrick. *Common Foundations of American and East Asian Modernization: From Alexander Hamilton to Junichero Koizumi.* Singapore: Select Books, 2009.

Banning, Lance. *The Jeffersonian Persuasion: Evolution of a Party Ideology.* Ithaca: Cornell University Press, 1978.

——. *The Sacred Fire of Liberty: James Madison and the Founding of the Federal Republic.* Ithaca: Cornell University Press, 1995.

Beard, Charles A. *An Economic Interpretation of the Constitution of the United States.* New York: Macmillan, 1962 [1913].

——. *Economic Origins of Jeffersonian Democracy.* New York: Free Press, 1965 [1915].

Bemis, Samuel Flagg. *Jay's Treaty: A Study in Commerce and Diplomacy.* New York: Macmillan, 1923.

Ben-Atar, Doron S. *Trade Secrets: Intellectual Property and the Origins of American Industrial Power.* New Haven: Yale University Press, 2004.

Bordewich, Fergus M. *The First Congress: How James Madison, George Washington, and a Group of Extraordinary Men Invented the Government.* New York: Simon & Schuster, 2016.

Brookhiser, Richard. *Alexander Hamilton, American.* New York: Free Press, 1999.

Brown, Roger H. *Redeeming the Republic: Federalists, Taxation, and the Origins of the Constitution.* Baltimore: Johns Hopkins University Press, 1993.

Carter, Susan B., et al., eds. *Historical Statistics of the United States: Earliest Times to the Present, Millennial Edition.* 5 vols. Cambridge: Cambridge University Press, 2006.

Chan, Michael D. *Aristotle and Hamilton on Commerce and Statesmanship.* Columbia: University of Missouri Press, 2006.

Chernow, Ron. *Alexander Hamilton.* New York: Penguin Press, 2004.

Cheney, Lynne. *James Madison: A Life Reconsidered.* New York: Viking, 2014.

Cowen, David Jack. *The Origins and Economic Impact of the First Bank of the United States, 1791–1797.* New York: Garland, 2000.

Davis, Joseph Stancliffe. *Essays in the Earlier History of American Corporations.* 2 vols. New York: Russell & Russell, 1965 [1917].

Dietze, Gottfried. *The Federalist: A Classic on Federalism and Free Government.* Baltimore: Johns Hopkins University Press, 1960.

Edling, Max M. *A Hercules in the Cradle: War, Money, and the American State, 1783–1867.* Chicago: University of Chicago Press, 2014.

——. *A Revolution in Favor of Government: Origins of the U.S. Constitution and the Making of the American State.* Oxford: Oxford University Press, 2003.

Einhorn, Robin L. *American Taxation, American Slavery.* Chicago: University of Chicago Press, 2006.

Elkins, Stanley, and Eric McKitrick. *The Age of Federalism: The Early American Republic, 1788–1800.* New York: Oxford University Press, 1993.

Ellis, Joseph J. *American Creation: Triumphs and Tragedies at the Founding of the Republic.* New York: Knopf, 2007.

——. *American Sphinx; The Character of Thomas Jefferson.* New York: Knopf, 1996.

——. *Founding Brothers: The Revolutionary Generation.* New York: Knopf, 2000.

——. *His Excellency George Washington.* New York: Knopf, 2004.

——. *The Quartet: Orchestrating the Second American Revolution, 1783-1789.* New York: Knopf, 2015.

Ferguson, E. James. *The Power of the Purse: A History of American Public Finance, 1776-1790.* Chapel Hill: University of North Carolina Press, 1961.

Fleming, Thomas. *A Disease in the Public Mind: A New Understanding of Why We Fought the Civil War.* New York: Da Capo Press, 2013.

——. *Duel: Alexander Hamilton, Aaron Burr, and the Future of America.* New York: Basic Books, 1999.

——. *The Intimate Lives of the Founding Fathers.* New York: Smithsonian Books, 2009.

——. *Washington's Secret War: The Hidden History of Valley Forge.* New York: Smithsonian Books, 2006 [2005].

Federici, Michael P. *The Political Philosophy of Alexander Hamilton.* Baltimore: Johns Hopkins University Press, 2012.

Flaumenhaft, Harvey. *The Effective Republic: Administration and Constitution in the Thought of Alexander Hamilton.* Durham: Duke University Press, 1992.

Flexner, James Thomas. *The Young Hamilton: A Biography.* Boston: Little, Brown, 1978.

Foner, Eric. *Gateway to Freedom: The Hidden History of the Underground Railroad.* New York: Norton, 2015.

Freeman, Joanne B. *Affairs of Honor: National Politics in the New Republic.* New Haven: Yale University Press, 2001.

Grant, James. *John Adams: Party of One.* New York: Farrar, Straus & Giroux, 2005.

Gordon, John Steele. *Hamilton's Blessing: The Extraordinary Life and Times of Our National Debt.* New York: Walker, 1997.

Hamilton, Allan McLane. *The Intimate Life of Alexander Hamilton.* London: Forgotten Books, 2015 [1910].

Hammond, Bray. *Banks and Politics in America, from the Revolution to the Civil War.* Princeton: Princeton University Press, 1957.

Hendrickson, David C. *Peace Pact: The Lost World of the American Founding.* Lawrence: University Press of Kansas, 2003.

Hendrickson, Robert. *Hamilton.* 2 vols. New York: Mason/Charter, 1976.

Hoffer, Peter Charles. *Rutgers v. Waddington: Alexander Hamilton, the End of the War for Independence, and the Origins of Judicial Review.* Lawrence: University Press of Kansas, 2016.

Hogeland, William. *Founding Finance: How Debt, Speculation, Foreclosures, Protests, and Crackdowns Made Us a Nation.* Austin: University of Texas Press, 2012.

——. *The Whiskey Rebellion: George Washington, Alexander Hamilton, and the Frontier Rebels Who Challenged America's Newfound Sovereignty.* New York: Scribner, 2006.

Irwin, Douglas A., and Richard Sylla, eds. *Founding Choices: American Economic Policy in the 1790s.* Chicago: University of Chicago Press, 2011.

Jefferson, Thomas. *Notes on the State of Virginia.* Chapel Hill: University of North Carolina Press, 1954.

Knott, Stephen F. *Alexander Hamilton and the Persistence of Myth.* Lawrence: University Press of Kansas, 2002.

Knott, Stephen F., and Tony Williams. *Washington and Hamilton: The Alliance That Forged America.* Naperville: Sourcebooks, 2015)

Kohn, Richard H. *Eagle and Sword: The Beginnings of the Military Establishment in America, 1783-1802.* New York: Free Press, 1975.

Larson, Edward J. *The Return of George Washington, 1783-1789.* New York: HarperCollins, 2014.

Lind, Michael, ed. *Hamilton's Republic: Readings in the American Democratic Nationalist Tradition.* New York: Free Press, 1997.

——. *Land of Promise: An Economic History of the United States.* New York: Harper, 2013 [2012].

Maier, Pauline. *Ratification: The People Debate the Constitution, 1787-1788.* Cambridge: Harvard University Press, 2010.

Miller, John C. *Alexander Hamilton and the Growth of the New Nation.* New Brunswick: Transaction, 2004 [1959].

McCoy, Drew R. *The Elusive Republic: Political Economy in Jeffersonian America.* Chapel Hill: University of North Carolina Press, 1980.

McCraw, Thomas K. *The Founders and Finance: How Hamilton, Gallatin, and Other Immigrants Forged a New Economy.* Cambridge: Harvard University Press, 2012.

McDonald, Forrest. *Alexander Hamilton: A Biography.* New York: Norton, 1982 [1979].

——. *Novus Ordo Seclorum: The Intellectual Origins of the Constitution.* Lawrence: University Press of Kansas, 1985.

McGuire, Robert A. *To Form a More Perfect Union: A New Economic Interpretation of the United States Constitution.* New York: Oxford University Press, 2003.

McNamara, Peter. *Political Economy and Statesmanship: Smith, Hamilton, and the Foundation of the Commercial Republic.* DeKalb: Northern Illinois University Press, 1998.

Melton, Buckner F., Jr. *Aaron Burr: Conspiracy to Treason.* New York: Wiley, 2002.

Mitchell, Broadus. *Alexander Hamilton: A Concise Biography.* New York: Barnes & Noble Books, 1999 [1976].

Morris, Richard B. *Alexander Hamilton and the Founding of the Nation.* New York: Dial Press, 1957.

Newton, Michael E. *Alexander Hamilton: The Formative Years.* N.p.: Eleftheria, 2015.

Oliver, F. S. *Alexander Hamilton: An Essay on American Union.* London: Thomas Nelson & Sons, 1906.

Perkins, Edwin J. *American Public Finance and Financial Services, 1700-1815.* Columbus: Ohio State University Press, 1994.

Peterson, Merrill D. *The Jefferson Image in the American Mind.* New York: Oxford University Press, 1960.

Rakove, Jack N. *Original Meanings: Politics and Ideas in the Making of the Constitution.* New York: Knopf, 1996.

Richards, Leonard L., *Shays's Rebellion: The American Revolution's Final Battle.* Philadelphia: University of Pennsylvania Press, 2002.

Rossiter, Clinton. *Alexander Hamilton and the Constitution.* New York: Harcourt, Brace & World, 1964.

Schockett, Andrew M. *Founding Corporate Power in Early National Philadelphia.* DeKalb: Northern Illinois University Press, 2007.

Sloan, Herbert E. *Principle and Interest: Thomas Jefferson and the Problem of Debt.* New York: Oxford University Press, 1995.

Smith, Jean Edward. *John Marshall: Definer of a Nation.* New York: Henry Holt, 1996.

Staloff, Darren. *Hamilton, Adams, Jefferson: The Politics of Enlightenment and the American Founding.* New York: Hill & Wang, 2005.

Tortajada, Ramón, ed. *The Economics of James Steuart.* London: Routledge, 1999.

Unger, Harlow Giles. *Noah Webster: The Life and Times of an American Patriot.* New York: Wiley, 1998.

Walling, Karl-Friedrich. *Republican Empire: Alexander Hamilton on War and Free Government.* Lawrence: University Press of Kansas, 1999.

White, Leonard D. *The Federalists: A Study in Administrative History.* New York: Macmillan, 1959 [1948].

Watkins, William J., Jr. *Reclaiming the American Revolution: The Kentucky and Virginia Resolutions and Their Legacy.* New York: Palgrave, 2004.

Wills, Garry. *Negro President: Jefferson and the Slave Power.* Boston: Houghton Mifflin, 2003.

Wood, Gordon S. *Empire of Liberty: A History of the Early Republic, 1789-1815.* New York: Oxford University Press, 2009.

——. *Revolutionary Characters: What Made the Founders Different.* New York: Penguin Press, 2006.

Wright, Robert E. *Corporation Nation.* Philadelphia: University of Pennsylvania Press, 2014.

——. *The First Wall Street: Chestnut Street, Philadelphia, and the Birth of American Finance.* Chicago: University of Chicago Press, 2005),

——. *Hamilton Unbound: Finance and the Creation of the American Republic.* Westport: Greenwood Press, 2002.

——. *One Nation Under Debt: Hamilton, Jefferson, and the History of What We Owe.* New York: McGraw-Hill, 2008.

——. *Origins of Commercial Banking in America, 1750-1800.* Lanham: Rowman & Littlefield, 2001.

——. *The Wealth of Nations Rediscovered: Integration and Expansion in American Financial Markets, 1780-1850.* Cambridge: Cambridge University Press, 2002.

Wright, Robert E., and David J. Cowen, *Financial Founding Fathers: The Men Who Made America Rich.* Chicago: University of Chicago Press, 2006.

Zane, John Maxcy. *The Story of Law.* 2nd ed. Indianapolis: Liberty Fund, 1998 [1927].

Articles

Davis, Joseph H. "An Annual Index of U.S. Industrial Production, 1790-1915." *Quarterly Journal of Economics* 119 (November 2004): 1177-1215.

Irwin, Douglas A. "The Aftermath of Hamilton's Report on Manufactures." *Journal of Economic History* 64 (2004): 800-21.

——. "Revenue or Reciprocity: Founding Feuds over U.S. Trade Policy." In Douglas Irwin and Richard Sylla, eds., *Founding Choices: American Economic Policy in the 1790s.* Chicago: University of Chicago Press, 2011, 89-120.

James, John A., and Richard Sylla. "The Changing Nature of American Public Debt, 1690-1835." In *La Dette Publique aux XVIIe et XIXe Siècles son Developpement sur le Plan Local, Regional et National.* Colloque International International Colloquium, Spa 12-16, IX 1978, Actes Handelingen. Brussels, 1980, 243-72.

McCraw, Thomas K. "The Strategic Vision of Alexander Hamilton." *American Scholar* 63 (Winter 1994): 31-57.

Rousseau, Peter L., and Richard Sylla. "Financial Systems, Economic Growth, and Globalization." In M. D. Bordo, A. M. Taylor, and J. G. Williamson, eds., *Globalization in Historical Perspective.* Chicago: University of Chicago Press, 2003, 373-413.

——. "Emerging Financial Markets and Early US Growth." *Explorations in Economic History* 42 (January 2005): 1-26.

Sylla, Richard. "Comparing the UK and US Financial Systems, 1790-1830." In Jeremy Atack and Larry Neal, eds., *The Origins and Development of Financial Markets and Institutions.* Cambridge: Cambridge University Press, 2009, 209-40.

——. "Emerging Markets in History: The United States, Japan, and Argentina." In R. Sato, R. V. Ramachandran, and K. Mino, eds., *Global Competition and Integration.* Boston: Kluwer Academic, 1999, 427-46.

——. "Financial Foundations: Public Credit, the National Bank, and Securities Markets." In Douglas Irwin and Richard Sylla, eds., *Founding Choices: American Economic Policy in the 1790s.* Chicago: University of Chicago Press, 2011, 59-88.

——. "Financial Systems and Economic Modernization." *Journal of Economic History* 62, no. 2 (June 2002): 279-92.

——. "Hamilton and the Federalist Financial Revolution, 1789-1795." *New York Journal of American History* 65, no. 3 (Spring 2004): 32-39.

——. "The Political Economy of Early US Financial Development." In Stephen Haber, Douglass C. North, and Barry Weingast, eds., *Political Institutions and Financial Development.* Stanford: Stanford University Press, 2008, 60-91.

——. "Reversing Financial Reversals: Government and the Financial System since 1789." In Price Fishback, ed., *Government and the American Economy from Colonial Times to the Present.* Chicago: University of Chicago Press, 2007, 115-47.

——. "Shaping the U.S. Financial System, 1690-1913: The Dominant Role of Public Finance." In R. Sylla, R. Tilly, and G. Tortella, eds., *The State, the Financial System, and Economic Modernization.* Cambridge: Cambridge University Press, 1999, 249-70.

——. "U.S. Securities Markets and the Banking System, 1790-1840." *Federal Reserve Bank of St. Louis Review* 80, no. 3 (May/June 1998): 83-103.

Sylla, Richard, Robert E. Wright, and David J. Cowen. "Alexander Hamilton, Central Banker: Crisis Management and the Lender of Last Resort during the US Panic of 1792." *Business History Review* 83 (Spring 2009): 61-86.

Wright, Robert E., and Richard Sylla. "Corporation Formation in the United States, 1790-1860: Law and Politics in Comparative Contexts." *Business History* 55, no. 4 (2013): 653-69.

[IMAGE CREDITS]

[INDEX]

Hamilton in militia of, 21, 23, 26, **28**, 30, 32, **34-35**, 37
infrastructure in, **232**
libel laws in, 207-8
and ratification of Constitution, 104, 106, 107-9, **108**, **109**, **110-11**, 224, 248
and *Rutgers v. Waddington* case, 83, 87
taxes in, 93
Vermont relations with, 89-90
New York Stock Exchange, 129, **129**
Newburgh Address, Washington's (1783), 78, **79**
Newburgh Conspiracy, 77, **80**, 189
Newton, Michael, 3*n*
Notes on the State of Virginia (Jefferson), 235

Oath of Allegiance, **42**, 43
Oliver, F.S., **250**
Orléans, Philippe d', 57
Orphan Asylum Society of New York City, 218
"Our Countrymen in Chains" (Whittier), **152**

Panic of 1792, 116, 133-35, **134**
paper money, 93-94, **94**, 226
Paterson, New Jersey: manufacturing in, 142, **143**
Paterson, William, 100, 142
Peale, Charles Willson, 14, **14**, **27**, 29, **29**, **32**, **118**, **151**
Pennsylvania
    American Revolution in, 39-40, 41-43, **41**
    and Annapolis Convention, 94
    Fries Rebellion in, 189, **190-91**, 193
    Whiskey Rebellion in, 138, 140
    See also Philadelphia, Pennsylvania
Pennsylvania Railroad, 232
People v. Croswell, 206-8
Perry, Matthew, 243
Philadelphia, Pennsylvania
    and American Revolutionary battles, 39, **39**, 40, 41, 42
    Bank of North America opening in, 70
    Constitutional Convention in, 66-67, 66*n*, 98, 100-104
    Continental Army surrounding of State House in, 78, **80**
    First Continental Congress in, 14, **18-19**
    Second Continental Congress in, 26, 39
    securities market in, **128**
    State House in, **72**, 78, **80**
    stock market in, **128**
    See also Bank of the United States
Pickering, Timothy, 165, **165**, 167, **167**, 197
Pinckney, Charles Cotesworth, 172, 180, 198, **199**, 200
Pitt, William, 135
Plutarch, 252
politics
    and financial system, 55-59
    and Hamilton's impact on world history, 248-49
Polk, Charles Peale, **27**
Postlethwayt, Malachy, 252
Powell (Colin) Doctrine, 193*n*
presidency
    powers of, 224
    See also executive branch; *specific person*
Princeton, Battle of, 32, 37, **37**, 38
Princeton, New Jersey: Confederation Congress meeting in, 78
Princeton University, 12-13, 37, 216*n*
private investors, 70, 87, 122, 123, 124, 224, 227
Providence Bank, 125
Provisional Army. *See* New Army
"Publius" (pseudonym). See *The Federalist* essays
Putnam, Israel, 40-41

Quakers, 153
Quasi War, **185**, 187, **187**, **192**, 226

railroads, 227
Randolph, Edmund, 124, **125**
Ranney, William Tylee, **37**
regulation, 140, 203, 242, 246
Rensselaer, Stephen van, 149*n*
Revolutionary War. *See* American Revolution
Reynolds affair, 172-76, **172**, **173**, **176**, **177**, 178, **179**, 207
Reynolds, James, 173-76, **177**, 178
Reynolds, Maria, 172-76, 178, 207
Rhode Island
    and Annapolis Convention, 94
    banks in, 125
    issuing of paper money by, 93, **94**
    and taxes, 77
Rochambeau, comte de (Jean-Baptiste de Vimeur), 44, **45**, 47, 51
Rossiter, Clinton, **92**
rule of law, 58, 81, 189
run-off election, of 1800, 199-200, **199**, **200**
Russia, 242-43
    See also Soviet Union
Rutgers v. Waddington (1784), 83, 87

Saratoga, Battle of, 40, 42, 43
Schuyler, Angelica. *See* Church, Angelica Schuyler
Schuyler, Elizabeth. *See* Hamilton, Elizabeth Schuyler (wife)
Schuyler (Philip) family, 47, 53, 144, 149, **149**, 174
Scott, John, **115**
Scrip Bubble, 133-34
Seabury, Samuel, 14, 15, 16, 20
Secretary of the Treasury, Hamilton as
    authority of, 114
    and Bank of the United States, 62, 89, 122-25
    and Dinner Table Bargain, 118, 120
    financial improprieties of, 172-76, **172**, **176**, 178, **179**, 206-7
    and Hamilton's goals and achievements, 55, 62, 113, 127, 129, 137, 144-45, 253
    and Hamilton's role in development of America, 226
    national currency and, 130-33
    national debt and, 115-18, 120, **121**, 122
    opposition to, 135, 147, 158, 169, 174
    and Panic of 1792, 133-35
    resignation of, 143-44, 147-48
    Reynolds affair and, 172-76, **172**, **176**, 178, **179**, 207
    and rise of American corporations, 129-30
    securities market and, 114, 122, 128-29, **128**
    slaves/slavery and, 147-48, 158
    taxes and, 116, 117, 122, 134, 138, 140
    and trade policies, 135
    and Whiskey Rebellion, 138, 140, 189
securities market
    and Board of Brokers, **128**
    corporations and, 130
    and financial history, 56
    and Hamilton as secretary of the Treasury, 114, 122, 128-29, **128**
    and Hamilton's impact on world history, 245
    and Hamilton's role in development of America, 226, 227
    Panic of 1792 and, 133-34
    and pillars of financial system, 59, 63
Sedgwick, Theodore, 180, **184**, 189, 193
Sedition Act. *See* Alien and Sedition Acts
Seven Years' War, 204
Shays Rebellion, **92**, 93, 95, 98, **98**, 189, **191**

"shock and awe" strategy, Hamilton's, 193
silver dollar, pattern for, **61**
Singapore, 246
sinking fund, 116
Sino-Japanese War, 245
The Slave Trade (Smith), **146**
slaves/slavery
    abolition/emancipation of, 147-67, 235-36
    and American Revolution, 151, **151**, 153
    anti-slavery societies and, 153
    British capture/return of, 158, 161
    colonization of, 235-36
    and Constitution, 199
    financial system and, 235
    and Haitian Revolution, 161-62, 165, 167
    and Hamilton as secretary of the Treasury, 147-78
    and Hamilton's eulogy for Greene, 156, **157**, 158
    and Hamilton's goals and achievements, 253
    of Hamilton's mother, 5-6, 7, 9, 147
    Hamilton's ownership of, 148-50
    and Hamilton's role in development of America, 223, 227, 235-36
    Hamilton's views about, 5-6, 7, 9, 15, 147, 151, 153, 156, 158, **159**, 235
    and Jay Treaty, 158, **159**, 161
    Louisiana Purchase and, 206
    and national unity, 235, 253
    and New York City slave market, **154-55**
    and opposition to Hamilton, 147-48
    of Schuyler family, 149, **150**
    and slave trade, **12**
    voting and, 199
    Whittier broadside about, **152**
Smart, John, **44**
Smith, Adam, **139**, 140, **141**, 203, 240, 246
Smith, John Raphael, **146**
Smith, Melancton, 107, 108, **108**
Society for Establishing Useful Manufactures, 142, **143**, 245
Sons of Liberty, 13, **15**, 27, **27**
South Carolina
    and Annapolis Convention, 94
    banks in, 127
    and ratification of Constitution, 107
    and slave battalions in American Revolution, 151, **151**, 153
    taxes in, 93
South Korea, 246
southerners
    and Civil War, 236
    and corporations, 130
    elections of 1800 and, 199
    and financial system, 117, 118, 120
    and Hamilton's eulogy for Greene, 156, 158
    and Louisiana Purchase, 206
    and slavery, 235
Soviet Union, 234, 248. *See also* Russia
Spain, 188, 234
St. Croix (West Indies), 5-7, 6*n*, 9, **10-11**, 12, 147, **148**
Standard Oil Company, 232
State House (Philadelphia), **72**, 78, **80**
states
    and Alien and Sedition Acts, 206
    bank charters by, 114, 125, 127, 226, 227
    boundaries of, 89-90, **90-91**
    and Constitutional Convention, 100-102
    currency of, 60, 63
    debts of, 115-16, 117-18, 120, 130
    federal relations with, 100-102
    and Hamilton as secretary of the Treasury, 114, 115-16, 130
    and Hamilton's accomplishments, 130

FLORIDA

GEORGIA

All alamaha R

Apalaxy

Fort Mobill

Pensacola

St Maria de Palaxy

St John R

F. St

St Deiphin St Josepha

Norleans

C. Samblas

Chandeleur I

St Pierre

R Misisipi now

R St Louis

Palaxy Bay

Yamasee

Mosqu

Fort Louis

St Bernards or

St Louis Bay

de l'Ascension

Bay del Spirito

Sancto

Ba

B.

Bah.

Lake Se

Joseph

NEW

LEON

NORTH R

Carlos Bay

Ponce Bay

Chanl of Florida

NEW

GALICIA

Panuco

GULF OF MEXICO

Negrillas

Alacranes

Cavanes R

Motance Bay

Sta Cruz

Havana

Bay Honda

CUB

Tortugas

C. Florida

la Bermeja

CS Antonio

G Corintos

C. Cotoche

I Pinos

Jardin

MEXICO

Mexico

Arcas

Merida

Cozumel

G Camanis

Villa

Rica

Sampoval R

C. Condusedo

YUCATAN

Campechy

La Camanis

Cabo de

Isle of Ixtoa

Juan d'Uloa

Triangles

Sacrifice I

de Ant. Lardo

CAMPECHY

Port Royal

Neg

St Marins Priest I

Chaubunal

Bay

Blew

TLASCALA

BAY

Cozumel

La Vera

Cruz

Pedro I

TABASCO

Salomanca

GULF of HONDURA

St Millan

Acapulco

Lignwood

Pedro I

Ruatun

I Guayana

C Honduras

Serra

Laguasial

Barmajos Points

Dolce G

C Camaron

Hayen I

Vera Pax

R Dulce

P de Sal

Trixillo

Viciosas

Socunusco

St Jage de

Guatimala

St Thomas

Gracioso Dios

St George

C Gratios Dios

S

B

MEXICO or NEW

HONDURAS

Carlago Bay

Honda

Bay

Mosq

la Trinidad

GUATIMALA

Valladolid

MOSKITOS

Catalina I

GREAT

Amapa

NICARAGUA

IParlos

St Andero

L of Nicaragua

I de Monglares

Nicaragua

Gulf of Amapalla

Leon

Nicaragua

Realejo

Granada

Nicaragua

St Lucar

COSTA

VERAGUA

SPAIN

DA

G Papagayo

Concepcion

Portobell

C Blanco

Puebla

Trinidad

Panama

SOUTH SEA

Gulf of Salinas

I Cano

Burica I

Isle of Ouicano

Bay of Panama

Pearl I

Quiba

Hyguera I

P Mala

P Pine